A PERSIAN SP

BY WILFRID BLUNT

★

WILFRID BLUNT

A Persian Spring

BARRIE

First published in 1957
by
JAMES BARRIE BOOKS LIMITED
3-4 CLEMENT'S INN LONDON W.C.2

Printed and bound in Great Britain by
THE GARDEN CITY PRESS LIMITED
LETCHWORTH, HERTFORDSHIRE

To my colleagues at Eton
in gratitude for twenty years of
kindness and forbearance

'I know only one thing sweeter than making a book, and that is, to project one.'

Jean Paul
Quintus Fixlein

CONTENTS

NOTE

*At the end of this book will be found a short
note on Iran which may be of use to readers
unfamiliar with the Persian background.*

vii

LIST OF ILLUSTRATIONS

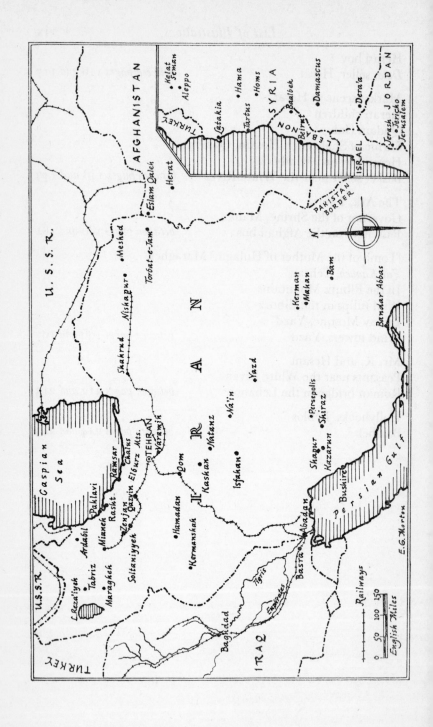

Preface

THOSE who travel in foreign lands for pleasure can for the most part be classed either as tourists or as explorers. The fourteen-week journey that I made to Iran and Afghanistan in the spring of 1956 fell, however, midway between tourism and exploration; it was more adventurous than a weekend in Boulogne, less adventurous than a year in the Gobi Desert. But travel in any form in the Near and Middle East is not at present easy; in some respects, indeed, it is harder now than it was nineteen hundred years ago. St. Paul, were he to make today those journeys which in his time were confined to the various provinces of the Roman Empire, would need *two* Turkish passports (one for use in Jordan, the other for Israel), endorsed for Great Britain, Italy, the Lebanon, Israel, Jordan and Greece, together with an incalculable number of exit and transit visas.

I can perhaps best describe myself as a tourist in lands not yet organized for tourism. The explorer makes light of his troubles. Half apologetically, he may let slip that the temperature was 120 degrees Fahrenheit, or that seven inches of rain washed away his tent in the night, that he lived for three weeks on whale blubber or was prostrate with beriberi; but he takes it for granted that illness and discomfort must be his lot. The tourist, on the other hand, is 'roasted' when the thermometer touches eighty-five, 'drowned' every time that it rains, and at death's door when he gets mild indigestion from overeating at a Grindelwald hotel. I have written as a tourist—hence my irritation at delays, my inability to become reconciled to oriental sanitation, my complaints of heat where a Persian Gulfer would be reaching for his overcoat. I beg my Persian friends to forgive my impatience.

I went to Persia to see many things—its landscape, its architecture, its flowers, its people. The mosques and the mountains I found more wonderful that I had dared to hope. With the flowers I was rather disappointed. But by far the most vivid impression that I brought back was that of the friendliness and hospitality of the Persian people. Their kindness, and that of the

European and American residents, form a recurrent theme of my book; I sincerely hope that nothing I have written will give offence to those whose hospitality I have enjoyed. I have purposely changed or omitted a few names and transplanted two incidents.

There are many people to whom I must extend my thanks. Mrs. Arthur Harrison, Mrs. George Sargeaunt, Mr. Sacheverell Sitwell, Mr. Graham Watson, Mr. Francis Cruso, Mr. Tom Lyon and Mr. Raef Payne kindly read my typescript and gave me much excellent advice. Lt.-Col. G. E. Wheeler, Director of the Central Asian Research Centre, made many helpful suggestions about the spelling of Persian and Arabic words—a perpetual headache for those who write about the Middle East; but I cannot hold him responsible for my errors. Moreover, I found it impracticable to follow his advice to employ the 'ā' for the Persian long 'a.' Mr. Alan Trott, who entertained me in the Lebanon, put me further in his debt by some useful suggestions. I would never be done were I to mention by name all those who befriended me. But I cannot leave unrecorded the outstanding kindness of everyone at the British Embassy in Tehran, from H.E. the British Ambassador and Lady Stevens down to the humblest clerk. Without the help of Mr. and Mrs. Tim Marten, I could hardly have achieved anything in Iran. I would also express my warmest thanks to Mr. and Mrs. Wiggin, Bishop and Mrs. Thompson, Dr. and Mrs. Coleman, Dr. and Mrs. Wild, Mr. Tom Cassilly, Dr. Wilke and Dr. and Herr Benjamin Amsel. I am grateful to Mr. Sheikh-ol-Islami for some very helpful Persian lessons; to Miss V. Thayre once again for her excellent typing; and to my nephew Simon Blunt, and Messrs. Greville of the Slough Trading Estate, for making the enlargements of my photographs used to illustrate this book. These photographs were taken with an Agfa Isolette kindly lent me by Mr. Charles Spencer. I know nothing about photography, and had not touched a camera for twenty years; if the results have any merit, it must be attributed to the clear air, the camera, and luck.

Last, but not least, I must express my gratitude to the Head Master of Eton for sanctioning my leave of absence and thus enabling me to realize the dream of a lifetime.

W. J. W. B.

Baldwin's Shore,
Eton College, *March 17th, 1957.*

I

Prelude

My leave had been granted. I opened my atlas and stared excitedly at the wide double sheet entitled 'ASIA, GENERAL,' though it managed to include Iceland and part of New Guinea.

It would be pleasant, I thought, to go to Persia by sea. But the sea was not co-operative. Gibraltar, Port Said, Aden, Bombay, Bushire . . . I hadn't the time. Should I then sail from Genoa to Beirut, take the Nairn coach to Baghdad, and fly from there to Tehran? The very word 'Baghdad' can still bind spells. I consulted a colleague who had been in Iraq.

'Baghdad? Why on earth do you want to go there? It's horrible.' He drew a book from his shelves and opened it. 'Listen to this. Of course it doesn't give you the faintest idea of what it's really like. Nothing could.' He began reading :

'Baghdad, with its extremes of climate, may rank among the most uncomfortable places in the world. It can take its place with Bokhara, where everyone from the emir downwards is afflicted with the tapeworm; with Muscat, where the whole population take refuge from the hot summer winds by standing in the sea, coming out after many hours with the ends of their noses blistered; with Oroya, where the newcomer bleeds at the nose and ears for weeks from the rarity of the atmosphere; with Hammerfest, where . . .'

'Stop!' I said. 'That's enough.'

I left my travel plans to simmer and set about trying to establish contact with someone in Persia.

'I know the very man,' said a friend. 'Consul in Isfahan. He's a charming fellow. You'd like him.'

'Do you think he'd put me up in Isfahan?'

'Not Isfahan; Bournemouth. He retired just before the war. As a matter of fact,' he added, 'I've just remembered something. He died two years ago.'

And so it continued. Promotion, retirement or death had

rendered one after another powerless to help me. Things began to look hopeless.

Then somebody said : 'I suppose you know the Martens?'

'The Martens?'

'He's a secretary at the Embassy in Tehran.'

I felt half inclined to ask if he were still alive. But he was indeed. And very courteously he invited me to spend the first fortnight of March with him; after that, he was going to England on leave. This clarified my plans : since I could not get away from Eton until the end of February, I would have to fly direct to Tehran. One problem, at all events, was settled.

It had rained; now it poured. Suddenly everyone whom I met was eager to furnish me with introductions—introductions to Anglican bishops and Persian lawyers; to botanists, bankers and business men; to archaeologists, museum officials and missionaries. I soon had more than I could ever hope to use.

Though I had read, at one time or another, a number of books dealing with early travel in Persia—and even, indeed, written one myself [1]—I was, as I realized, not too well acquainted on the contemporary scene. I had a nodding acquaintance with Curzon's two monumental volumes, now more than sixty years old but not yet superseded; I had browsed in Sykes's History and extravagantly purchased Upham Pope's six splendid folios; I had read Edward Browne's classic *A Year amongst the Persians* and Morier's imperishable *Hajji Baba*; but I had little idea as to how one travelled nowadays through the country, what luggage one would need, what one could safely eat and drink, what precautions one should take against illness. I went to the London Library.

Certainly there was no dearth of material. I gazed bewildered at the crowded shelves, scanning the titles. *By Camel and Car to the Peacock Throne*; *The Land of the Lion and the Sun*; *In the Land of the Lion and the Sun*; *Persia: Romance and Reality*; *Behind the Veil in Persia*; *A Lady Doctor in Bakhtiari Land*; *Persian Pilgrimage*; *Queer Things about Persia* (by the author of *Queer Things about Japan*). I pulled out a volume by a lady writer—a volume with chapter sub-headings such as 'Peeps into some hareems,' or 'Astonishment of natives at sight

[1] *Pietro's Pilgrimage* (James Barrie, 1953).

of hairpins.' And so I passed from book to book, reading a page here and a page there, marvelling at the diversity of their authors. There were the tough explorers—men, and women who roughed it like men. There were the archaeologists, sniffing out buried treasure like truffle-hounds and piling fact upon fact to puncture the hard-won reputations of their predecessors. There were the diplomats, medical missionaries and philanthropists; the globe-trotters, adventurers and soldiers; the artists, botanists and orientalists. And lastly, there were the hirsute young men who travelled in jeeps called 'Lizzie' and perpetually photographed one another mending punctures ('with Friday Mosque in background').

I seized a random handful, added to it what was said to be the most recent guide-book,[1] and returned home.

Murray's *Handbook for travellers in Asia Minor, Trans-caucasia, Persia, etc.*, edited by Sir Charles Wilson, was published in 1895 and reprinted ten years later. I did not find it very helpful, for 'Persia etc.' was dismissed very summarily, almost apologetically.

The equipment advocated by Sir Charles for the journey suggested a full-scale Victorian invasion of the Orient. The traveller was recommended to carry round with him 'Russian top boots two sizes too large for the foot, galoshes for visits to grandees, and a black frock coat if visits are contemplated to royal personages.' Camping equipment—'good stout *tents*, each about half a horseload; a tent *carpet, camp-bed, cork mattress, folding table, indiarubber bath*,' etc. etc.—was essential. There were the 'large *English hunting saddle*, with plenty of Ds., and an English *crop and lash* (for fighting off the formidable native dogs).' Delicacies such as *Harvey sauce* and Liebig's *extractum carnis* must be taken on the journey, for Sir Charles attached great importance to 'good living, *provided it be not carried beyond the bounds of temperance.*' There was the standard pharmacopoeia, supplemented by *Warburg's mixture, Dover's powder, Cockle's pills*, and the indispensable *cholera belt*. There were eye lotion, binoculars and other gifts for 'establishing

[1] I did not then know of G. H. Ebtahaj's almost unobtainable and rather sketchy *Guide Book on Iran*, of which three editions, all undated, were published between 1930 and 1940.

friendly relations with the natives.' There were mathematical instruments and drawing equipment, heelball and squeeze paper, rifles and revolvers, and finally 'the *Levinge bag*, that gives complete protection against vermin of every description that abound in all parts of the East.' But, alas, the *Levinge bag* 'takes up room and is troublesome to manage'; the traveller might, after all, be compelled to dispense with it. . . .

I closed the book sadly and turned to the travelogues.

The more I read, the more depressed I became. Could there, I wondered, be anything new left to say about Persia? And even if there were, how should I, a mere tourist, here today and gone tomorrow, be able to say it? The glories of Isfahan, Meshed and Persepolis had been sung a hundred times, and in words that were sometimes suspiciously similar. Yet not all these authors were in agreement. For example, some found Shiraz a glorious city of roses, nightingales and wine, whereas others pronounced the roses negligible, the nightingales non-existent, and the wine undrinkable. It made me wonder whether one found in Persia only what one went to find.

But what most struck me, and most alarmed me, in these books was the fact that every traveller in the Near or Middle East became, sooner or later, the prey to sickness or disaster. 'Having fallen a victim to a sharp, painful illness well known as "gippy tummy",' wrote one who spent three weeks in agony. 'Christopher was ill when he woke up, from the fleas,' said another; adding later: 'C. is in a sad state. His legs are swollen up to the knee and covered with water blisters.' That was the notorious Azarbayjan flea—no joke, yet a poor thing by comparison with the red-spotted Mianeh bug or the deadly black scorpion of Kashan.

Nor could the fanaticism of Islam be discounted. These travellers told of stoning, robbery, imprisonment, and worse. There were, too, the dangers of the road—of repeated breakdowns in remote places, of fatal disasters among the precipitous mountains.

Add to these tangible perils the more ghostly menace of the *pa-lis*, *nasnas*, *ghul* and *al*. The *pa-lis*, or 'foot-licker,' is a form of vampire that drains away the life-blood of a sleeping man by licking the soles of his feet. It is, however, a creature of low

Lotfollah Mosque, Isfahan
(p. 68)

Friday Mosque,
Isfahan. North-west
portal
(p. 39)

In the Bazaar,
Isfahan
(p. 42)

Khaju Bridge, Isfahan
(p. 80)

Chehel Sotun, Isfahan
(p. 73)

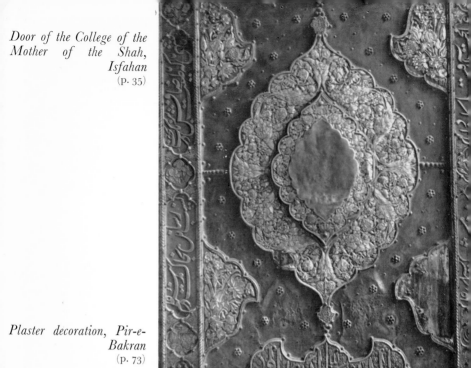

Door of the College of the Mother of the Shah, Isfahan
(p. 35)

Plaster decoration, Pir-e-Bakran
(p. 73)

intelligence, and—as two Isfahani muleteers were the first to discover—can readily be fooled by the traveller sleeping feet to feet with a companion.

Gashte-am hazar u si u seh dareh,
Amma na-dide-am mard-e-du sereh

muttered the simple soul as it crept thirstily away :

I have wandered through a thousand and thirty-
three valleys,
But never yet saw a two-headed man !

The *nasnas* poses as an elderly invalid begging a lift across a river; but in mid-stream it shows its true colours and strangles its benefactor. The *ghul*—equivalent of our will-o'-the-wisp— assumes the voice of a friend or relation and, crying for help, lures the traveller away from the caravan and murders him. But of the *al* I was certainly not afraid; this flaxen-haired gourmet feeds solely upon the livers of young mothers.

But however little I might fear ghostly perils, those other dangers were real enough. I thought again of my comfortable arm-chair, my cosy fire, the punctual and appetizing meals, the congenial company that I would leave behind; of those pleasant hours at the Drawing Schools and at Baldwin's Shore. I was no longer young. I was never tough. How rash a venture !

Next came the question of language.

To travel in a European country where one cannot talk to the local inhabitants in their own tongue is to miss much. But it rarely leads to serious inconvenience; the native eager to air his English or his French is never far to seek. In the wilder parts of Persia and Afghanistan, however, the tongue-tied traveller might well find himself in a predicament. I decided that I must learn some Persian.

For the beginner of, say, Italian, a plethora of elementary readers, grammars and vocabularies is available, graded to suit every age, intelligence and taste. There are picture-books show- ing the family at work and at play, with *Il padre fumando la pipa* and *La madre leggendo il libro*; there are books with parallel Italian and English texts; there are excellent Lingua- phone records; there is, when all else fails, the Italian housemaid next door. The path to Persian is not so primrose.

True, there is Miss Lambton's magnificent Grammar; but it is too formidable a work for the casual and unaided student. There are also language records—of which more presently. There are several 'teach-yourself' Persian books, but these are for the most part inadequate and out of date, and each has its own system of transliterating that lovely but defeating script. None the less, to make a start I armed myself with a couple of them.

The Persian language belongs to the Indo-European group— and with what satisfaction one discovers *madar*, mother; *baradar*, brother; *bad*, bad; *behtar*, better, and the like! But there is soon an end to such close similarities. Unfortunately also, Persian has taken over, along with the Arabic script, a very large number of Arabic words; and Arabic is a notoriously difficult language. Moreover, though one might not unreasonably hope to identify, say, *garaj* as 'garage' when thus transliterated, how long would it take to recognize it when written گاراج. I amused myself for a fortnight or so, in a desultory kind of a way, with these two books. They must be a nice people, I thought, who call a bed *takht-e-khab*—'throne of sleep'; you wouldn't catch a Frenchman calling it that. It was a rich language; for I remembered having read somewhere that there were sixty-five words for 'girl,' one of which was reserved for 'a young girl pretty enough to be able to dispense with jewellery.' Yet it appeared to be in other ways economical, many words bearing two or more quite distinct meanings. *Shir*, for example, might mean 'milk,' 'lion' or 'water-tap.' An ankle, I learned, was *moch-e-pa* (foot-wrist) and an egg *tokhm-e-morgh*[1] (hen-seed)— constructions that recalled the German. I liked *sarbaz* (head-loser) for 'soldier.' It was pleasant to come upon old friends such as *jangal* (forest), *payjama*, *khaki* (earth-coloured) and *shal* (shawl). But I did not feel that I was really getting anywhere.

And in particular, I was worried about the pronunciation. For instance, that of the letters usually transliterated 'q' and 'gh' could obviously not be learned from a book; nor did there seem to be any general agreement as to how they should be pronounced, beyond that they were now pronounced identically. The sound, writes Sir Wolseley Haig, 'bears the same relation to the sound of "g" in "log" as "ch" in "loch" bears to "ck"

[1] Known to our troops during the war as 'tuppenny mugs.'

in "lock." Some may not at first find it easy to acquire. . . . It is a guttural, and must not be converted into the letter "r," as some, to avoid a difficulty, pronounce it.' Mr. E. Hawker, on the other hand, says : 'The pronunciation is quite easy : place the tip of the tongue against the lower lip and make the sound of gargling. The sound is exactly that of a Parisian *r*.'

Or take the letter *ain*, usually transliterated as a reversed apostrophe—pronounced, says Mr. Hawker, like the hiatus between 'my' and 'aunt' when one says 'my aunt,' and compared by Sir Wolseley to the check in the voice of a Cockney saying 'Clapham'—i.e. 'Cla'am.' But how should one pronounce an initial *ain*—as, say, in the word 'Abbas'?

Most of the other letters seemed fairly straightforward. One could not really trill an 'r,' Sir Wolseley maintained, without studying gramophone records of Sir Harry Lauder singing. But Scotsmen are notoriously clannish; I was content to muddle along in my own poor Sassenach way.

None the less, there still remained the three unpronounceable letters, and the whole question of stress and accent. Unless I could find a Persian teacher in London there could only be one answer : gramophone records.

'Are you in oil?' said the photogenic young lady.

'I don't think so.'

'Then why do you wish to learn Persian? Would you care to hear our new Modern Hebrew records?'

'But I am going to Persia, not to Israel.'

She yielded with some reluctance, took down the box of Persian records from the shelf and handed me the textbook. I opened it and read : 'The diseases of domesticated animals are as follows: glanders, *yāmān*, *mishmishé*, colic, sandcracks, *qaraqush* (splint), and thrush. . . .'

Perhaps she noticed that I was smiling, for she said severely, 'Turn to page twelve, please. I will now play the opening phrase of the record. Follow very carefully.'

'Khāné-ye dūst-e bandé dar dāmane-ye kūh vāqi' ast'

('The house of my friend is at the foot of the hill'), said the book.

'*Honey-yea doosty bunday dar damunayay koo . . .*' cooed the record; then it uttered a 'v' followed by a sound like the last dregs of bath-water vanishing down the waste-pipe.

'Excuse me, would you mind playing that phrase again.'

My ears had not deceived me; the v-gurgle was exactly repeated.

'My book,' I said, 'has *vaqi*' *ast*, but on the record it sounds different. Is this sort of thing explained anywhere?'

'No doubt there is a little footnote. In our Modern Hebrew records . . .'

'But where is this little footnote?'

She flicked through the pages, but could find nothing. 'No doubt it is somewhere in the Grammar. You see, these Persian records were made before the war. Now in our Hebrew recordings . . .'

However, I bought the records, and I must admit that they were worth the money. If I have not succeeded in making very good use of them, the fault is partly mine. For the sad truth is that, at the age of fifty-five, the brain is no longer a basin but a colander. If I learned ten words, a couple of days later I had forgotten eight or nine of them. It is a salutary thing for a teacher to be reminded from time to time of the difficulty of learning.

After I had worked at the records for a few weeks, I felt that the moment had come to try out my Persian on a native. I happened one evening to be dining with a friend at an Indian restaurant in London, and by good fortune our waiter, as I discovered towards the end of dinner, proved to be a Persian.

'*Farsi harf mizanid?*' he said.

'I beg your pardon?'

He repeated the phrase more slowly, and I guessed he must be asking if I spoke Persian. 'Oh well, I'm rather a beginner,' I said modestly.

'Say something in Persian, please.'

It was lucky that we were just ready for our coffee; I had the very sentence for the occasion.

'*Lotfan qahveh biyavarid,*' I said.

'I do not understand.'

I repeated the phrase, taking infinite pains with the 'q.'

'I understand that you wish me to bring you something. But *qahveh*? There is no such word.'

'*Qahveh*,' I repeated; '*qahveh*.'

'No, no. Say it please in English, sair.'

'Coffee.'

'Ah! You mean *qahveh*!'

'That's what I said. *Qahveh*.'

' 'Scuse me, sair, you said *qahveh*.'

And not the minutest shade of difference could I detect between his 'q' and mine. It was disheartening, and my friend had the bad taste to smile.

Now comes the strangest part of the story. I can hardly expect you to believe it: 'Man,' said Wilde, 'will believe the impossible, but not the improbable.' At this very instant there was a commotion at the next table: the leg of a chair had given way, bringing its occupant heavily to the ground. I sprang to my feet. '*An sandali shekasteh ast*,' I cried; '*najjar-ra biyavarid*' —'That chair is broken; fetch the carpenter.' That unpromising phrase from Lesson 4 had come unexpectedly into its own.

The waiter was delighted. '*Vairy* good, sair; *vairy* good! You speak Persian *par*fectly, sair.'

My friend stopped smiling and admitted that he was impressed. 'But it was odd,' he added ungenerously, 'that he didn't get that bit about the coffee.'

'Not really,' I said. 'To tell the truth, I didn't think much of his accent.'

2

London to Tehran

A MONTH today I shall be in Tehran. . . .

Three weeks today I shall be in Tehran. . . .

Today fortnight . . .

I feel as excited as a boy of fourteen crossing to Dieppe for the first time, excited as though I had never been abroad before, as though no one had ever been abroad before.

Like a stick nearing a cataract, *accelerando sempre*, the days rush madly by. They say the dying man will often glimpse the world beyond. So I, though corporeally still at Eton, am spiritually on the central Asian plateau. The daily scene is unreal, distorted, as though I were drugged. Everything seems exaggerated, unfamiliar.

'When are you off, sir?'

'Send me a postcard from Istanbul, sir.' (Go down two places!)

'Sir! When are you off, sir?'

'Send me a picture of the Taj Mahal, sir.' (Go down to bottom!)

'Sir! Sir! When are you off, sir?'

'But you *are* coming back, sir?' (Go to the top!)

In ten days' time I shall be . . .

A Sunday paper announces that I am going to Persia and Afghanistan under the aegis of the Royal Horticultural Society, to collect and reintroduce into Europe the lost *Iris persica*. (Thus is the casual gossip of a dinner-table caught up and magnified by the Press). Yes—I promised to keep an eye open for that iris, though heaven knows if I shall recognize it. But now I am believed to be a regular botanical expedition. By every post, letters arrive from irisophiles imploring me to search for improbable irises in impossible places. They invite an exchange of plants I shall never find for plants I could never grow. They urge me to take trowels and crowbars and polythene bags. The hue and cry is taken up by others too: 'Dear Sir, When you are in Afghanistan, would you be so kind as to observe what Russian books are selling in the bookshops of Kabul....'

Three days, two days, one day ...
Last night, I dreamed that I was being chased downhill by a flock of No. 27 buses.

February 28th

London Airport; the hour of Early School.
'Are you travelling with that gentleman, sir?'
The porter thumbed a large, red-faced man of about fifty, dressed in loud checks, who was propping up (or possibly being propped by; it was hard to tell which) a stout sack of golfing instruments. In his buttonhole he wore—rather superfluously, it seemed to me—a little circular metal badge decorated with the Union Jack. For he was something that, wherever he went —among Frogs and Wogs and Dagoes—would be for ever England.
'I hope ... I mean ... No.'
He was not what I was travelling *with*; he stood, indeed, for everything that I was travelling *from*, as fast as the fastest plane could take me.

'Weather conditions at Orly' delayed our departure, and two hours after taking off we found ourselves dumped without warning at Le Bourget. Six swarthy women bound for Madrid and Barcelona, who thus missed their connection, set up an Iberian wail and clamoured for the blood of Air France.
'*Mais, Mesdames, vous savez ce qu'on dit? "Air France, Air Chance."* There will be another plane tomorrow. And the day after. Paris is so beautiful. ...'
But not in this weather. An arctic blast cut through clothes as a knife cuts ripe Camembert. The Spaniards, lacking that rich complement of arms supplied by thoughtful Nature to Indian goddesses, grappled hopelessly with hats and coats and skirts and miscellaneous impedimenta. I, having no skirt, and with a good hour in which to reach Orly, was more fortunate.

Snowbound France, like a crinkled tablecloth, like a piece of white *batik*, spread below us—so lovely that we had no eyes for the air hostess who demonstrated the correct way to inflate a life-jacket, no ears for the air host (or whatever they call him) who lauded the remoter beauties of 'Mong Blong.'

Then clouds enveloped us. I turned to the bunch of pamphlets that Pan American provide for the amusement or edification of their clients. 'Pan American World Airways,' I read, 'is the recipient of many safety awards, but it is only sensible to face the fact that everyone who travels should be acquainted with emergency equipment and procedures.

'YOUR ROLE IN A WATER LANDING

'Loosen your collar and tie—remove glasses, pencils, pens or other sharp objects—ladies, take off those high-heeled shoes—KEEP ALL CLOTHING ON. . . .'

I searched myself in vain for any object sharper than a Biro.
'A short time before landing you will hear the command "Brace for ditching". . .'
Inspiring words! And how tame, by comparison, was the French equivalent. *'Préparez-vous pour l'amerissage'!*

The clouds dispersed, disclosing brown hillsides sparsely sprinkled with snow and looking like cabinet puddings sugared by an economical cook. Then the snow vanished, and the brown gave place to a gentler green—Italy. The air host was busy broadcasting the life story of Jason, who once did something or other on the coast at our feet. But I was thinking of all those Italian postmen who, according to our newspapers, were being daily devoured by wolves almost to the very gates of Rome.

There were no wolves at the Rome airport—only sunshine and unfamiliar warmth. I beguiled the forty-minute halt by conversing with a Czech priest who had graduated via Mount Athos to New York and was now on his way to Holy Week in the Holy Land. He wore the usual inverted coal-scuttle hat and patriarchal white beard, and his dusty stomach was enlivened by a large conch suspended from a rosary.

'Tell me, Father, did you like it on Athos?'

'I like better New York. And you, my son, you are a diplomat?'

We rose again into the darkening sky. Sunset gilded gloriously the cloud-tops a moment; then the world turned grey—a cold, aluminium grey that seemed a mere extension of the fuselage. The male passengers were reading *Life*, ordering martinis (at half a dollar a time), counting travellers' cheques and beginning to exchange autobiographies; a woman was doing something necessary but disagreeable to a baby. I preferred to think on Gissing and Douglas, who loved this Calabrian coast.

The Ionian Sea. Would there be light enough, would it be cloudless enough, to see the Isles of Greece? Alas, no! Not even a twinkle from the rocks.

At Beirut, where for the first time I put foot on Asian soil, the *Salle d'Attente* was decorated with murals of surf-bathers in bikinis and scenes from the Trojan War, newly painted by a local artist in a style fashionable in Paris in the early twenties. The figures were as wooden as the Horse of Troy.

Damascus. As we walked towards the airport buildings, my restless proof-reader's eye was disturbed by a giant notice which read, 'NO PHOTOGRAHING.' It would be hard to imagine anything drearier than the airport's *café chantant*, in which we were imprisoned for an hour. Its ceiling was festooned with paper streamers and lanterns, and the walls were painted with pictures in execrable taste; the subdued lighting suggested economy rather than romance; the waiters looked miserable, and the crooner was unspeakable. For only company there were two high-ranking American officers and their families, to whom I tried to be amiable and was monosyllabically snubbed. I had never before met rude Americans. I drank my tea in silence, awaiting release.

Then Damascus lay below us with its myriad lights. The moon, but two days past its full, was shining in a cloudless sky, and red tongues of flame spurted from the plane's engines. Alone now in the tourist-class cabin, I envied the Americans the comfort of their luxury seats. Someone turned down the lights. In the moonlight, the unending Syrian desert, like melted butter, stood motionless at my feet. Dozing fitfully, I missed both Euphrates and Tigris. At last the Zagros Mountains became visible ahead of us, their silver crests barring the approach to Persia.

Fantastic peaks, cold and cruel as in a lunar landscape, swift-moving after the sluggish desert, rose up to meet us. It might have been somewhere near Hamadan that black cloud squadrons advanced to blot out this grim picture; but over our heads the tranquil moon still shone. Then I must have slept; for suddenly I became conscious that the lights had been turned up and that the plane was losing height. I looked at my watch : it was just four o'clock. And it was snowing heavily; in a silent hail of white bullets, the big flakes bombarded the machine. Only a few hundred feet below us, two pale and blurred strings of light revealed that we were approaching the runway. I fastened my safety-belt, clutched my medal of St. Christopher, and braced myself for ditching.

But the pilot, liking the weather as little as I did, decided against landing. Not until he had three times circled the aerodrome did he finally take the plunge, to bring the machine faultlessly down upon the runway.

And thus, with the snowflakes whirling blindingly about me, shivering in the chill of an unwelcoming dawn, I entered the Land of the Lion and the Sun.

3

Tehran

AND Tim Marten was there, in a deer-stalker, to meet me! In such weather, at such an hour, to collect a total stranger; could kindness be carried further? It could, as I was soon to discover; the whole British Embassy in Tehran might have had no other *raison d'être* than to minister to my comfort and smooth my stony pathway across Iran.

Through such crowded snow as in Europe only falls in those pretty toys you shake, Tim [1] drove me to the flat of Max Peirotti, the British consul, who will put me up until there is room in the Embassy. This big kind welcoming man rose into a blue Chinese dressing-gown, plied me with coffee, and then sent me to bed until lunch-time. Reluctant I was, but too tired to protest.

On the wall of my bedroom was a Japanese nature-printed fish. [2]

It was still trying to snow as I summoned a taxi and drove round to the Embassy. Finding myself thus for the first time closeted with a real live local inhabitant, I decided to try the effect of my Persian on him. After careful rehearsal I said (with little immediate truth):

'The spring in Persia is very beautiful.'

(But what I really wanted to say was: 'Why does this taxi smell as though five goats have spent the night in it?')

There followed a copious reply, of which I only caught 'Spring . . . Tehran . . . sun . . . flowers . . . hot.' None the less, the general tenor of his answer was clear enough. In other words, I could understand Persian.

I followed up my success with: 'Tehran is a very beautiful

[1] I found it difficult to decide whether to refer to my friends by their Christian names or by their surnames. I came to the conclusion that it was best to write in each case what came most naturally. In using a Christian name, I am not attempting to emulate the forced heartiness of Television or the vulgarity of the cheap Press.

[2] Pressed flowers and leaves can be rolled with an inky roller, and a paper-print taken from them. Presumably one can do the same with a kipper.

city.' (But what I wanted to say was: 'No sane man would have attempted to overtake that Cadillac round a blind corner; for heaven's sake drive more carefully.')

The driver, suspecting now that he was dealing with a cretin whose mental age was about six, limited his reply to a monosyllable. I tried again:

'But Isfahan is more beautiful than Tehran.'

This apparently harmless remark must have got his patriotic goat. His foot flat down on the accelerator, he embarked upon an impassioned monologue of which I only caught the oft-repeated words: Tehran, Isfahan, Shah. Carried away by his own eloquence, he failed to notice a large pot-hole in the road. . . .

The British Embassy buildings stand in a large compound, in the stateliest imaginable grove of white-boled, white-stemmed, white-twigged oriental planes of fabulous beauty—improbable as the silvered branches of a Christmas florist. Avice Marten welcomed me in a drawing-room which Mayfair had engendered and Iran embellished: English cretonnes and Persian rugs, water-colours of the placid English countryside and miniatures of bloody Iranian battles, whisky from Scotland and pottery from Soltanabad—the British lion lying peacefully down with the Persian lamb. There was coffee and brandy; Avice sat on a low stool—fitting compromise, as it were, between Western chair and Eastern rug—and her kind bright laughter tinkled among the coffee-cups.

I am to move into the house on Friday.

Some social duty called Avice, and Tehran called me. For three hours, shivering, slithering in slush, I wandered at random through the heart of the city.

Modern Tehran is the creation of Reza Shah. The Shah, though he had never been farther afield than Ankara, had very clear ideas as to what a big European city was like. And Tehran must follow suit. 'An Opera House, a Stock Exchange, and *no camels*!' he thundered. But the Opera House, faultily conceived by an Iranian architect, could never be completed; the Stock Exchange was never begun. The camels, however, vanished—together with much that the Qajars built. For it was Agha Mohammad Khan, the eunuch founder of the Qajar dynasty, who in 1785 made Tehran the capital of Persia, and his nephew and successor, Fath Ali Shah, who continued to embellish it. Reza Shah's clearance included the twelve garishly tiled city gates, and also the ramparts which had been erected in 1871, in imitation of the Paris fortifications and chiefly with money sent from Europe for the Persian Famine Relief Fund. Now there are wide avenues that, but for the state of the macadam, recall South Kensington and are thronged with cars which seem to be practising for the *Mille Miglia*. The architecture—again one thinks of South Kensington—is varied and mostly unsatisfactory: oriental 'art nouveau,' mild flirtations with the Bauhaus, *mésalliances* with Persepolis and Ctesiphon, and the crumbling shell of the Germanic Opera House rub shoulders with a few really good modern Western buildings such as the white freestone and grey marble National Bank in the Avenue Ferdausi.

The main square (Maidan-e-Sepah) is a museum-piece of architectural disasters ranging from imitations of Italianate gothic and renaissance, by way of the Alhambra and the Grand Palais, to the neo-Classical and 'art nouveau.' In the centre of the square, on a pedestal decorated with bull-head capitals and reliefs of top-heavy Achaemenid warriors clutching large spears, is a statue of modern Iran's god, Reza Shah. Making all allowance for corruption, it is hard to see how the much-lauded railway station could have cost a million pounds. The police headquarters, in Achaemenid style, has provoked a popular joke about 'Persé-police.' These are the growing pains of an oriental city which is attempting simultaneously to 'go Western' and to foster the national architectural heritage.

Yet, leave the main thoroughfares, and there is still something to charm. There are balconied houses, sixty or seventy years old perhaps, which show that the Qajar style has a certain distinction; indeed, Qajar bric-à-brac must sooner or later inevitably find its patrons, as has Victorian bric-à-brac in London. Perhaps there will even be a revival of the Fath Ali Shah wasp-waist and beard. ('My dear, isn't it *Qajar*!')

The street scene is no longer 'colourful.' Nine-tenths of the population wear an approximation to European dress, and even in the bazaars, those last strongholds of the oriental way of life, the West perpetually encroaches. Many shop signs and advertisements are written in English and Persian, and, as in Greece, there is the perpetually diverting game of transliterating, say, 'Scholl's Foot Comfort' or 'Huntley and Palmer's Biscuits' (but in Greece the alphabet does at least meet one half-way). The people are friendly and polite. They do not stare, though one must look odd; they beg but little, for there are no tourists. Let us be thankful.

Perhaps the two things which most strike the traveller fresh from Europe are the stupendous street-end views of the snow-wall of the Elburz mountains, and the *'jubs,'* or open drains, which run along both sides of the principal streets like exaggerated and more perilous versions of Hobson's Conduit in Cambridge. Into these *jubs*, which serve the double purpose of collecting Tehran's refuse and providing most of its drinking water, it is not difficult to fall, and carelessly driven cars (as I was soon to discover) sometimes suffer the same fate. The British Embassy water, it should be explained, comes direct from the Elburz, hence the popular legend that the Persian for 'drinking water' is 'britishembassy.'

Such are my first impressions of Tehran; I had been told not to expect too much.

March 1st

The National Museum, disguised as a Sasanian palace, houses a superb collection of antiquities which is beautifully displayed in spacious halls. There was only one other visitor when I arrived; yet when I attempted to walk a few paces back in order to compare two objects, officious officials rushed up and stopped me. This kind of red tape makes me mad. As with Reza Shah's innumerable roundabouts, clockwise motion is presumably believed to be Western, and hence 'progressive'; the traffic, however, still goes the shortest way round.

Most exciting of the exhibits are the pots, a great chunk of Persepolis the colour of fried mushrooms, and the recently discovered gold plates—bright as new sovereigns—which record the foundation of Persepolis by Darius.

After tea, Tim took me the round of the antique shops near the Embassy—and very tempting they are. Magnificent pottery —the turquoise, lustre and polychrome bowls of Rai, the striped wares of Gorgan and the lustres of Kashan and Soltanabad—is

being dug up all the time, and sells at prices which, by Great
Russell Street standards, are absurdly low. (If only our one-
track-minded English studio-potters would give the Far East a
rest and turn for a change to Persia for inspiration!)

Manuscripts and miniatures, as I had already been warned,
are few here, poor and dear. There is some hideous modern
stuff, on paper so repulsive that even the blind could tell
it was worthless. The carpets—we had a great many out and
made knowing remarks about warp and woof and knots—did
not for the most part excite my cupidity. With overweight so
savagely charged, this is just as well.

But the pots! I shall dream of them tonight and pursue them
again tomorrow. Or rather, on Saturday; I have still to get used
to Friday being 'Sunday.'

March 2nd

Avice, the perfect hostess, in her goodness invited for drinks
three Persians who could be of help to me. First, Dr. Allevi, who
cured the eyes of certain immensely important *mollas*[1] at
Meshed. He has promised me introductions to the four most
influential men there; if they cannot get me inside the Gauhar
Shad Mosque, probably the finest surviving building in all Islam,
then no one can. Dr. Parsa, whom I had met at Kew, is Iran's
leading botanist; he will tell me where I can hope to find *Iris
persica*, and also give me a recipe for making sherbet. Mr.
Hannibal, in a smart dinner-jacket, is Russian by birth, though
now more Persian than the Persians. Already familiar to me
from the pages of Robert Byron, 'he is descended, like Pushkin,
from Peter the Great's negro, and is thereby cousin to certain
English royalties.' Mr. Hannibal will show me the Ethnological
Museum, of which he is Director; the royal Golestan Palace,
which eats out of his hand; and the ancient town of Qazvin,
which is so much his preserve that it is hard to believe that he
did not build it.

March 3rd

There is no guide-book to Tehran, though there are a few
pages on the sights of the town in Ebtehaj's unpurchasable

[1] Formerly a *molla* might be anyone versed in Islamic law; today he has
to have studied religion at an authorized theological school.

Guide Book on Iran, which I consulted in the Embassy library. Eventually I succeeded in buying a town plan—of a sort. The enormous value of Baedekers, tourist offices, bus and railway time-tables and so on—things which in Europe we take for granted—becomes daily more apparent. Without the help of the Embassy I really do not know how one could find anything, get anywhere.

I do not consider myself wholly imbecile, and I do know a few words of Persian; yet this morning, determined not to be helpless, I spent a full hour *failing* to buy a stamp. Then, finding I was completely lost, I took a taxi to the Ethnological Museum.

Mr. Hannibal greeted me at the door as though he were receiving royalty. With him was a tame dervish who appears to be part of the collection; he is the last snake-charmer in Tehran, but, unfortunately, had temporarily mislaid his snake. Nor did I have my camera with me. He would have made a splendid portrait.

Ethnological museums can be as depressing as English station waiting-rooms or—as in Munich—they can be thrilling. Mr. Hannibal has neither the space nor the money to make his museum immediately attractive : the rooms are dark, the exhibits crowded; had I been alone I would not have stopped long. But, with his infinite store of miscellaneous knowledge, he was able to bring the objects excitingly to life. The dervish went round with us, and in front of a large banner portraying the death of Hosain recited the interminable verses inscribed upon it. His engaging toothless smile, his tentative little chucklings, I shall not easily forget. But I wish he had had his snake.

The Martens being involved in a high-power diplomatic luncheon, I had promised to be out. I had hoped that Mr. Hannibal would be my guest, but he was already engaged. I therefore asked him to recommend me a native restaurant.

With its 'arty' tablecloths, its European chairs, tables and crockery, the place might have been an English suburban tea-shop. I plunged for a *kebab* and rice, which came garnished with garlic, eggs, fragments of a dry orange, and pieces of brown paper that turned out to be bread. I rejected Pepsi-Cola ('bottled by the Zamzam Bottling Company') in favour of *dugh*—the buttermilk that is universally drunk; it is thirst-quenching, and

Tilework in the Friday Mosque, Isfahan

Waiting for the doctor, Zangiabad

sufficiently nasty for one to feel that it must be doing one good. A blaring wireless emitted local music, followed by prayers; then Big Ben struck, and we were treated to selections from *Faust* and *Cavalleria Rusticana*. On the wall above my head was a picture that appeared to represent the Archbishop of Canterbury proposing to a Persian princess.

The bill came to the equivalent of three shillings and sixpence.

The antique shops called me.

I returned to one that had particularly aroused my curiosity; for I had noticed, tucked away in a pocket at the back of a portfolio, a handful of drawings that were obviously being withheld from me.

'They would not interest you,' said the dealer when I asked to see them. Knowing that fine pieces are often set aside for special clients, I insisted.

They were not what I had expected.

'What do you call such drawings in English?'

'Pornographic—very.'

I watched him write 'ponografikveri' in his notebook, for future reference. 'Is that O.K.?' he asked.

I let it stand. It was still an understatement.

'. . . An *iris*? They told me you were looking for an *heiress*!'

It was at a diplomatic cocktail party at Shemran, in a drawing-room furnished regardless of expense and taste. Two hundred people, perhaps, in this Tower of Babel, where French is spoken with an Italian accent; English with a Persian accent, a Swiss accent; German with American, Dutch, Swedish accents. . . . Every language except Persian. Everyone seemed madly delighted to find everyone else there. '*Ma chérie, comme tu es jolie ce soir* . . .' (kiss). 'Darling, how *absolutely* wonderful . . .' (double kiss). The total number of osculations exchanged must have run into four figures; the total quantity of gin consumed into dozens of gallons.

'What does England think about oil?' said an intense American woman to me, in American.

I had no idea. I can never bring myself to pretend to a knowledge of national or international topics of this kind. I told my *Américaine* that only one Englishman in a hundred thousand

was capable of thinking about oil, and that I was not one of
that brilliant minority. She then proceeded to tell me, at greatest
length, what I *ought* to think about oil. I turned off my mind
at the main, letting my surface thoughts wander among fields of
white lilies.

Near me I could hear a Pole saying to what might have been
a Spaniard : 'Never trust a man who wears green pants. . . .'

'Excuse me, I do not understand.'

'Er—*méfiez-vous toujours de quelqu'un qui porte le caleçon
vert.*'

'*Ah oui, mon ami—vous avez bien raison!*'

March 4th

I must describe these mornings, so improbable in their beauty.

The sky assumes (non-botanists, forgive me !) the precise blue
of *Gentiana Macaulayi*, the remembered blue of the 'morning
glory,' a colour approached—if at all—in English skies only by
an inch or two topping a rare sunset. And this astonishing shade
it retains the whole day through. The air is so rarefied that the
Elburz stands, a vertical whitewashed wall, barring the streets;
it is so invigorating that I feel I would like to walk a mile—
and that is twice what I ever feel like walking in England. The
loveliness of the white tracery, delicate as coral, of the oriental
planes against that gentian blue passes belief; no wonder that
Xerxes fell in love with one.[1]

From Xerxes to Hannibal. . . .

True to his word, Mr. Hannibal met me at the Golestan to
show me over the Palace.

I waited for him beside the garden throne-room. This is a
large veranda, open upon one side, discreetly glittering with glass
mosaic; more tasteful than a fun-fair though less so than the
Amalienburg, but sharing the gaiety common to those two otherwise disparate objects. The building is Qajar and dates from the
early part of the nineteenth century. The throne itself—it is
more like a 'throne of sleep'—is a lush affair in translucent
butter-coloured Yazd marble and upheld, like Solomon's, by
jins. Typical Qajar tilework—pastel-shaded and pretty in colour

---

[1] It seems he really did—see Aelian, Herodotus, and the text of Handel's
only-too-celebrated 'Largo.'

as a Marie Laurencin—decorates the façade of the wings of the veranda. The more I see of Qajar work, the more I like it; but no doubt Isfahan will cure me of a taste for what is, after all, unimportant and decadent, however superficially charming.

Passing through gardens ornamented with pools and cypresses we reached the Palace itself. A more gaudily flashing entrance hall and an unimposing stairway led us to the New Museum, built by Nasr-ed-Din Shah on his return, in 1873, from his first visit to Europe. The room is large and rather ugly, broken by bays faced with glass cases in which miscellaneous bric-à-brac, chiefly objects presented to the Shahs by Western monarchs, is displayed. Here porcelain jars and Swiss musical boxes jostle for breathing-space with meteorites and jewelled swords. Among the innumerable clocks is one of the cuckoo variety, the place of the bird being taken by a skimpily dressed houri who emerges at the hours to stomach-dance and buttock-waggle.

Many of the objects are such as are manufactured for the seduction of the feebler-minded kind of tourist visiting the European capitals and art centres—for example, miniature-mosaic views of Rome and Venice. From others, one felt that the words 'A Present from Brighton' must have been surreptitiously erased before dispatch. There are pompous gold-plated entrée dishes and ink-stands that ought to have come from City Companies (the ugliest and costliest of all, I noticed, was in fact the gift of the Corporation of the City of London). But there are rare things too.

Towards the end of the room hang some royal portraits, including an almost entirely blue one of Reza Shah by Mak (pronounced 'muck'). Hereabouts the Museum becomes transformed into an Aladdin's cave, the *pièce de résistance* of which is the famous Peacock Throne. Curzon considered it 'wrong'; I cannot remember, and do not greatly care, whether it is at the moment believed to be the genuine article or not. Genuine certainly is a large terrestrial sphere entirely encrusted with precious stones : Africa with rubies, India with amethysts, etc. It was said sixty years ago to be worth a million pounds.

Beneath the New Museum is a vaulted hall containing porcelain and some interesting work by Qajar artists. I wish I had made a note of the name of the painter of a splendid picture of a portly eunuch leading two tiny children by the hand.

The lofty twin-towered pavilion called Shems-el-Emaret is really better seen from the street, as I discovered later on my way to the bazaars. There I wandered for an hour, watching the ebb and flow of native life and regretting the growing intrusion of the West; for the real thing I must wait until Isfahan, Shiraz and—if my luck holds—Herat.

Walking homewards through a little-Westernized quarter I saw the public letter-writers plying their trade, the sellers of *kebabs* roasting their skewered meat-scraps over glowing charcoal, and the makers of bread throwing the floury paste upon red-hot pebbles. Here more of the women were in native dress —the blue, white-spotted *chador* which envelops them almost completely, a corner held in the mouth concealing all but a fraction of the face. I came also upon two savage street-fights, which seemed at least one too many for a shortish walk.

I was farther from home than I realized; eventually, no taxi being visible, I found and bravely took a bus, though I have a feeling that this method of transport is not considered quite proper in Embassy circles. I was interested to see that men gave up their seats to women, and would have done so myself had standing been possible for someone of my height.

The British Embassy has exactly the appearance of a lesser English public school. Designed some eighty years ago by Major Pierson, R.E., of the Indo-European Telegraph Department, the houses are constructed of faded apricot brick in that Victorian Romanesque style which so cunningly combines piety with economy. The chancery, with its insistent clock tower, must of course be the school chapel. High enclosing walls, and lodge gates guarded by a vigilant porter, complete the illusion.

In their privet-hedged maisonettes live the housemasters, their wives (but how can they dress so well on those slender salaries?) and their children. Eager young assistant masters and school messengers with sheaves of examination papers in their hands rush backwards and forwards across the plane-shaded quadrangle. A Rolls-Royce is drawn up outside what is clearly the headmaster's house. It must be term time.

But where are the boys?

It set me thinking—this boyless academy—of the similarities and dissimilarities of the worlds of diplomacy and education.

Why, for example, should diplomats be perpetually on the move, whereas schoolmasters and dons remain stationary or even stagnant? How good for us might it not be if every four or five years we were ruthlessly winkled out of our cosy shells!

How good. But how distasteful!

March 5th

Two immense bearded Americans straight off an Assyrian bas-relief, and a little English maiden—incongruous trio!—have arrived here from Herat. The Americans spoke of the incredible isolation of the place and the terrifying aspect of its inhabitants —immense bearded men, they said. Their car broke down at nightfall near the Afghan frontier and they were obliged to beg shelter (it was wet and bitterly cold) in a black tent where they woke next morning to find themselves chiefly among camels. The maiden—needless to say she is writing a book—is dashing back to Buckingham Palace to be presented.

I am now more than ever determined to get to Herat.

Thought for today: 'Payments for marks are a chief source of income to [Persian] professors' (Groseclose, *An Introduction to Iran*).

March 6th

Avice drove me this morning up to Golahek, where, in a delightful wood about seven miles from Tehran and seven hundred feet higher than the capital, the British Embassy has its summer quarters. In the good old days the Embassy moved up here *en bloc* at the beginning of June; now the ruinous state of certain houses in both compounds makes this impossible, and most of the secretaries are obliged to choose a permanent home in one or the other. To fry in summer, or to shiver in winter? Electric fans and refrigerators have done much to mitigate the discomfort of hot days in the capital, and the nights there are always cool. On this turquoise morning, air crisp and a silver sun, the charms of Golahek may well seem almost irresistible. But I know neither Golahek in January nor Tehran in August.

Dr. Parsa came to dinner with his wife and son. The Doctor babbles amiably; having consulted his own book, he reports upon the habitat of *Iris persica*, which should grow in the very suburbs of Tehran. His family have not half a dozen words of English between them.

Parsa brought with him the promised recipe for making sherbet, which I give in his own words :

SHARBAT

1. To take the Juice of the fruit
2. To boil the shugar or cane
3. To clean the sugar by the white of egg; the impurity of the sugar (liquid) will be absorbed by the white of egg
4. The froth is gathered & thrown away
5. Before cistallisation of sugar (when it is going to be elastic) Juice of fruit is added to it
6. Little vanilla is added too

March 7th

The cricket nets are out in the Embassy compound. It is time that I left. . . .

4

Isfahan

March 8th

Vers Ispahan—by air!

Iranian Airways are manned by Americans. The planes—I
forget their make—are American also; since they are not
equipped to be 'talked' up or down, they can only take off or
land when weather conditions are perfect. Nor are they
pressurized.

My plane was delayed in starting. I sat in the airport waiting-
room, studying a map of Iran upon which an optimistic
draughtsman had inscribed a network of imaginary air-lines, and
trying with little success to decipher the Persian notices. My
fingers clutched three luggage tickets bearing the legend 'This
is *not* the luggage ticket/baggage check described by the
Warsaw Convention article 4.'

Even after we had boarded the plane, there was some further
delay while a young American mechanic, armed with a hammer,
scrambled about the wings. But at last everyone appeared satisfied, and the homely little machine scuttled down the runway
and took the air.

There below us, as we sucked the ritual acid drop, lay the
wide tawny plains and the lavender mountains and, to our north,
the white barrier of the Elburz and the distant, prim little cone
of mighty Demavend. Now for the first time I saw the shaft-
heads of the famous *qanats* (underground water-conduits),
punctuating the plain like perforations in paper.

The colours were incessantly changing. Now a grape-bloom
descended upon the hills, now came golden sand; here and there
a fleck of emerald accompanied the brown thread of a water-
course. We traversed a salt-lake twice the size of Hampshire and
headed for a range of snow-covered mountains. The plane
cleared them by a few lazy feet, to reach a buff mud-flat
upon which a billion golf balls had been neatly laid at nine-inch

intervals. Then little rectangles of green began to reappear, with
scattered mud huts and the criss-cross lines of cultivation.

'You ought soon to be able to see the dome of the Masjed-e-
Shah [Royal Mosque],' said my neighbour.

I turned sharply in my seat and strained impatiently forward
to catch my first view of the longed-for city. As I did so, I felt
a sudden, piercing pain in the small of my back. When, five
minutes later, we landed, I found that I could barely
move.

It is undignified to make one's first entry into an unknown
hotel almost on all fours, but there was no alternative. When
they discovered that I was human, and not some escapee from
the Tehran zoo, the staff of the Irantour were kind and understanding. Thinking that I might be able to send round to the
chemist for medicine, I asked the manager (who speaks good
English) what the Persian for 'lumbago' was. He had no idea;
obviously he had never seen a man in this posture before.
I crawled to my suitcase and got out Miss Lambton's dictionary. Miss Lambton must suffer from rude health: she
gives no word for 'lumbago,' 'rheumatism,' 'sciatica,' or any
of the complaints from which ordinary mortals intermittently
suffer. Even 'plague' she refers to 'pestilence,' and many
a victim may well have died before he could bring himself to
make that extra effort. Diarrhoea, that distressing but almost
universal complaint in Iran, is conspicuous in her pages by its
absence (lucky Miss Lambton!). How gladly would one exchange
'pigeon-fancier,' 'parasitologist' or even 'milch-cow' for information of a more practical kind!

Seeing that I was getting nowhere, I ordered a taxi—into
which I was half pulled, half pushed—and set off for the nearest
chemist. Hardly had I grovelled into the shop before I found
myself possessed of an English remedy, '——'s Lumbago
Plaster,' which, though it temporarily relieved the pain, had
within a few hours also relieved me of most of the skin on my
back.

Encouraged now by the glowing warmth that the plaster
engendered, I told the taxi to proceed to the Maidan, the great
central Square of Isfahan, where it deposited me, more dead
than alive, beside the entrance to the Royal Mosque.

A digression—and why not?

I once knew two old spinster sisters who lived in Cambridge. They were very poor. They lived on air and memories, and it seemed that nothing more exciting was ever likely to happen to them than to be accorded a passing mention in a book by Gwen Raverat. And then, quite unexpectedly, they were left a little legacy. It wasn't really enough to invest, even in an annuity: just enough for a 'fling.' So they decided to blue the lot and achieve their lifelong ambition : to see the Niagara Falls.

I lunched with them soon after they got back.

'Well, how was it—I mean, how were they?' I said.

Kate, as always, was the spokeswoman. 'We looked, and we looked,' she answered sadly, 'and we were only surprised that it wasn't bigger.'

They were both dead before the year was up. Niagara killed them, just as surely as it killed those tight-rope walkers and barrel-rollers who plunged into its icy waters.

I had often wondered if Isfahan would be like that. For so long had I dreamed of its blue domes and glittering tiled portals; would I be disappointed? It was a moment of intense excitement.

I would not yet look at the Maidan, nor even at the great *ivan* (portal) that gives access to the Mosque; I wanted my first impression to be that of the court itself—for this, before all else, was what I had come to Persia to see. Still bowed with pain, I passed beneath the high portal into the flowery-domed vestibule, turned to the right (for I knew the way by heart), emerged in the court, agonizingly straightened my back and looked about me.

The prospect surpassed in splendour my wildest imaginings (can it be that physical pain enhances aesthetic sensibility?). Whatever I may see hereafter in Iran that shall be purer in form (the Friday Mosque here?), richer in colour (the Gauhar Shad Mosque at Meshed?) or more brashly glittering (the Shrine at Qom?)—nothing can provoke greater ecstasy than I experienced at that moment. The dream of a lifetime had been realized.

Let me try to keep calm, be factual. Built in the early years of the seventeenth century, the Royal Mosque is the crowning architectural achievement of Shah Abbas (the great monarch who made Isfahan his capital and transformed a relatively unimportant Persian city into the most magnificent metropolis

of his day. The four sides of the rectangular court are walled by
two-storeyed arcades broken in the centre by towering portals;
the largest of these—that in the south-west wall—is flanked by
two minarets and leads to the sanctuary, above which rises the
immense turquoise dome. The entire surface of the walls and
portals is tiled, and though many colours have been used, the
dominant tone is a soft blue—the French powder-blue of love-
in-a-mist. They stood, these intricately arabesqued walls, like the
pages of some gigantic illuminated manuscript, the sunlight
falling upon them and throwing into mysterious shadow the
arched vaulting of the portals and the chambers beyond; and in
the tank where the pilgrims were performing their ritual ablutions the whole blue miracle was softly repeated.

Again I am being carried away. Facts! Eighteen million bricks,
half a million tiles. . . . But such figures are meaningless here—
cannot convey the magnitude, the bravura, the pomp of it all.
And this, according to Robert Byron, is the 'huge acreage of
coarse floral tilework' which forms 'just that kind of "oriental"
scenery so dear to the Omar Khayyam fiends'! To admit
admiration for the Royal Mosque, to lavish praise upon
Mendelssohn's fiddle concerto, is to confess oneself a hopeless
romantic, blind or deaf to the higher merits of classical form.
So let it be: I will go my own perverse, unfashionable way.
When I have seen the more respectable Mongol and Timurid
buildings, then it will be time enough to confess that my first
fine raptures were misplaced.

The axis of the Maidan is north-south; that of the Mosque
must lie north-east and south-west in order that the *mehrab*
(prayer niche) may be in alignment with Mecca. This change of
direction, brilliantly manipulated here, gives variety to what
might otherwise be—and in many mosques indeed is—an excessive symmetry. Thus the view from the entrance hall strikes
diagonally across the turquoise-floored oratory and the court,
and from the Maidan no part of the court is visible—as visitors
to Isfahan in earlier, more fanatical days knew to their regret.

The unexpected beauty of this angular view from the entrance
hall detained me when at last I tore myself away from the
glories of the court. I stopped also to admire—who could not?
—the portal that faces the Maidan: an arch nearly ninety feet
high, hung with clustered stalactites glittering with reflected sun-

light (for it faces due north). Then I passed into the Maidan.

To anyone who has read about Isfahan, the first sight of the Maidan is bound to come as something of a shock. Here Shah Abbas and his courtiers played polo (the goal-posts still stand), and for three centuries it had remained a vast, dusty, open Square—perhaps the largest in the world. Now some dead municipal hand with itching Western fingers has planted it with geraniums and begonias, and set it about with seats that might have—perhaps did—come straight from Woods of Taplow, and ought to have

> *Speak not—whisper not;*
> *Here bloweth thyme and bergamot*

inscribed on them.[1]

Yet I ought not to be too ungrateful, for I crawled and sank into one of those not uncomfortable seats (rare commodities in a land of heel-squatters) and, once more painfully lifting my eyes above begonia level, took stock of the scene before me.

The Square—it is, in fact, a very elongated rectangle—is enormous, the perimeter being little short of a mile. On the west side rises the Ali Qapu—the pavilion, leading to the royal palace, from whose shady terrace Abbas and his courtiers used to watch the pageantry of the Maidan; to the east is the Shaikh Lotfollah Mosque, built by Abbas to the glory of his saintly father-in-law; to the south stands the entrance to the bazaar; all these I shall visit as soon as I am well. For the moment, I contemplate with pleasure the Lotfollah's buff and turquoise saucer-dome, the slender columns of the Ali Qapu, and the double-tiered white-and-blue arcade that runs the whole circuit of the Square. The Maidan of Isfahan has been described as the most impressive Square in the world; it is hard to suggest a rival.

My reflections were interrupted by the arrival of a group of boys released from a nearby school. They wore, as do most students, an approximation to Western dress. Crowding amiably round me, they showed me their botany textbooks and their English primers. One proceeded to recite Gray's 'Elegy';

[1] Mr. Christopher Sykes has since told me that the authorities originally planned to build large blocks of flats in the centre of the Maidan. This outrage was prevented by M. André Godard, the French Director of Antiquities, to whom Iran owes so much. The municipal garden was a compromise.

another was entangled in Wells's *The Country of the Blind*, and asked for enlightenment. I did what I could; though a one-eyed man, here I was King.

They were pleasant, ingenuous boys, and I hoped I should meet them again. In fact I did not. But throughout my time in Persia I was to see much of its youth. This was the result rather of their initiative than of mine, for foreigners are still sufficiently rare to have remained objects of considerable interest. But I would not have had it otherwise; I like the young. My chief regret was the impossibility of ever exchanging a single word with Persian girls. Of the few Persian women whom I met, only two or three had even a smattering of any European tongue.

Bishop Thompson, Anglican Bishop of Iran, lives in the Mission compound, which is only a fit man's stone-throw from the Irantour Hotel. I surprised him reading *Pietro's Pilgrimage*, which served as a better introduction, perhaps, than my letter from a friend of a friend of the Bishop's. He and Mrs. Thompson made me very welcome; but his house is full, and I must return for the present to the Irantour.

On my way back to the hotel, a man tried to sell me two white hens.

By European standards the Irantour is simple, and Baedeker would not accord it many asterisks; for Iran it is no doubt well above average, and its garden is charming. The rooms are spacious and clean, and though the lavatories are of Sasanian simplicity there are actually some that boast a throne; the rest involve a technique that the feeble-kneed and lumbaginous can never satisfactorily master. Ebtehaj's statement, that a 'modern sanitary system has not been completely installed in the country,' is less than the truth, as the least fastidious traveller will soon discover. As for the food, I would rather describe it as 'interesting' and leave it at that. The American visitors too, of whom there are several, must find it all a change from the motherland.

March 9th

It is not every morning that one wakes to see a bishop at one's bedside. Or rather, to sense the episcopal presence, for I had taken so many sleeping pills to ease the pain that I was still three-quarters doped. When I had struggled into my clothes, I went along to his house to fix an appointment with the English mission doctor, Peter Wild. If he fails me, I shall advertise for a witch-doctor.

The Bishop's garden was full of yellow jonquils, primroses (from Mazandaran), and almond just breaking into flower. As I sat on the veranda, drinking in the beauty of the spring morning, a young Persian convert appeared and extracted ten *tomans* from me for the '*colporteurs* of the Gospel' (quick work!). I had always thought that *colporteurs* were persons who man-handled large crates at Covent Garden market, and was sorry to meet no more than one of their collecting agents.

Swift on his heels came another youthful convert, Akbar Navid, who is, he tells me, half-way through *Lorna Doone*. Brave fellow! That is a good deal farther than I ever got.

Then the Bishop appeared and conducted me across the complicated courtyards of the compound to Dr. Wild's house.

I have frequently been told that readers of travelogues do not wish to hear of the sufferings endured by their authors. I cannot agree. To learn, as I sit with a book in a comfortable arm-chair by the fireside, that its author has icicles in his beard and is about to be eaten by wolves, quite doubles my pleasure. And in any case, having undergone so much on their behalf, an author is surely entitled to linger over his anguish as long as he chooses.

But of mine there is little more to relate. Wild is by general consent a first-rate doctor and a brilliant surgeon. I could tell by the way he ripped off that plaster that he knew his job. He re-established my self-confidence by assuring me that I had not, as I half feared, slipped a disc; then, with a couple of swift and painlessly administered injections, he restored me immediately to a state in which I could stand almost as vertical as *pithecanthropus erectus*.

Wild has been fourteen years in Persia, eleven of them at Kerman. Like Marco Polo,[1] he has some alarming stories to tell of the properties of Kerman water. And Kerman is on my itinerary!

[1] *Travels*. Everyman ed., p. 69.

I found myself wondering, as I stood once again this afternoon in the blue glory of the Royal Mosque, how I should feel if I suddenly received news that the College Library at Eton had been burnt to the ground or that the N.S.P.C.C. had cajoled Parliament into decreeing the Wall Game illegal; I mean, some major cataclysm at home. Would I still be able to digest my lunch? Would I sleep the less?

I only know that distance induces a curious detachment. When, safely in England, one reads of famine in China, flood and desolation in the Ganges Valley, death and destruction in Bolivia, these things seem so much less real than a bicyclist killed in Maidenhead or a burglary accomplished in Slough. It is precisely the creating of this state of detachment that is so rejuvenating. It is why I wanted to get away.

March 10th

Navid, the young Doone fan, has firmly attached himself to me. After breakfast, he came round to the Irantour to take me to see the Shaking Minarets. He also brought a kind note from Mrs. Thompson, inviting me to move into their house this evening.

Navid's enthusiasm to learn (though combined with a certain stubbornness) is fantastic. Hard to imagine an English boy of seventeen so eager. Before I can wish him (in my best Persian) a good morning, he asks, 'What is a philomath, please?'

'A philomath? Oh, well—someone who loves—(Greek $\phi\iota\lambda\omega$, I love)—who loves . . . well, mathematics, do you think?'

'No—I do not.'

'It isn't a very common word. Where did you come across it?'

'In this ah-tickle. I will now read to you. "The introduction of inoculation . . ." '

'One moment,' I said. 'It is "árticle," not "ah-tickle." '

'This ah-tickle says: "The introduction of inoculation . . ." '

The lesson at an end, we set out in a taxi for the Shaking Minarets. I noticed that a photograph of the driver's son obscured the speedometer. Car-drivers in Isfahan are utterly reckless, and immense 'safety first' posters showing a giant Death, in a burnous, banging two little cars together and shaking out the victims into a sea of blood, apparently do nothing to help.

Never was there a drearier tourists' 'stunt' than these two
ugly little turrets which crown a mosque on a dusty road expen-
sively far from the town. (Visitors, save your money!) A man goes
a few feet up one turret and wriggles a bit, and the other turret
shakes; then he rushes down again and demands a huge tip. It
is no more of a miracle than finding that a large rocking-horse
rocks. Navid is disappointed at my lack of enthusiasm. But his
mind is chiefly on higher things. 'What,' he asks, 'is the meaning
of "tintinnabulation"?'

Half-way along the Chahar Bagh—the magnificent avenue,
lined with four rows of plane trees, that Abbas drove through
the heart of his capital—stands the College of the Mother of the
Shah, built by Soltan Hosain at the beginning of the eighteenth
century. Being 'late,' and therefore 'decadent,' it has received
less than its fair share of praise, though Curzon considered it
'one of the stateliest ruins,' and Mr. Upham Pope 'the last construction that in any sense deserves the qualification "great",'
in Persia. It has now been admirably restored as a national
monument, and though no longer in use as a college is still open
for prayer.

With its four portals and turquoise-domed sanctuary, the
College follows the usual mosque plan. The rooms of the students
overlook the court, those of the officers of the College being
situated in four minor courts at the corners of it. The tilework
is light-hearted but not vulgar, and there is some enchantingly
delicate tracery in the arcades. The main doors are covered with
embossed silver plaques, partly gilded. But the feature which
gives the College its peculiar charm is the splendid group of
white-stemmed plane trees, whose still leafless twigs, a silver
filigree against the velvet darkness of the prayer chambers, are
reflected in the long marble tank. The College is smaller and less
magnificent than the Royal Mosque, but it has more 'atmosphere'; one could sit for hours (and I shall) in its calm silent
court, so near to—yet so sheltered from—the clamorous bustle
of the Chahar Bagh.

While dodging, in a clockwise direction, round the bole of a
large plane tree to get a photograph unobserved, I bumped
shoulders with a young German who was up to the same trick

but rotating widdershins. He carried me off to meet the friend with whom he is bicycling round the world. They gave me their card:

ALL OVER THE WORLD	AUTOUR DU MONDE
WALTER HAMANN	
MERCHANT AND JOURNALISTE	
HAGEN RODER	
ELECTRICAL ENGINEERING AND PHOTOREPORTER	
GERMANY-ALLEMAGNE	
Malente-Gremsmühlen	Mülheim-Ruhr
Postf. 3.	Bergstr. 18

They have been four months on the road, and are allowing themselves four years for five continents. They carry a type-writer, sleeping-bags, tents and heaven knows what else on their specially designed bicycles (which unfortunately I did not see). Charming, good-looking young men—well dressed, well washed, well shaven. How do they manage to remain so spick and span with such slender resources? No doubt we shall hear more of them—if they ever get back alive. But how can they hope (as they do) to write about it all? If they complete the course, their book could be nothing more than a string of place names—a mere gazetteer.

Bicycling across Asia is nothing new. In 1886, Major Yate met an American in Herat whose 'iron horse' so alarmed the Afghans that they put him back over the Persian border. Almost every year, the Embassies of Tehran are besieged by legless motorists and female tricyclists on their way to Calcutta or Hong Kong.

The Bishop's house is a spacious, airy building, agreeably cool in summer but I suspect a bit draughty in January.

> *Do not grumble, do not grouse;*
> *After all, it's not your house.*

Someone had told me that I should find this inspiring couplet framed in my bedroom, but I did not; no doubt it was in one of the other spare rooms. In any case, no one who stays with the Bishop and Mrs. Thompson could have the slightest desire to complain. Their kindness and hospitality are in the best traditions of both Christianity and Islam. The Bishop, who is seventy (says *Crockford*, so we may suppose it is no secret), began life as an Indian Army engineer. He has worked in Persia for more than forty years, and his wife was born in the country; they have both given themselves unsparingly to the furtherance of Christianity in Iran.

It cannot have been easy for the missionaries, for Islam does not welcome proselytism and converts find life difficult. (This is only to be expected; had I, for instance, become a Moslem my own career would obviously have suffered.) I do not know how many converts have been made, nor what admixture of motives may have governed their conversion; but I imagine that the number is very small, and that the example of Christian lives has been the primary stimulus. Whatever one's views may be as to the advisability, or desirability, of attempting to proselytize in a land where the national religion has served it well for thirteen centuries, one cannot fail to be impressed by the integrity and devotion of the missionaries themselves. But I could not help wondering whether these converts imagine that the English and the Christian way of life are identical, and that they are seeing a representative cross-section of it. Do they, for example, suppose that family prayers, grace before meals, church twice on Sundays, teetotalism and abstinence from tobacco are the rule in every English household? Do they realize that the best strawberries have been put on the top of the basket? A visit to London might be a disillusioning experience.

The Mission, after innumerable postponements, celebrated Christmas this evening with a fork supper followed by paper games. The Bishop scraped home to win the 'Hidden Books' competition, though he failed to spot 'Hosea' in the picture of a young man displaying a pair of socks. Miss Mills was indignant when 'One Pair of Feet' was disallowed. The 'Pairs' game proved easier; 'Fortnum and ——,' the missing word to be supplied and the judges' decision final. 'Mustard and Pepper,' with no marks for 'Mustard and Cress,' seemed a little hard, and there was sympathy for the Bishop's clerical Iranian son-in-law, who had put 'Mustard and Faith.' A merry evening. Three cheers for the winners, and so to bed.

March 11th

I set off in a droshky for the Friday Mosque, which lies at the farthest end of the bazaar.

Looking at these ancient vehicles, one might imagine that all the cabs of Edwardian London had come to Isfahan to die. But how brave and smiling a face they put on death! The trappings are tattered but gaudy; the steeds are parti-stained a gay orange with henna, and their harnesses—of course they will die in harness—glitter and jingle with metal studs and little bells. I thought of those painted old harridans with dyed hair and a plethora of bangles who tinkle up and down Jermyn Street.

There is a flat charge of a shilling.

The Friday[1] Mosque in any Persian city will usually be found to be the earliest in date, the largest, and not infrequently the most interesting; that in Isfahan is an epitome of Persian architectural development over a period of little less than a millennium.

And perhaps even longer. But whatever vestiges may survive of earlier foundations, for practical purposes the two brick dome-chambers, both dating from the end of the eleventh century, are among the oldest remaining parts of the Mosque. Drab, dusty, crumbling, they make no immediate appeal to the lover of the picturesque; but even the uninitiated will soon sense something of the serenity of the structure, the perfect resolution (especially in the smaller dome-chamber) of the problem of setting a circular dome upon a square base. Mr. Eric Schroeder[2] well estimates the magnitude of the achievement of these Seljuq architects:

'European dome-builders never approached their skill. How ingeniously the Western builder compensated his ignorance of

[1] Strictly speaking, the 'enveloping' (i.e., the principal) mosque. The closely related word for 'Friday,' the day when all the people are 'enveloped' in the mosque, is frequently used in its place. I am indebted to Mr. Alan Trott for this information.

[2] *A Survey of Persian Art*, ed. by Upham Pope; p. 1008.

the mechanics of dome-construction is attested by the ten chains round the base of St. Peter's, and the concealed cone which fastens the haunch of St. Paul's. But engineers could not hope to prescribe an ideally light dome of plain masonry before Newton's work on the calculus.

'The Seljuqs, however, had *solved* the difficulties which Wren *avoided*. Not that they knew anything of the calculus : their knowledge was empirical. But by courageous experiment and intelligent observation of failure the Seljuqs built in the twelfth century what is practically the ideal dome, made possible by the advance of mathematical science in the eighteenth.'

The Mongol contribution is best studied in the brilliant incised plasterwork of the *mehrab* (dated 1310) in the sanctuary of Uljaitu. Both this and the dome-chambers are hidden in the immense vaulted labyrinth which spreads in all directions around the court—a court larger than that of the Royal Mosque. No real conception of the enormous area covered by the buildings is possible without a full explanation of this forest of pillars, of which Mr. Upham Pope provides an excellent plan.

The buildings round the court, it has recently been discovered, are structurally of the twelfth century, but all that is visible is Timurid and Safavid, with who can tell how much of reconstruction and repair. One enters from the street by way of a dark, mean little tunnel, to emerge suddenly into the vast sunlit courtyard, richly tiled, a-flutter with doves. The worshippers, except on a Friday, will be few; there is a sense of infinite peace. I came here this morning with Mr. Honafar, the Director of the Chehel Sotun and a leading authority on the buildings of Isfahan. With us was a party of Iranians, and explanations were in Persian; no doubt I missed much, but nothing could diminish my enjoyment of the silent loveliness of the place. A shower had fallen, adding lustre to the tilework and undreamed-of beauty to the translucent Yazd marble, perhaps the most exquisite building material in the world.

I was on my way back from the Friday Mosque when he accosted me.

'I say, you alone?'

He looked like a rather seedy version of Haile Selassie. His eyes had a dangerous glint.

'I say, you alone?'

'I don't want anything, thank you.'

'I don't want to give you nothing, sir. I nephew of Arch-bishop of ——, late Archbishop. I like English peoples, I like talking English peoples, I teach English to boys, terrible boys, I like Longfellow, "Life is real, life is earnest," Longfellow better than Omar-e-Khayam, Omar-e-Khayam all drink all women dirty book, Armenians do not like talk about Omar-e-Khayam. . . .' As he spoke, he clutched the lapel of my coat, brushed dust from my shoulder, patted my arm, poked me playfully in the stomach. A crowd began to collect.

'Let's go and drink a cup of tea somewhere,' I said desperately.

He knew the very place, which proved to be the hotel in which he was living. He led me upstairs to a room containing nothing but four beds, dirtier than any *rubai* of Omar Khayyam known to me. A small table, two chairs, two cups of tea and a pot of carnations were brought for us.

It was education that he wished to discuss, and when he discovered that I was a schoolmaster he was enchanted.

'What is your school?'

'Eton College.'

He had not heard of it. 'Big school?' he inquired.

'Yes—eleven hundred and fifty boys.'

'And how much girls?'

His contention—his turban-bee—was that Persian youths sent abroad for their education went to France, Germany, Switzer-land and America, but never to England. Were they sent to England, then all Anglo-Iranian problems would be solved for ever. He implored me to go at once (there was nothing I more wished to do) and write two letters to England: one to the Prime Minister in general terms, the other to the Head Master of Eton telling him that he must take a hundred Persian boys into the school next autumn. They would, of course, receive their education free; why haggle over a few thousand pounds when the whole future of Great Britain in the Middle East was at stake?

'If only I were Prime Minister . . .' he said.

A waiter, dressed in blue-and-white striped pyjamas, pre-sented the bill and seemed to demand immediate settlement.

'Probably you will wish to pay,' said the late Archbishop's nephew.

Probably I did.

In the afternoon I visited with the Bishop the School of Arts and Crafts—an impressive modern building in which a handful of boys were being instructed along lines current in academic Paris studios fifty years ago : endless copying, laboriously hatched shading. The teacher's own work—miniatures in the Safavid manner—served for the most part as models and remained his major interest. When I tried to look at what his boys were doing I was perpetually diverted by an 'Attend, please! This also is mine.' He would like me to recommend some books on teaching art; but I doubt whether books would help. A couple of years in London or Paris *might* do the trick. . . .

Contemporary Persian art consists almost exclusively of pastiches of Timurid and Safavid miniatures; sloppy water-colour landscapes and architectural scenes on very rough paper, in the French manner, and excruciating oil-paintings executed in crudest colours with the help of black-and-white reproductions in nineteenth-century *Salon* catalogues. Odd how a great tradition can decline into such sterility. It is the same in Japan, except that Japanese artists are more skilful in plundering the West.

The evening service in the little mission church—for today is Sunday—was in Persian. I caught a few words here and there, including my own name and those of Dr. and Mrs. Cochrane, American Presbyterian missionaries from Meshed who have also just arrived to stay with the Bishop. Missionary work in Persia is partitioned : American Presbyterians in the north, C.M.S. in the south.

It is rather on my conscience that I cut the English service and the Bishop's sermon this morning.

March 12th

Bath in a hip-bath, filled from Ali Baba jars, at 7 a.m. It took me back to my childhood.

After breakfast came family prayers in the Prayer Room—

another link with the past. Formal prayers and readings from the Bible were followed by extempore prayers by the Bishop ('for our brethren in Egypt') and Mrs. Thompson, then by Dr. and Mrs. Cochrane. This is not really my line, and it was with some apprehension that I heard Mrs. Cochrane perorate, realizing that my turn came next. The Bishop, with perfect episcopal tact, allowed exactly the right interval to elapse : an interval long enough for me to extemporize if I so wished, yet not so long as to create an embarrassing vacuum. I was grateful.

When I was a child, the word 'bazaar' connoted something inexpressibly tedious that my grandmother had just opened, where with the half-crown I had been given to spend I was soon cajoled into buying a shilling object that I did not want. But comes a happier moment when the overtones of the word assume the romance of the Orient.

Bazaar life is much the same throughout Islam, and the bazaars of Isfahan differ no more from those of Fez than does one English public school from another. The clothes, the funny hats may vary from place to place, but the ethos, the pattern of existence are everywhere alike. What is here written of the bazaars of Isfahan will doubtless also serve for those that I hope to see elsewhere.

A labyrinth of dusky, high-vaulted tunnels, illuminated only by shafts of light falling through circular apertures in the roofs. Falling? They *stand*, it seems—solid as Norman pillars. Eyes soon grow accustomed to this cool twilight, and ears at last to clamour. And there is much work for the nose : the smell of spices, of leather, of calicoes, of camel dung, of charcoal braziers, of herbs, of paper notebooks, of grilled meat, of cheese, of linseed oil, of humanity.

'Mind your backs!' (but no one says it) as a man with twenty-seven chairs on his shoulders pushes his way through the crowd.

In little recesses the size of large dog-kennels the merchants are bowed over their illegible accounts. Children dirty but beautiful, tiny as gnats, hammer great cauldrons in the bazaar of the coppersmiths; the noise is like Stravinsky's *Rites of Spring* heard over an Italian loud-speaker. Tiny figures in inner darkness, little black eyes straining to blindness, create the rugs that you and I tread unthinking underfoot. The bakers are throwing the slobbering paste upon an ocean of red-hot pebbles, to draw out sheets of bread like thin cork bath-mats.

You will be sneezing your way through the spice bazaar, and —'Mind your backs!' This time a camel maybe, laden to the last straw; a string of incorrigible mules; a Western bicycle, reckless and bell-less, scattering the harmless crowd.

A dizzy pile of pomegranates. A pyramid of glittering pink candy that might be a king's ransom. Three large blue-and-white dishes, fit for a palace, charged with some sticky beastliness and abandoned to the flies. Ali Baba jars, printed calicoes, a thousand teapots, ten thousand slippers.

The people. Men with henna-dyed beards and too old to be true; men dressed in the tattered remnants of carpets. Baggy once-white cotton trousers and sweeping *abas*. Turbans blue, black, white and green. A dervish with his begging-bowl. Some theological students, black-robed with white turbans. Women wrapped up as if they were in transit in the parcel post. And the children—so many of them—bent so seriously over their adult labours, with barely time for a remembered smile.

In an enormous old ramshackle barn, down a little midnight alley hard to find, is the last blindfold camel that grinds linseed between two huge millstones. Such light as there is filters through a negligible hole in the high-vaulted roof. A Doré illustration to Dante's *Inferno*, a Rembrandt come to life. There are other alleys that lead to little mosques where, perched on the top of library steps, a *molla* may be preaching. Yet others open into spacious caravanserais stacked with bales of merchandise and brightened by an almond tree that sheds its fragile pink blossom into a blue-tiled pool. In a back alley where the gutters run blue, dyers are at work, and the dull, heavy thud of the textile-printers forms a *basso ostinato* to the distant percussion of the coppersmiths and the shrill clamour of the crowd.

All this, and more, I saw and heard—and smelled—when I went to the bazaars this morning with Mrs. Thompson, Mrs. Cochrane, and the ghost of Hajji Baba.

The Bishop is a staunch teetotaller. Feeling the need of a drink, I slipped stealthily out of the house (may he forgive me) and round to the bar of the Irantour for a vodka. The bar is, of course, decorated with (vile) illustrations of Omar Khayyam's

Rubaiyat, supported by home-made translations in 'arty' lettering.

Some American Point Four men were there, and snatches of their conversation reached me :

'What the heck is there to do in this old hole?'

(Concerning Persepolis): 'I ain't going south to see a lot o' ruddy stones. I'm good right here.'

How infinitely preferable is this honest philistinism to pretentious, dutiful sightseeing! Nothing is more depressing than the sight of those English Continental tourists who in London obviously never set foot in a picture gallery 'doing' the Prado or the Uffizi in order not to lose face when they get home.

Here is another example of agreeable honesty. At a reception given recently by the Queen Mother in Tehran, the guests assembled in the 'library.' In the vast bookcases not a book was to be seen. How easy it would have been for Her Majesty to order a hundred yards of red leather bindings and fifty yards of blue, as they do, I am told, in America!

She too was American, and perhaps fifteen: very gay, very pretty, amazingly unsophisticated. She was on her way to Baghdad with her parents, I have no idea why—nor why she should come and seat herself at my table to entertain an old and unknown fogey so charmingly.

'Will you put me in your book? I've always wanted to come in a book.'

'Certainly.'

'I bet you won't. Oh! I oughtn't to have said that; Mummy says it's wrong to bet.'

'I bet—if your mother will excuse the expression—I will.'

'Promise?'

'Promise.'

5

Shiraz

March 13th

The plane carried me, this radiant morning, to Shiraz—a bumpy journey over desperate, desolate wastes and mountains powdered with fresh-fallen snow; a journey into the wide-open arms of Spring.

Mr. Sharp, the English chaplain, had been unable to book me a room at either of the European hotels; he therefore escorted me to the native Hotel Z, which better suited my buoyant vernal mood. (I could, however, wish that the clock in the hall did not have the Big Ben chimes.) The bedrooms, which are all on the ground floor, open upon a flowery courtyard. In the centre of this is a large oval pool of green, stagnant water in which the hotel crockery was being washed up. Around the pool are orange trees still hung with fruit, two tall eucalyptuses, beds of stocks, and rose-bushes just breaking into flower. Provided that one remains at a sensible distance from the pool and other hazards, no more agreeable place to sit could well be imagined. And in a thus carefully selected corner I am at this very moment lunching off *pilau* and yoghourt. The wireless, which had newly been calling us to prayer, has suddenly relented and struck up the 'Ride of the Valkyries.' The sun is shining. There is a freshening breeze. The temperature is exactly right. Bliss it is; and how glad I am not to be with the Americans up at the Hotel Park Sa'di!

The hotel manager's brother, Ali, made himself known to me after lunch and invited me to go with him later to see the tombs of Hafez and Sa'di, which lie outside the town. Both have recently been entirely reconstructed, and need a hundred years of neglect before they acquire the necessary patina. The little blue-capped Sa'diyeh will never look more than comical and gawky; there is, however, potential charm in the colonnaded pavilion and well-planted gardens of the Hafeziyeh. (But even

Tooting would look bewitching on this most exquisite of all evenings.) The violet hills are spread like a backcloth behind marble turned by setting sun to gold; below lies Shiraz with its flamboyant cypresses. The air is fresh and calm. It is good to be alive. The years are dropping from me.

The body of Hafez lies in a tomb of yellow Yazd marble inscribed with two of his odes. With Ali's help I read the lines that I already knew :

> *Though I am old, hold me all night in your arms,*
> *So that at dawn, drunk with youth and fire, I arise.*

It is customary, in the Hafeziyeh, to have resort to divination. A copy of the Odes was fetched and I jabbed my finger at random, lighting upon Ode 105; in it is a famous reference to Jesus. The editor of a Shiraz weekly newspaper, who happened to be present, was struck by the coincidence and asked me if he might 'write me up' in his paper. Never averse from the most improbable publicity, I give him permission and my photograph. I did not see the results—if any—of his labours.

Ali having insisted upon paying for the taxi, I made return by inviting him to come and drink some Shiraz wine with me. He knew, he said, a tavern. It proved to be a sordid little hole, windowless, tucked guiltily away, like some fourth-rate cafeteria off Leicester Square. Nor did I care for the wine. Two professional boozers—old boon-companions of Ali—were already in possession and attached themselves to us. Ali acted as interpreter :

'This gentleman he say, what you do here?'

'This gentleman he say, wine very good, *arak* very better.'

As soon as I possibly could, I made my escape. I don't think I much care for Ali—or for his friends.

Back at the hotel, a little flushed perhaps with the indifferent vintage of Shiraz, I sat down on my bed to read Hafez.

In English, of course. And in English it just will not do. FitzGerald alone has transmuted Persian poetry into English poetry. With Hafez, Gertrude Bell came the nearest to succeeding; she was hardly more than a girl at the time, and her Swinburnian translations have at least a youthful fire.

Where love poetry is in question, part of the trouble comes

from the Persian ideal of beauty, and the similes used to express it, being too remote from our own.[1] Take the chin. The Persians admire a dimpled chin with a drop of moisture in the middle: 'Thou whose chin contains a well-pit,' as Hafez puts it. In the West, the dry chin is usually considered preferable. Or the lips. The West encourages comparison to cherries and coral; it allows rosy, crimson, ruby, and vermeil-tinctur'd (Milton) as epithets. Hafez calls them *wine-dropping* and *sugar-dropping* rubies. Where we might say, 'Let me feed upon your lips,' he writes:

> *On thy sugar-dropping rubies*
> *Let me for life's food rely.*

Dribbling, in fact.

I dare say the vicar's daughter would not take offence if you said that her figure reminded you of 'a silver-shanked cypress' or 'a shade-reared box-tree.' She might be no more than mystified at your comparing her hair to polo sticks, her eyebrows to prayer niches and her eyes to 'tipsy narcissi.' But what if you were to tell her, as Hafez tells his beloved, that her face was like a polo ball and her mouth resembled a small pistachio nut; that the hair on her upper lip put you in mind of sprouting corn and her gait of a strutting partridge?

No—Hafez still awaits his FitzGerald. Until he appears, we must either learn Persian or take him on trust.

And then, not knowing that Shiraz possessed the only drinking water in all Persia, I cleaned my teeth in Pepsi-Cola.

March 14th

Another radiant morning. As I dressed, I read, with the help of a crib, the lines from Sa'di's *Golestan* that describe the coming of spring:

'He hath commanded the chamberlain of the morning breeze to spread the emerald carpet over the land, and bidden the foster-mother of the spring cloud to suckle the daughters of the meadow in the cradle of the earth; He hath clothed the trees with a garment of green leaves, to be a robe of honour for the

---

[1] The translators of the Bible were confronted with the same problem —e.g., 'Thy navel is like a round goblet, which wanteth not liquor: thy belly is like an heap of wheat set about with lilies, etc.' (*Song of Solomon,* vii, 20.)

New Year, and with the coming of spring hath crowned the heads of their children, the branches, with blossom. . . .'

Some part, at any rate, of the beauty of Persian prose survives even my translation.

After Isfahan, Shiraz is a disappointment, for little remains that is more than two hundred years old. It was Karim Khan Zand—the Vakil, or 'Regent,' as he modestly preferred to be called—who in the second half of the eighteenth century restored a certain metropolitan dignity to a city that had declined into dreary provincialism. The Vakil built town walls, caravanserais, mosques, *madrasehs* and bazaars, and—incidentally—ruled his people with a tenderness unique in Persian history.

Shiraz, which soon after the Vakil's death fell once more on evil days, has, however, now again raised its head. It has set out to become—more, it has succeeded in becoming—the most up-to-date town in Iran. It possesses one of the best hotels and the only filtered drinking water in the country and, what is far more remarkable, the best-equipped hospital in the world. Let them do what they like to Shiraz : let them build skyscrapers and funiculars, let them erect as many statues of Reza Shah, make as many roundabouts and Avenue Pahlavis as they wish —so long as they keep their hands off Isfahan.

The architecture of Shiraz strikes a very different note from that of Isfahan. The domes of the mosques are onion-shaped and stridently decorated; they reminded me of the Cathedral of St. Basil in Moscow, or of their exact contemporary—the balloon of the brothers Montgolfier; but I see that one writer prefers to compare them to the tips of large stalks of asparagus. The flowery pink-and-yellow tilework is pretty enough, but of coarse quality.

The Shah Cheragh Mosque has a glittering mirror-mosaic entrance which I tried to photograph. But a son of the eighth Imam is buried inside, and I was therefore stopped by a policeman, who made me show my passport and then clung to me like a leech. Eventually I dodged into a doorway and so gave him the slip; it was pleasant to watch his unhappy and fruitless search for me, and I was particularly delighted at getting, unobserved, a photograph of him looking quite his silliest.

The Friday Mosque was built in the ninth century, but has been often and excessively rebuilt and restored. The most remarkable object in it is a small tabernacle in the centre of the main court; erected in 1450, it is said to be a copy of the Ka'ba at Mecca. Robert Byron considered the combination of marble and intense turquoise blue tiles a mistake; certainly it is unusual, but I thought it successful as used here. The Madraseh-ye-Khan is charmingly decayed, but there are signs that scaffolding will soon make life intolerable for the happy, harmless hollyhocks. Upham Pope gives a picture of the entrance lodge, which dates from the time of Shah Abbas; it is decorated with excellent tilework that serves as a reminder that so much in Shiraz is in fact second-rate. The New Mosque (actually one of the oldest) is very large and very dull, but some stately old plane trees help to relieve its gloom.

Having drunk my fill of the mosques, I took a taxi to the Mission, where I was to lunch with Sharp. There is a flat rate of sixpence throughout the town, and no tipping—a pleasant change after the high charges of the London taxi service. Sharp is a remarkable man : orientalist, architect and musician as well as priest. The English church, which he himself designed, closely follows the pattern of the Shiraz bazaars—a vaulted building in straw-coloured brick picked out with turquoise tiles : a sensible and successful experiment. It is rapidly becoming known as a rival to Persepolis among the sights of the Shiraz neighbourhood.

The afternoon found me watching, to the strains of the 'Blue Danube,' the brisk finals of a hospital tennis tournament. There followed tea with a Harley Street specialist at the Park Sa'di. The hotel has a fine position and an enviable garden (a special feature of which is a pair of enormous osier baskets planted with hundreds of 'progressive' pansies); but it has that nondescript, cosmopolitan atmosphere which invariably attends Western comfort abroad. I was still glad to be at the Hotel Z.

I wound up the day with a Persian lesson and further and inescapable carousing with Ali. The word *boland* (pronounced 'blunt') means, he tells me, 'tall' and 'noisy.' Shiraz wine is little worse, though a shade more expensive, than the cheap Médoc one buys for mildly festive occasions.

March 15th

A garden or two, with their tall cypresses and scattered beds of roses, and a stroll through the bazaars, passed the morning agreeably enough. The Vakil's bazaar is, from an architectural standpoint, the most impressive I have yet seen. The gardens disappoint. Near the bazaars is the eighteenth-century Vakil Mosque, one of the largest and best preserved in the city. I was able to wander unmolested round its spacious court, and even to get a photograph of the *shabestan* (corresponding to the nave of a church), whose massive spiral pillars are, *with their capitals, monoliths.*

At last I have met a Bahai—a member of that tormented religious sect whose founder, known as the 'Bab,' was executed at Tabriz in 1850.[1]

The young man introduced himself to me while I was lunching in the garden, and sat for a few minutes at my table. 'I am,' he said in English, 'a Bahai.' Such an admission, made to a complete stranger, was surprising and not a little indiscreet; for every man's hand is still against the followers of the Bab.

Persecution, he said, had broken out afresh a year or two ago. 'In Yazd, they take a Bahai and burn his beard and his arse.'

'Oh dear, I'm sorry!'

'They are angry that he ride it in the street.'

'Ah—now I understand.'

Coleman, the English mission doctor, has been invited to the wedding of the son of the *kadkhoda* (headman) of Pudenak—a small village near Shiraz where he has started a clinic. He suggested that I might like to go with him.

We arrived about four o'clock at Pudenak—a cluster of squalid mud hovels—just as the procession was leaving the bride's house. The bride—she was ten—and another child of about the same age were mounted upon a henna-stained grey horse. Confronting them, propped upon the shoulders of the animal and held in place by two men who walked beside it, was a large mirror. Drums were beating, and a trumpeter with

[1] Impossible to discuss the Babis and Bahais here. The curious may consult E. G. Browne's *A Year amongst the Persians.*

cheeks expandable to the size of grapefruit blew raucous blasts that echoed and re-echoed among the mud walls. The women and girls of Pudenak, dressed in all their finery, waved gossamer bright scarves that fluttered gently as falling petals; they might have been flower maidens in *Parsifal*.

Thus processing along the ankle-breaking alley that served for the village street, past stagnant pools which reflected this kaleidoscope of colour, we reached a little square, where we were conducted to seats of honour upon a terrace above one of the houses.

The bride was now carried off to the *hammam* for the ceremonial bath, and from somewhere among the crowd there emerged the bridegroom—a young man in the middle twenties, also on horseback. A troupe of hired entertainers arrived— comedians in Ruritanian uniforms and grotesque moustaches, a man dressed as a pregnant woman, two epicene child acrobats, and a fiddler. Their performance was slow-moving, and by Western standards equivocal. There was singing too, and shrill ululations of applause from the women crowded together at one end of the square, on the roof-tops, on the walls. The men, who held the centre of the arena, fell to a game not unlike single- sticks, which ended in the inevitable brawl. The uproar was tremendous.

These games at an end, the bridegroom was ceremonially shaved. This was a long business, and while it continued a col- lection was taken to help defray the cost of the wedding (little less, I later learned, than two hundred pounds). Wanting a change of scene, I climbed over the roof-tops till I could look down upon the empty shell of the village and beyond it to the boundless plain. The setting sun was gilding the walls; far away a salt-marsh glittered. There was not a soul in sight save one old crone, tending her donkey in a little yard and babbling to herself. Before me stretched an infinite silence; at my back there rose, as from the soundbox of an immense gramophone, the confused murmur of the square.

I returned to find the shaving at an end, and the bridegroom's friends busy tying scarves round his arm. All the men—Coleman and I among them—were then lined up, and the bridegroom passed down the rank to receive the kiss of each in turn. What was I to do? I had become separated from Coleman, and ahead of him in the queue; I could not ask his advice. I felt as ill at ease as a shy guest at a fine dinner, confronted with a vast uncut unpredictable pudding. Would I insult him, bring him bad luck perhaps, if I did not kiss him? Would I be ruining for ever the prestige of the English in Pudenak if I did?

I decided that, whatever might be the rules of Rome, in Pudenak one need not do as the Pudenaki. So, seizing his hand in both mine, I gave it a seven-pound squeeze and said, '*Kebrit-e-ziad*.' Unfortunately this means 'lots of boxes of matches'; in my embarrassment I had confused *kebrit* and *tabrik* (congratulations).

Apparently unshaken by this curious salutation, the bridegroom leaped upon a henna-dyed grey and we all set off in procession to the gates of the village, where, accompanied by a handful of his friends, he galloped brilliantly away over the plain to pray at the shrine of a local saint.

The crowd broke up and went about its own business until the feast—for which, unfortunately, we could not stay—was ready to begin. Before we left, the headman showed us over the public bath. A low, dark and muddy passage, narrow and winding, led to the sultry, pitch-black hole, not more than eight feet in diameter, that constituted the *hammam* of Pudenak. In this fearful prison the poor child had been made ready for the embraces of the virile, unknown young man who had been allotted to her by her parents. Coleman spoke, from wide experience, of the harmful results of the consummation of such marriages.

Dinner with a Persian doctor, Dr. Ghadimi, and his German wife, to meet a Persian woman who is anxious to send her son to Eton. She has written three times, she says, without response —so unreliable must be the Persian postal service. She inquired the fees, and was horrified to find how *low* they were. Thinking that she might not grasp the value of the pound sterling, I translated the sum into *tomans*.

'I understand perfectly. But why is it so *cheap*? Is there *nowhere* more expensive?'

To reassure her, I promised her that we would do our level best to pile on the extras. She still felt, however, that she could

Royal Mosque,
Isfahan
(p. 30)

Vakil Mosque,
Shiraz
(p. 50)

Namazeh Hospital, Shiraz
(p. 61)

Porch of Xerxes, Persepolis
(p. 55)

Gauhar Shad Mosque, Meshed
(p. 105)

(Left) In the Copper-smiths' Bazaar, Isfahan

(Right) Brothers, Herat

not really be getting anything worth while for less than a thousand a year. If only I could collect together a little group of such delightful parents, how gladly would I open, for their adorable children, a school whose fees would be entirely to their satisfaction!

But alas! we shall never, at any price, have little Hassan among us; for he is already eight, and were he the Shah's own son could barely hope for a place at this late hour.

I have been thinking about this rose-and-nightingale business.

Obviously, most travellers find what they have repeatedly been told is there; it is the insidious power of advertisement.

Take, for example, the Author whose book is before me now, and who was in Shiraz in the spring of 1949. He is something of a poet; he writes evocatively, and with gusto, though in stating that the distance from Shiraz to Persepolis is eighty miles, whereas the map makes it thirty-five, he seems to give rash rein to his poetic fancy. I felt pretty sure that I could count on his discovering a nice show of roses in Shiraz.

And I was not disappointed. It was roses, roses, all the way for him. 'The roses,' he says, 'were in floods.' There were 'dark scarlet roses which glowed savagely.' There were 'trellises on which solid sheets of roses clung.' Roses even endangered the traffic: 'Every motor-car was full of them, so many roses plastered on the windscreen that you wondered how the driver could see through them.' Needless to say, the air was laden with the scent of roses. In the bazaars, boys filled his hands with roses because 'there was no other way of getting rid of them.' In one garden our Author saw 'perhaps a quarter of a million roses' and 'thirty or forty gardeners, all snipping feverishly.' When I read that this particular garden seemed to him 'a firework display eternally wheeling in procession,' I could not help wondering whether some mischievous garden-boy had not laced that favourite rose-spice cordial of his with heady Shiraz wine.

Our Author became something of an expert on roses before he left Shiraz. For example, he learnt the useful trick of telling the time of day by the varying scent of their petals. He discovered, too, an interesting variety that 'threw off a heat which came in gusts.' No wonder that he was reduced to a state of 'the wildest excitement' by it all.

Now every gardener knows, from bitter experience, that roses flower better some years than others. 1949 was, quite obviously, a bumper year, and 1956 may well be an exceptionally poor one. I cannot pretend to have inspected every rose-bush in Shiraz; and I had to leave before the flowers were at their best. But I would be prepared to bet my bottom *toman* that all the roses that I saw in the town would not unduly overcrowd Queen Mary's Rose Garden in Regent's Park.

And the nightingales?

I thought that our Author would inevitably have run into quite a flock of these in Shiraz. I thought they would have swarmed in the streets like locusts, bringing traffic to a standstill. I felt almost sure that, somehow or other, he would have learnt to tell the time by them. I hoped that one or two of them might even have nested in his beard.

But what do we find? One single, prosaic reference, in his description of the tomb of Hafez: 'The nightingales sing there.' That is all.

How can we account for this reticence? Had no one warned him to look out for nightingales? Or did he strike a 'bad' year?

March 16th

Two Englishwomen who are staying in Shiraz—Miss Quinn (a missionary) and her friend Miss Chalmers-Cox—suggested that we should share a car for Persepolis. 'It'll be so much cheaper with three,' said Miss Quinn.

Passing through the Allahu-Akbar gate, with its oft-sung view of Shiraz, the road to Persepolis follows for a while the course of the little, frolicking Ruknabad stream beloved of Hafez, tops the pass and then descends into the swampy plain of Mervdasht. We made a halt beside a lake, so that the ladies could study waterfowl.

'Avocets,' said Miss Quinn.

'Stilts,' corrected Miss Chalmers-Cox.

On a distant hillside a large flock of animals was visible. 'Oh, look at all those sheep!' said Miss Chalmers-Cox.

'Goats,' corrected Miss Quinn.

There was much putting on of long-distance specs, followed by the undeniable recognition of sheep *and* goats.

'I always think it was such hard luck on those goats in the Bible,' said Miss Quinn. 'Goats are so much nicer than sheep, and so much cleverer.'

What have the theologians to say to that?

Persepolis first becomes visible as a handful of little match-sticks standing upon a faintly etched horizontal line at the foot of a wall of buff limestone mountains; it appears utterly insignificant. But as one draws closer, the match-sticks grow to nine-pins, to pygmy pillars, and finally to towering columns set upon a vast stone-faced platform poised fifty feet above the plain. We made and remade all the right cultural noises as this curious, but not unreasonable, transformation was unfolded before our eyes; then, paying our sixpences, we climbed the two broad flights of gently graded stairs and made ready to walk in triumph through Persepolis.

The great ceremonial palaces where the Achaemenid kings spent each year the fresh weeks of early spring and the vernal equinox—those palaces which Darius and Xerxes built and Alexander burned—have been described by a hundred writers. Some, like Mr. Robert Payne (who was lucky enough to meet a wolf on the platform), are quite carried away by their ecstasy. At the other end of the scale there is Robert Byron, who considered that in its prime Persepolis must have looked like a Hollywood set,[1] and whose immediate reaction to the great Apadana stairway was, 'How much did this cost?' Between those two extremes comes the bulk of the writers, who soberly extol the grandeur of the ruins while admitting that much of the detail is aesthetically unsatisfactory.

Like Robert Byron, I had come to Persia attuned to Islamic architecture, and with only three sadly grey hours at my disposal I could but 'do' Persepolis *à l'Américaine*; my opinions, therefore, are both ignorant and prejudiced. But I must confess that of the two Roberts I found myself more in sympathy with Byron than with Payne. The Entrance Hall of Xerxes, with its heroic reliefs of winged, animal-bodied deities? 'How

[1] Compare the greater Byron's comment on first seeing the Parthenon (in 1810): 'How like the Mansion House!'

impressive!' The Apadana stairway, fronted by long processions of tribute-bearers? 'How wonderfully preserved!' The sixty-foot columns of the Apadana porches, once crowned with capitals in the form of two-headed bulls and lions? 'How astonishing!' But where, if anywhere, could one truthfully say, 'How beautiful!'? I could nowhere feel, as in the mosques of Isfahan, that consummate ecstasy which love or beauty alone can engender.

As I was studying a relief that appeared to represent Darius performing a *pas de deux* with a unicorn, the voice of Miss Quinn was heard crying in that wilderness. Time pressed. The sunless day was already waning; the Achaemenid tombs and Sasanian rock carvings at nearby Naqsh-e-Rostam had still to be visited.

Four cruciform, gigantic tombs of Achaemenid kings, cut in the sheer rock-face, dominate Naqsh-e-Rostam. Small entrances in the pillared façades lead the energetic to the bat-infested tomb-chambers, now stripped of everything but the empty sarcophagi; we took these gloomy vaults on trust, and turned to the series of seven Sasanian reliefs carved in the lower surface of the rock. Here are represented, heroic-sized, Shapur receiving homage from the captive Roman Emperor Valerian, and other triumphs and investitures of the Sasanian monarchs. There is something undeniably comic about the immense balloon head-dresses and what Byron calls the 'muslin cowboy trousers' of these proud kings, perched on their wooden, stocky horses; about the symbolic rings that seem to be doing service in a royal game of equestrian deck-quoits. Roman stolidity is there, but with a foretaste of more frivolous baroque.

There was only time for a swift glance at the square Achaemenid tomb-house, known as the tomb of Zoroaster, which stands nearby, and neither time nor light for us to go on to Pasargadae, where Cyrus is buried. Regretfully, we turned our faces towards Shiraz.

The charge for the car was sixty *tomans*. I drew a twenty-*toman* note from my pocket. Miss Quinn gave it an almost imperceptible glance and said brightly, 'Sixty *tomans*; that makes thirty *tomans* each: thirty for you and thirty for us.' I dived again into my pocket.

This curious system of arithmetic is, I was to discover, taught in certain American schools also.

Dinner with the Colemans. Besides myself, two Persians with practically no English were present. Afterwards Coleman showed us a mixed batch of his colour photographs.

'This is the court of the Friday Mosque at Isfahan; a bit under-exposed, I'm afraid. Oh, and here are the children at Margate; that's my mother-in-law in the green hat. This one of the bazaar I'm rather pleased with. . . .'

Then suddenly there appeared on the screen what looked like an aerial view of Vesuvius in full eruption. 'Ah, now *this*,' said Coleman with pride, 'was a rather unusual little stomach operation. . . .'

I shut my eyes, thus very nearly missing an excellent picture of Bakhtiari tribesmen.

Coleman is hoping to take me to Shapur tomorrow to see the Sasanian rock-carvings there, and thinks he has succeeded in borrowing a car. It will involve a spectacular six-hour journey each way, and a night at Kazerun.

March 17th

Obeying orders, I went round at eight o'clock to find Coleman. Rashly, I had had no breakfast; I thought we were merely fixing a time to leave for Shapur.

But the hoped-for car had not materialized, and we set out in search of another.

'I think I know a chap who might lend us a Land Rover,' said Coleman.

He was out.

'There's a man who has a jeep. . . .'

He had gone to Isfahan.

'Let's try Tabatabai' (I forget the real name).

His car had hit a tree the day before.

The doctor looked at his watch; both it and my stomach registered eleven o'clock. 'Heavens!' he said. 'I'd no idea it was so late. I must fly. I'll be back in a few minutes. Can you amuse yourself while I'm away? I've just got to cut off a leg.'

'To WHAT?'

'An amputation. I never like amputations, but they have to be done. And then we'll go round and see that Oil chap. . . .'

Mrs. Coleman plied me with coffee and biscuits. But I could hardly swallow them : I kept thinking of that axe or saw or whatever they use. And all over in a few minutes! I had imagined a major amputation to be a full day's work; it was horrible to be able to do it so quickly.

That 'Oil chap' was in; he had a Chevrolet and a chauffeur; and he generously offered us the use of both. But the car, he said, would not be available until five o'clock. This was unfortunate, for it meant that we would have to do the last and best part of the outward journey in darkness.

Moreover, night-driving in Persia is highly alarming, for cars are not equipped with—or at all events do not use—dip-switches. Lights ablaze, they drive full tilt at one another until they are about fifty yards apart, when first the one, then the other, turns off its lights altogether.

'I suppose you realize,' said Sharp, whom I ran into on my way home—'I suppose you realize that there isn't a hotel at Kazerun? Where are you going to spend the night? You'd better get a letter from the Ministry of Education to the local Education Officer. And cards? I imagine you've got visiting cards? They're almost essential out here.'

With his help I got cards (in English and Persian) printed in a couple of hours, and from the Ministry a letter so potent that one would have thought that education in England must be at a standstill in my absence.

The sunset into which we were driving looked hostile, and soon after leaving the plain rain set in. Then night fell, and our view became bounded by the rocks that bordered the way, and by blossoming shrubs that shone a lurid pink in the glare of our headlights. From time to time, mammoth oil-tankers from Bushire bore down upon us, forcing us dangerously near the precipice's edge. Others lay derelict by the wayside; for this terrible road takes a heavy toll, and serious accidents are not uncommon. At one point a lorry lay overturned, so obstructing the road that we had to get out and guide the car past it. On the back of it was inscribed (Coleman translating for me) : 'Go forward in the hope of God.'

Surmounting the Pass of the Old Woman—7,400 feet—we descended rapidly a road crazily rough and winding, to make the briefer ascent to the Pass of the Daughter. Curzon, who rode this way over the old and precipitous bridle-path, has some pretty catty things to say about elderly Persian females and their only too similar daughters; even today, neither mother nor child seems particularly lovable, and the plunging descent from the summit of the Daughter to the plain of Kazerun is perhaps the most perilous stage of the whole journey.

One of the most remarkable things about Coleman, I discovered, was that he knew everyone everywhere. Though he had never before been to Kazerun, no sooner had we arrived in the town than he was greeted by several of his former patients, all eager to conduct us to the house of Kazerun's Director of Education.

The Director looked exactly like Peter Ustinov. The poor man had already gone to bed : or so I supposed, for he appeared in pyjamas; but Coleman assured me that this might well be his notion of informal evening dress. I handed him my card and glowing academic testimonial. He welcomed us warmly, and without a moment's hesitation offered to give us and our chauffeur lodging for the night.

His servant was roused to produce an excellent dinner. Then bedding was fetched and laid upon the floor : mattresses covered by two widespread sheets and two small yellow quilts till they looked like a pair of poached eggs sitting side by side on toast. And there, so far as the howling of the jackals permitted, we slept.

March 18th

The deutero-Ustinov gave us a delicious breakfast. As we left his hospitable house, I could not help wondering what kind of a welcome two Persian gentlemen arriving at ten o'clock at night with a chauffeur and a highly bogus letter of introduction might hope to receive from me at Eton. Our host offered us, not the bare minimum, but the best that he could provide. He did it with the utmost courtesy. At the time, there was no possible way

of marking our gratitude; later, however, I made such amends
as I could by sending him a book. This uncalculating kindness,
which I was to meet again and again, made a deeper impression
upon me than anything else in Persia.

In exchanging Shiraz for Kazerun we had exchanged spring
for summer. The countryside, with its white houses and waving
palm trees, its hot sunlight and fertile soil, reminded me of
Algeria, and the ten-mile drive to Shapur was sheer delight.

Even had Shapur been deprived of its Sasanian monuments,
the beauty of the mountain gorge on whose rock-face they are
inscribed would have been reward enough for the long journey
from Shiraz. The reliefs themselves added little to what Naqsh-
e-Rostam had already shown; indeed, for the most part they are
inferior and less well preserved. But their romantic setting and
the summer sun, the green willows and rushing torrent, combined to make me think more kindly of the Sasanians.

In a cave high up in the mountain-side lies the famous fallen
heroic statue of Shapur the Great—almost the only surviving
piece of Sasanian sculpture in the round. It looked a stiff climb
to the cave, and I was grateful that I could avoid, on the plea
of lack of time, that which I felt little inclination in any case to
undertake. A bore to put one's knee out in this remote spot!

There are ruins at Shapur of an ancient city. But I was better
pleased by a shepherd boy, perched decoratively with his flock
upon a megalithic wall, who fled in tears before my camera,
and by a splendid clump of the cherry-red and white *Tulipa
Clusiana*. This pretty flower, sometimes known as the Lady
Tulip, occurs at intervals between Spain and Tibet; though it
is said to be fairly common in the olive groves of southern
France and northern Italy, I had never found it before.

I shall not easily forget the excitement of the return journey
from Kazerun to Shiraz, the incomparable beauty of mountains
which in so short a space ran the whole gamut of form, colour
and texture. Now they were as austere as north Wales, or
dappled with camel-thorn till they looked like an Innes; sometimes from rock more purple than Scotch heather a blood-red
stream would break; or the foreground hills might step aside a
moment to disclose a distant blue prospect of sheer snow-capped

Alps. And such a blue! If *Prussian* blue, why not *Persian* blue also?

This ever-changing panorama diverted our attention from the dangers of the road and more than reconciled us to the interminable jolting. As we stopped to admire the broad valley below us, a boy—almost black he was—appeared from nowhere and thrust into our white hands a bunch of whitest jonquils outscenting the most expensive hair-oils. We took our lunch at a wayside teahouse in a high-lying village named, I think, Dajestan, where, at the foot of a little waterfall and among a labyrinth of runnels, a grove of willows flourished. The air was so mountain-fresh that we were soon driven inside to seek the warmth of the stove.

Then the buff plains were ours again, and soon a speck of green announced still-distant Shiraz. By five o'clock I was sitting at Mrs. Coleman's hospitable table, back as it were in England and trying to remember whether I liked one lump of sugar in my tea, or two.

Evening service at the Mission church. The congregation barely numbered a dozen, of which our own party constituted the half. The protean Sharp flitted from reading desk to lectern, from organ to pulpit, preached a scholarly sermon, and served us coffee after. Coleman had some harrowing stories of the horrors of dysentery, which put me yet further off an already off-putting hotel supper. To stimulate an appetite I ordered, on my return, a bottle of wine, but was told that I might only drink it if I closeted myself in my bedroom. This is really too complicated.

I now know everybody in this hotel, but get them hopelessly mixed up. That man with the silly moustache, for example, is he the one who is buying carpets, or is he the law student from Tehran? And that shapeless black Cyclops—is it she who makes eye (one only) at me when we meet? For if so, I must prepare to make one or two back.

March 19th

Owen Hawes, who is in charge of the waterworks, showed me this morning over the new Namazeh hospital, built at the expense of one of Shiraz's wealthiest citizens and by general consent the most up-to-date hospital in the world. It is a remarkable institution to find anywhere—of all places, in Iran.

The New York architect, Whiting, designed the long, white buildings, which are 'modern' in the best sense of the word: simple, yet wholly free from affectation. One day the hospital will accommodate five hundred patients; at present, owing to staff and other difficulties (which it is *hoped* are only temporary), not more than sixty beds are ready for use.

Even a layman of medicine cannot fail to be deeply impressed. The wards—none of which contains more than four beds—will be kept warm in winter by radiant coils, and cool in summer by thirty-five miles of water-pipes, set in the ceilings. The roofs can be flooded in hot weather, and the roof garden watered by the turn of a single tap. 'Earthquake joints' make the fabric virtually indestructible by shock. The fittings and equipment have been fetched from all corners of the globe: sanitary ware from Paisley, cutlery from Japan, doors from Finland, light installations from Germany. The use of static sparks (whatever they are) prevents the possibility of explosions in the splendid operating theatres. There is a central supply for all surgical equipment. There are automatic tray-conveyors to carry meals to every floor. There are pressure sterilizers, 'Burn automatic rubber-glove conditioners,' and heaven knows what else besides. And of course there is air-conditioning in every room. Even the notices discouraging spitting—EXPECTORATION FORBIDDEN—have an up-to-date ring.

Lawns ever green, groves of forsythias and beds of stocks provide a fit setting for this Utopian institution, and one learns without surprise that nearly a quarter of a million gallons of Mr. Hawes's water are used daily in the summer.

But when the visitor has recovered from the first shock of astonishment, he may well find himself asking, as did I, 'Was the construction of this fantastically expensive hospital the best possible use to which Mr. Namazeh's millions could have been put? Ought we to give a small child a very costly watch? Would not a hundred cheap watches have made a hundred children equally happy?' What I was to see that very afternoon convinced me that, in a land so full of sickness and so inadequately

provided with medical services, the real need is for the establishment of small clinics in the villages.

But it was Mr. Namazeh's money, not mine; and he wanted
it that way. We can only hope that his hospital will set a standard that will raise the status of medicine and surgery throughout the whole country; that it will not suffer the fate of too
many ambitious Persian enterprises, and that its patients will
not solely be drawn from among those rich society *malades
imaginaires* who find it 'interesting' to undergo the latest fashionable treatment for the latest fashionable malady.

Coleman picked me up at the hospital to take me to lunch at
Zangiabad, a small village, not far from Persepolis, where he
has also started a clinic. With us went three native nurses—all
Moslems, and a blind Armenian evangelist who spoke passable
German.

We sang hymns most of the way—strange words to familiar
tunes, and falling strangely from infidel lips. The evangelist led
us, his worn but resolute voice straining to the higher notes and
his interminable monologue crowding every moment of the brief
interludes in our singing. Thus chanting to the Christian God,
we passed the mighty pagan ruins of Persepolis and soon after,
abandoning what had still considered itself a road, headed direct
across the flat stony plain towards a distant village of low, mud-
built houses. Outside the village we stopped for prayer.

The headman welcomed us and conducted us to the house of
the owner of the village, in whose absence he was acting as host.
The house, though also fashioned of mud, stood out four-square
and solid among its crazily crumbling neighbours, its pretty
walled garden, planted with fruit trees and poplars and watered
by little runnels, giving promise of welcome shade in the summer
heats.

We lunched upon the floor, the headman courteously plucking
choice morsels for me from the communal dishes and turning
a politely blind eye when my clumsy fingers scattered the rice
upon a once spotless cloth, or my endless legs, refusing to remain
telescoped, became entangled in a bowl of yoghourt. It was a
good meal, cleanly served and washed down with many little
cups of fragrant tea.

A clamour outside the garden gate put paid to any hope of a

siesta; and soon after, what appeared to be the entire population of the village swarmed into the garden and surrounded the veranda upon which the doctor was setting up his surgery. I wandered about, talking with the patients as far as I was able and photographing those who were willing. A more charming, well-mannered and friendly crowd it would be impossible to imagine.

I quoted my only Persian couplet :

> *Agar ferdaus bar ruye zamin ast,*
> *Hamin ast u hamin ast u hamin ast*[1]

and asked if anyone could tell me the name of the author. No one knew; but it was generally agreed that the man, if not actually a Zangiabadi, must certainly be a Shirazi.

Except for the doctor I was probably the only European whom most of them had ever seen, for several men to whom I spoke confessed that they had never been so far as Persepolis. At all events, I was a nine days' wonder. There was a sensation when I drew my puny little European pipe from my pocket and lit it—for the doctor is a non-smoker. Someone who was sucking grimly at a native pipe the size of a bassoon insisted upon a temporary exchange—an experiment that gave poor satisfaction to both parties but vast entertainment to the spectators.

After a while I went up on to the veranda to discover how the doctor was faring. I edged my way through the crowd, past the evangelist who was reading aloud from a braille copy of the Gospels, till I could see the doctor and his patient. I could not have chosen a sadder moment. Lying face downwards in its mother's lap was a naked infant perhaps five months old. Its buttocks were hideously burnt. The tiny body was quivering with the piteous, almost voiceless sobbing of an anguish beyond human endurance. The mother showed no signs of emotion; she held the child as unconcernedly as if it were a shopping basket. I turned away, half afraid that I was going to vomit. . . .

When the clinic was over, we walked into the village to visit one or two patients who were too ill to leave their beds. Unable to get the picture of that charred flesh out of my mind, I asked

[1] If Paradise is on earth,
It is this, it is this, it is this.
I found later that the Meshedi, Yazdi, Kermani and Isfahani were all equally eager to claim the anonymous poet as a compatriot.

the doctor whether there was any hope of the child living; it seemed unbelievable that so agonizing a wound could heal.

'None. If we could get it to the hospital it's possible we could save it. But the mother won't let it come. It's always happening : they make their fires in holes in the floor and the children crawl into them. When I first came out here, this kind of thing used to keep me awake at night. Now I'm hardened to it. I couldn't carry on if I weren't. One does what one can; one can't do more. But it's heartbreaking all the same. . . .'

Accompanied by a crowd of villagers, we passed down the deeply rutted channel of caked mud that was the village street. Coleman had a kindly word, a friendly smile, a hand-on-shoulder greeting for everyone. One and all they adored him. He stopped outside a mud hovel, through whose open door I could see the prostrate figure of a dying man; his face was grey and he was moaning softly. He was dying as they do in Persia, his friends and relations drinking tea, chatting and smoking all around him.

'Come inside !' said the doctor as I held back. But I refused; I knew that I could not take it.

Farther down the street we came upon an old man who, as soon as he saw us, tried to make his escape.

'Stop him !' cried the doctor. 'He hasn't paid for his medicine.'

He was soon captured and brought before us, vehemently protesting that he hadn't a penny. 'It's pure nonsense,' said the doctor to me. 'He's very well off; he can easily afford it.'

'Come on, old man ! Pay up !' cried the crowd. But he still refused.

'Search his pockets,' ordered the doctor, taking the law into his own hands.

The delighted villagers set on him—not unkindly—and soon produced the trifling sum demanded.

'Let this be a lesson to you, old man,' said the doctor as he pocketed the money. 'Next time I shall charge you the full amount.'

And seeing that he had been outwitted, the victim joined amiably in the general laughter.

When all the patients had been visited, the village headman took us to the public bath which, simple though it was, was vastly superior to that at Pudenak. It is used by women on four days of the week, by men on the remaining three. A dark, winding passage led to a single, domed chamber with a pool in the centre. The room was full, the air thick with steam. In one corner, and raised considerably above the level of the floor, was a sort of outsize font which seemed to be reserved for the cleansing and delectation of the youth of Zangiabad, whose golden heads and shoulders, crowded like tulips in a bowl, clustered happily in the misty half-light.

We returned to Shiraz with two patients (one with hernia and a boisterous hen in part advance-payment for treatment), singing our homeward way among the darkening hills. And as we journeyed, I remembered, in deep humility, what I had seen that afternoon. Such selfless devotion is true Christianity.

6

Isfahan

March 20th

I paid my modest hotel bill, made out to Mr. Bulnyth, and drove off to the airport. I would have liked more time at Shiraz, but I had been advised not to be on the move during the first days of the *Nau Ruz* (New Year's Day) holiday, which begins tomorrow.

In a land where the internal letter post is inexplicably slow and carriers and parcel post do not exist, the traveller is expected to act the postman. The officials at the airport were so amazed by the child's tricycle, which I am therefore taking to the blind children of Isfahan from the Shiraz missionaries, that they forgot to charge me overweight on it.

The Irantour Hotel is full, and the Sirus can give me a bed for one night only. Once again the kind Thompsons have offered to come to my rescue.

March 21st

I breakfasted on the roof of the hotel.
'Tabrik-e-Nau Ruz!'
'Tabrik-e-Nau Ruz!'
'Congratulations on the New Year!' We say it again and again. Everyone except myself is wearing his best clothes; I return to my room and put on my only (still fairly) presentable suit. The sun is shining; the garden of the Irantour opposite is a riot of almond, peach and cherry blossom. I cannot remember why we celebrate New Year's Day among January's snow and ice, but it is a rotten idea.

No one more wholeheartedly agrees with me on this point than Mr. Heshmatullah Dowlatshahi (Heshmatus = sultan) Ataollah Shahabpur = Ali Ashraf Keshawarz. Or so he subscribes himself; perhaps some portion of it is his address.

67

Mr. Heshmatullah (for short) wrote to me last Christmas, out of the Persian blue, on the subject of the NEW UNIVERSAL UNION (of which he is presumably the President) and to congratulate me 'for the birth of our prophet Jesus Christ'; it was a kindly, if an unexpected gesture. We all, says Mr. H. (for shorter), worship the same 'Unparalleled God' (Zadig would have been in full accord). If we can only agree upon a universal New Year's Day, all our differences will vanish and 'a door will be opened from the earth to the Paradise.' We shall all become one great big happy family, with peace for ever more.

Which shall the Day be? 'Mother Nature,' says Mr. H., 'has led us to the first day of Spring, which coincides with March 22nd. Why do we call this the most suitable day for a universal calebration [*sic*]? It is because on this day not only the human beings, but ALL BEINGS OF THE EARTH share with us in our celebration. Not only the young and the old, the white and the black, the rich and the poor approve this day . . . but all animals, plants, the stones, the water and even the air have a happy time then. . . .'

When we learn that Mr. H.'s project has the unqualified support of Mrs. Ludmille L. Holt of Cleveland, Ohio, who herself 'responds instinctively to Spring's resurgence with spiritual and physical hopes,' how can we withhold our support? For full particulars apply to the NEW UNIVERSAL UNION. Tehran —IRAN. P.O. Box 335.

A New Year's box of matches to you all!

Byron has pronounced the Shaikh Lotfollah Mosque one of the four finest buildings in Persia, though he admits that, unlike the small dome-chamber in the Friday Mosque, it will be found acceptable to the Omar Khayyam brigade also. Here structure is concealed, surface pattern triumphant. The tilework—blue, of course, predominates, though there is an unusual amount of buff —is of incredible richness and complexity; nowhere, perhaps, is calligraphy—white lettering on a ground of midnight blue— more dramatically used. Technically the building is a miracle. Yet it did not altogether please me. One might easily suffer from claustrophobia in this blue twilit prison, drown perhaps in its aqueous depths. I came out gladly again into the sunlight, to sit awhile upon the translucent greenish-yellow Yazd marble ledge beneath the portal and gaze at the beloved vulgarities of the Royal Mosque.

And at what Byron irreverently dismisses as 'that brick boot-box'—in other words, the Ali Qapu, or Sublime Porte. This sacred gateway, through which Shah Abbas himself would not ride, is crowned by a great veranda supported by twelve tall wooden columns. From this the finest grandstand in the world there is a magnificent prospect of the Maidan, the Royal and Shaikh Lotfollah Mosques, and the tawny amphitheatre of mountains that surrounds the city. Here Shah Abbas watched the games and spectacles staged in the arena below, and each year at *Nau Ruz*—this very day—gave audience to foreign diplomats and received their gifts.

The back of the Ali Qapu rises to six storeys in a labyrinth of small rooms approached by narrow spiral staircases. Immediately behind the veranda there is a small vaulted audience hall. These rooms are delightfully decorated with flowers, birds and arabesques that William Morris could almost have painted, and with figure subjects that he most certainly could not. In the top storey is a series of 'porcelain chambers' whose walls are fretted with little niches cut to the shape of the vases they once contained.

Such is the Ali Qapu: clumsy, ill-proportioned—yet charming. And more charged with memories of the Safavid kings than any other building in Isfahan. I sat for a while beside the now empty pool in the veranda, alone with my thoughts, so sunk in the pomps of yesteryear that had Shah Abbas suddenly stepped out from the audience hall and invited me to join him in a goblet of snow-cooled Shiraz wine I would hardly have been surprised.

At the north end of the Maidan is an open-air teahouse where I have become a regular, and I believe a welcome, guest. Under the shade of an ancient plane tree one can sit (on a real though rickety chair) and observe the life that eddies around the entrance to the bazaar. There is a table set with a dozen or more pots of purple stocks in full flower, deliciously scented. A small, earnest-faced child with a squint and an axe breaks up sugar-cones by the hour, and turns a sidelong envious glance at certain idle boys who sail paper boats and splash one another in the nearby pool. I have got to know one or two of the other 'regulars,' and exchange a few words with them, in particular with a gloomy soldier who looks as though he had lost several wars single-handed. Life, he says, is bad. Why? He tells me, but I cannot understand. Everyone is friendly, everyone polite.

At noon, the wireless blasts the muezzin's call, and a few of the guests rise to perform the complicated gymnastics of Moslem prayer. (Islam is certainly a keep-fit religion : no praying with lumbago.) No one is embarrassed : neither those who pray nor those who shirk.

This afternoon, as I sat there, I was joined by a patriarchal figure in a tremendous turban. 'I am,' he introduced himself in Persian, 'a *sha'er*.'

'A what? I don't understand.'

'Hafez, Sa'di, Khayyam—and myself,' he said modestly.

'Ah! a poet.'

'Let me read you my poem on the New Year.'

A crowd collected. The reading was applauded. The poet bowed, produced a green Biro and inscribed in my notebook an extempore couplet in praise of the beauties of the Maidan.

On my way home a youth who was studying an English book as he walked (for the Persian student is a born peripatetic) stopped me and pointed to a word in it.

'Please how you say this?'

'Repercussion.'

'Reep-kujjen?'

'No, "Repercussion."'

'Reep-kujjen, I thank you.'

Wild took me later to see Dr. Minasian, an Armenian collector. He plied us with comfits and red Jolfa wine, and showed us amongst other things two charming portraits, painted on glass, of Fath Ali Shah's handsome sons.

March 22nd

I slipped round after breakfast to the Irantour to see whether any letters had arrived for me—and so got caught.

She was sitting on the hotel veranda, drinking Pepsi-Cola,

sighing for the motherland, bored stiff. She was pretty—in a dumb, American sort of way.

She immediately addressed me. She was so bored she would have attempted conversation with an ostrich.

She had arrived, it seemed, by the Tehran plane at lunch-time yesterday, and had been told that the return plane was leaving at ten this morning. And now they said that it didn't go till three! She had *done* Isfahan yesterday afternoon. What could she do? What *was* there to do in this god-forsaken hole?

'I'm bored, bored, bored,' she moaned *crescendo*.

She said she wished that a good-looking young American boy would come along right now and whisk her off somewhere in a sports car. I was not a little relieved to find myself disqualified on all counts from serving as her escort.

Her conversation was stimulating and unusual:

She said: 'The trouble about black-and-white photos, I always think, is that you don't get the colour.'

She said: 'I don't like to see the men in Persia kissing each other; it looks so *queer* somehow.'

She said that coming from Tehran she had sat on the left-hand side of the aeroplane, and she was going back on the right-hand side so as to get the other view.

She had been to Damascus; and when she found that I had not, she was full of commiseration. It was far older, far quainter, than Isfahan. St. Paul had been there too, and it was still *vurry, vurry* much the same. Aleppo? No? A pity: it, too, was *vurry* old, and *vurry* cute.

Now why, I asked myself, did she find Damascus and Aleppo so delightful, and Isfahan so dull? Chiefly, I suspect, because she had been there and I had not. Partly, perhaps, because she had managed to escape from each as soon as her two hours' ration of sightseeing was over. Or had there been that good-looking young American boy with the sports car. . . ?

But now I, too, was 'bored, bored, bored.' I looked at my watch and sprang up. 'I'm sorry; I'd no idea how late it was. Will you please excuse me? I've got to go and see a man about . . . about a camel.'

Many years ago, I heard a sermon on the subject of Thoroughness. The preacher had once, he told us, visited a

Roman Catholic church in Italy. Everything *seemed* very magnificent, and in particular an elaborately carved and gilded statue of the Virgin, set in a niche, had greatly impressed him. But when he squeezed in behind and examined the back of the figure, what did he find? Nothing! The sculptor had not bothered to carve or gild the back *because it did not show*! God, however, saw everything : the things we meant Him to see, and the things we did not. How different was the attitude of the old *English* monks! For when the floor-tiles in the Abbey of—I forget the name—were being repaired, it was found that the under-sides had been as carefully decorated as the surfaces that were exposed to view. That, he said, was the kind of thoroughness that God expected of us.

This simple moral tale has stuck in my memory when much wisdom has slipped away. I would not mention it now, but that I chanced to think of it when I approached the Royal Mosque by a back alley, and saw how the great entrance portal, that smiles so fairly upon the Maidan, is backed by nothing more than a pile of children's bricks. And so are they all : mere film sets, erected regardless of cost. Baroque at its most daring never carried façade architecture so far as this.

March 23rd

Once again I am woken by the camel bells. And this time I am wide enough awake to rise and watch from my window the long procession wind past in the grey light of dawn. Then from a nearby mosque we are informed that Allah is great and Mohammad his Prophet. . . .

At breakfast (with porridge and a Parsee) Miss Mills comes in to borrow a copy of Archbishop Temple's *Readings in St. John's Gospel*.

Such is Iran, land of contrasts.

Wanting to sample a pomegranate, and knowing of its explosive habits, I bought one and took it to the bank of the River Zendeh Rud to eat. In very hot weather it may possibly be worth the mess and the trouble. A tattered child joyfully relieved me of the remaining half.

After all the lush descriptions in books, Persian fruit is a disappointment. Or rather, at the moment it is virtually non-existent. Nothing is forced or bottled, or even imported; to taste the famous Khorasan melons, one must be in Iran in melon-time. I am sorry also to miss the white melons of Isfahan, which sometimes weigh as much as seventy pounds and, when ripe, burst if one gallops by; but I dare say they aren't so responsive to pedestrians. I am told that melons sell by weight, and that ditch-water is therefore syringed into them to make them heavier. Perhaps it is just as well that I am spared temptation.

March 24th

With the Cochranes to Oshtorjan and Pir-e-Bakran—two early fourteenth-century mosques accessible from Isfahan by car.

The features of Oshtorjan are the delicate plasterwork in the dome and, in a portal at the back of the building, the brightest gentian-blue tiles I have yet seen. Pir-e-Bakran lies among rugged mountains some twenty miles from Isfahan, a fitting hermitage for a saint and a mystic. Here too is exquisitely fretted plasterwork, and a splendid portal—turned towards Mecca 'in order that the soul of the departed saint might more freely communicate with the holy city.' The building is chiefly of stone, and has a Sasanian quality. I missed the hoof-prints of Ali's horse; no doubt they were twice the regulation size.

We drove back across the desert at sunset, among mountains the deep, incredible tomato-red that Lear found in Egypt. The moon was almost full and ridiculously large. Here and there a ruined pigeon-tower stood gaunt against a sky gently gradated from cerulean to primrose.

March 25th

Between the Ali Qapu and the Chahar Bagh, in what remains of the royal gardens, stands the Chehel Sotun or Hall of the Forty Columns—one of the verandahed throne-rooms where Shah Abbas gave audience to his ministers and foreign ambassadors.

The vast veranda, whose roof rests upon twenty tall and slender red-painted wooden pillars some of which stand upon groups of stone lions, is reflected in a long rectangular pool. (Hence, some say, the Hall of the Forty Columns; but 'forty' is often used in a general sense to suggest size and splendour.)

Behind this lies the throne-room, glittering with mosaic mirror-work—a technique invented, I now learn, to save wastage of the countless mirrors that arrived broken after their long journey from Europe. At the back of the building, and running its full breadth, comes the picture gallery, gloriously roofed in blue, red and green and walled with six huge mural paintings showing scenes of Safavid festivity and combat. As recently as 1890, Curzon commented upon the 'extraordinary vividness' of the colours and gilding of these paintings, which date from the middle of the eighteenth century. What has happened to them since? Today, though they still remain a valuable record for the student of Safavid court life, they are gloomy and dis-coloured. In the picture gallery is arranged a small collection of manuscripts, pottery and textiles.

The Chehel Sotun was built by Shah Abbas; but a century later, a part of the building was destroyed by fire, Shah Soltan Hosain refusing to interfere with God's purpose by allowing any attempt to extinguish the flames. (We may laugh. But at a later date the Church opposed the introduction of lightning-con-ductors into England on the same grounds.) How much of the present structure is original, it is not easy to say. Fragments of frescoes which are now being freed of the whitewash with which piety and prudery had covered them, certainly appear to date from the seventeenth century. These show dancers, cup-bearers, and mildly erotic scenes such as figure in miniatures of the period, and some delicate blue and old rose arabesques.

At all events, in spite of much vandalism and neglect the Chehel Sotun still retains very considerable charm. I envy Robert Byron his good fortune in having been able, on the occasion of Reza Shah's birthday, to attend a state reception there, for the mirrored throne-room must be a dazzling sight when lit by 'pyramids of lamps.' How enjoyable and impressive the reception was is attested by the fact that it made Byron 'feel quite affectionate towards the old monster' who figures through-out the pages of *The Road to Oxiana* as Public Enemy Number One.

The 'old monster,' though he was forced to abdicate in 1941 and has been dead these twelve years, is still very much alive in the memory of his people. His statue greets the English traveller with embarrassing frequency in the streets, his 'reforms'—though modified after his abdication—are visible at every turn, and legend is busy with his career. Like most dictators he did a certain amount of good, a great deal of harm, behaved with the utmost brutality when it so suited him, and finally came the customary crash.

Colonel Reza, of the Persian Cossack Brigade, was forty-seven when in 1925 he drove the last effete Qajar monarch from the throne and assumed the grandiloquent title of Shahinshah— King of Kings. In his attempt to modernize Iran, the Shah soon encountered the opposition of the *mollas*. Western dress provided the apparently trivial pretext for the greatest battles. When the (second) Empress was refused admission to the shrine at Qom because she was inadequately veiled, Reza Shah, summoned by telephone, rushed to the scene in a fast car and horsewhipped the principal *molla* in the mosque itself. The at that time compulsory 'Pahlavi' hat—a ridiculous peaked cap like those worn by French postmen—was alleged to make prayer impossible since the wearer could not touch the ground with his forehead. Reza Shah's simple remedy—to wear it back to front when praying—did not appeal to the *mollas*, who staged a demonstration of protest in the shrine at Meshed, whereupon the Shah sent his troops into the mosque and machine-gunned the rebels. When the *chador* was forbidden, the police received orders to tear them from the faces of the women who disobeyed; many elderly women, feeling as naked without a veil as would a man without his trousers, never again left the house. Women, suddenly provided with Western hats, could be seen taking them off to one another in the street.

Defiance of the *mollas* had cost Amanullah his Afghan throne; Reza Shah, like Kemal Atatürk, triumphed. He acted promptly, and ruthlessly. If the *mollas* staged a religious procession, the Shah put on a free cinematograph show to coincide with it. When the *mollas* complained that a factory in the outskirts of Meshed overtopped the golden dome of the Shrine of Imam Reza, the Shah ordered an additional storey to be built. Part of the vast wealth of the Shrines of Meshed and Qom was appropriated for education or the construction of hospitals.

Reza Shah terrified his people. The greatest generals trembled in his antechamber; his ministers, awaiting the advent of the royal plane, dared not so much as to light a cigarette lest his hawk eye should spot from the air a puff of smoke, or subsequently observe upon the ground a stubbed end. Officials of a small town in Mazandaran, unable to acquire the compulsory top-hats in time for a sudden imperial visitation, were obliged to have them knocked up by the local blacksmith out of painted tin—a subterfuge that was betrayed by the heavy hailstorm that greeted the monarch's arrival.

Sometimes, however, he was successfully deceived. When making a ceremonial journey on his beloved trans-Iranian railway, he failed to notice beside the line a telltale pile of sand which had been hastily heaped to conceal an overturned engine. Nor did he discover—so it is said—that the series of schools that he unexpectedly elected to visit in Mazandaran was in reality but a single (indeed the only) school, whose pupils and blackboards were rapidly whisked to the next village while he was receiving loyal addresses from the inhabitants of the last.

A final story—from his early days. Reza Shah, as a private, was posted on sentry duty outside the National Bank in Tehran. Here he managed to get across a young messenger from the British Embassy who, losing his temper, vigorously kicked the seat that was later to grace a throne. Reza did not forget, and on his accession not unnaturally ordered the man's immediate expulsion from Iran.

These are the more frivolous aspects of his career (for this is a light-hearted book). His serious economic and social achievements are described in several partisan biographies written while he was still in power.[1] An impartial appraisal of his life and work remains to be written.

Sermon by the Bishop this evening. I was present, and hope thereby to have made amends for last week's defaulting.

March 26th

Ali Sajjadi is Isfahan's most renowned miniature painter. But far more interesting to me was his small son of nine, Jalil, who is studying calligraphy and already writes the Sweet Persian Hand very prettily. He was sitting on a low stool in the corner

[1] In particular, *Reza Shah,* by M. Essad-Bey (pseudonym); Hutchinson, 1938. The present Shah has also written a chapter about his father.

of his father's shop-cum-studio, seemingly hardly bigger than his pen, bent over the paper that rested on his knees and concentrating as though his little life depended upon it. I got him to write a few lines for me. Ali Sajjadi, thirsting for praise, was disappointed at my showing more interest in his son's work than in his own; but what can one say about these tepid *réchauffés* of Behzad and Reza Abbasi?

صبح   جبیلی سجّادی

شب تاریک رفت و آمد روز   وه چه روزی چو بخت من فیروز

پادشاه ستارگان امروز   ازافق سر برون کرده بهو ز

باز شد دیدگان من از خواب

به به از آفتاب عالتاب

یک طرف ناله فردوسی سهو   باکنک العدوا کبر ازبکسر

ازصدای نوازسفی ما در   وزسفیها ی دلپند بر بدر

باز شد دیدگان من از خواب

به به از آفتاب عالمتاب

از افق صبح مسفید دمید   آسمات بجو نئز کننت سفید

باتگوه و جلال و جاه رسید   پادشا ه ستارگان خورشید

باز شد دیدگان من از خواب

به به از آفتاب عالمتاب

The Bishop took me to tea with the Governor of Isfahan, to whom I had a letter of introduction. His palace lies behind the Ali Qapu and overlooks the royal gardens.

We found him receiving a small but distinguished company. Near the tea-tables were four identical, vacant chairs. After shaking hands with us, the Governor, with a gracious wave of the hand, indicated that one of these was for my use, and I, ignorant of the etiquette, not only accepted it but seated myself on the very middle of it. Then he did the same to the Bishop.

The Bishop took two steps towards it, then suddenly recoiled as though he had trodden upon a scorpion. The Governor implored him to advance and sit down; the Bishop appeared to say that the honour of sitting upon so splendid and important a chair was not for the likes of him. The Governor gazed disgustedly at the chair as if he were about to make an unreasonably inadequate bid for it in an antique shop, brushed some imaginary dust from it, and with little deprecating gestures conveyed the shame he felt at offering so distinguished a guest such unworthy accommodation. Finally the Bishop plucked up his courage, advanced daintily, and seated himself with the utmost humility bolt upright on the very edge of it. I was having my first lesson in *ta'arof*—the elaborate etiquette that makes it almost impossible for two Persians to get through a door in less than four and a half minutes.

I found myself next a mute general hung with medals; I later gathered that he was the Governor's brother and the Deputy Prime Minister. Such conversation as there was was carried on in Persian. I *khaili khub*bed and *khaili qashang*ed[1] for all I was worth, but it was heavy going. The Governor created a diversion by announcing that he had once spent a week in England, the most treasured recollection of his visit being a hockey match at Folkestone. Tea was brought in, and sticky sweets to bear sticky conversation company. I let my eyes wander round the room— to the mantelpiece upon which stood two vases full of paper tulips and a pot of dead hyacinths; to the wall above it, where hung a highly polychrome portrait of the Shah; to the french windows which overlooked a long tank that reflected the slender columns of the Chehel Sotun.

At last the Bishop rose. The Governor immediately seized him by the shoulder and forced him back into his chair. The Bishop seemed to be saying that the Governor must be the busiest man in Iran; the Governor appeared to answer that he had absolutely nothing to do for the next fortnight. 'Besides,' he added, 'I want to talk to Mr. Blunt.' Whereupon he crossed the room and sat down in the chair on my left.

In desperation, I said, '*Est-ce que Votre Excellence parle français?*'

'*Mais assurément. Et vous?*'

I said I did.

---

[1] *Khaili khub*, very good; *khaili qashang*, very pretty.

'Then why the devil,' said the Governor, crossly but in excellent French, 'didn't you say so an hour ago?'

This was hardly fair. But at all events the situation was saved. Conversation flowed easily now. The Governor spoke of 'our' great city, 'our' royal mosque, till he seemed in my eyes to become Shah Abbas himself, who had created all this magnificence.

'If there is anything I can do for you,' he said graciously, 'you must let me know.'

The Bishop rose once more, and this time he was not gainsaid. For, after all, the Governor *was* a very busy man.

March 27th

During the last few days I have been searching out a number of the less well-known mosques—no easy matter without a map (what hours a Baedeker would save!). In a slum district not far from the Maidan is the little Maqsud Beg Mosque, whose pretty Safavid portal I have three times tried in vain to enter. At the farther end of the bazaar, near the Friday Mosque, is that of Baba Qasem, built in the fourteenth century and later much restored. According to the seventeenth-century traveller John Chardin, witnesses who testified falsely on Baba Qasem's tomb 'suddenly burst, and their bowels gushed out.' This tomb has now vanished, and I did not think that that of a bath-towel manufacturer, which still remains, would afford a fair test of Chardin's veracity. In 1928, the building was being used as a stable for the neighbouring grocer's donkey, but the beast has since been expelled. The Mosque's tree-shaded portal is picturesque and photogenic, but unimportant.

Well worth the labour of discovery is the Mosque of Harun-e-Vilaya (A.D. 1513), with a tile-mosaic portal of the finest quality. Christians are not too popular here, nor in the Mosque of Shah Zaid, grandson of Imam Hosain—a building remarkable for the mural paintings which, contrary to the tenets of Islam, portray figures—lifesize and gruesome—and animals. Unfortunately it was too dark for more than a general impression of martyrdom and dripping blood.

The Zendeh Rud, or 'Living river,' Isfahan's proud waterway, rises in the Bakhtiara Mountains and vanishes in the marshes of Gavkhaneh; a hundred miles or so in all, serious only in its middle reaches and only when spring melts the mountain snows.

Today it deserved its name, its waters lashing themselves into a frenzy against the pillars of the Shahrestan bridge, near which, with the Bishop and Mrs. Thompson, I picnicked in the hot sun. Two or three miles downstream from the town, this is the most picturesque of Isfahan's five bridges: an Islamic brick structure on Sasanian stone pillars, crumbling as a child's sand castle whose walls the incoming tide has lapped.

Most attractive of them all, though not the most famous, is the Khaju bridge, built by Shah Abbas II to connect Isfahan with the former Zoroastrian settlement of Gabrestan. This is at once a bridge and a dam. Elegant hexagonal pavilions break the monotony of the long two-storey arcading and in spring tempt the Isfahani to the enjoyment of the silent pool above the dam and the raging torrent below it.

The Allahverdi Khan bridge—usually known as the Pol-e-si-u-seh, or 'Thirty-three [arch] bridge'—is a continuation of the Chahar Bagh and joins Isfahan to the Armenian suburb of Jolfa. It is the work of Shah Abbas's famous generalissimo. 'This beautiful structure, in all probability the stateliest bridge in the world, is alone worth a visit to Isfahan to see,' wrote Lord Curzon. More than three hundred yards in length, double-tiered, noble in conception, it none the less lacks—in my humble opinion—the variety of outline that gives such distinction to the Khaju bridge.

(New) Jolfa was founded by Shah Abbas as a settlement for the Armenians of Jolfa, on the Araxes, who were thus rescued from the dangers of Turkish attack and brought to set an example of industry to the inhabitants of the Shah's new capital. Until relatively recently, all European residents were compelled to live in this suburb. Jolfa cathedral, built in the reign of Shah Abbas II, has a domed roof *painted* with gold arabesques on a blue ground, delicate as the border of a Safavid miniature. A 'Last Judgment' whose pincers and boiling oil turned the stomach of Dr. Julian Huxley, and other gloomy oil-paintings, adorn the walls.

I was too idle to go to the cemetery, beyond the town, to see the graves of the Europeans there, and in particular that of the young Swiss watchmaker, Rodolph Stadler, who was at first honoured but ultimately put to death by Shah Sefi. The headstone of his tomb bears the simple legend, *CY GIT RODOLFE.*

The Shiah sect of Islam, to which the Persians belong, believes that the twelfth Imam, who disappeared in A.D. 873, still lives and will reappear in the Gauhar Shad Mosque at Meshed on the Day of Judgment. Tonight, the eve of his birth-day, the town is illuminated in his honour; there are flags on the droshkies and trams and an atmosphere of restrained hilarity in the streets.

After supper, therefore, I took a No. 1 bus, which circles most of the city, to see the fun. Isfahan bus-conductors depend for their wages upon the number of passengers who can be enticed into their vehicles; unlike their London counterparts, therefore, they perpetually lean out and implore one to step inside. The ordinary fare is about a penny; the complete circuit of this particular bus, which takes an hour, costs twopence.

At the nearest point to the Maidan I alighted and went on foot to the Royal Mosque. In contrast to the rest of the town, here all was strangely silent and half deserted. There was no floodlighting or Western vulgarity—only festoons of little lamps that spangled the velvet night without robbing it of mystery. A moon one day past full, still too low in the sky to light the square, streaked domes and minarets with bars of liquid silver. I stood a while in a shadowy archway, watching the solitary flitting figures that darkness surrendered a moment and too soon reclaimed; of lovers there were none. From those regrettable but now forgiven flower-beds came the hot white scent of tobacco plants.

Not for anything would I have missed the perfection of that moment.

March 28th

It has been said that travellers in Persia see more dawns than anyone else in the world; with the exception of assistant masters at Eton, this may well be true.

I left for Tehran at half past five—my first experience of a long-distance Persian bus. The company had sold my front seat twice over, the other purchaser being a *lederhose*d young German. But, first come, first served: I refused to budge. My neighbour was a garrulous Jew who spoke English:

'What is your country?'

'What is your religion?'

'What is your work?'

'What is your salary?'

'What is your age?'

'How many children have you?'

'Why are you not married?'

'If you do not know, who knows?' (This, I find, is the set riposte to 'I don't know.')

Rashly, I asked him about himself. This released a pent-up flood of grievances and injustices. He had been in prison. They had stolen his money—two million *tomans*: they had seized his land. . . .

'What did you pay for your bus ticket?' he asked suddenly. I told him.

'That was far too much.'

'But do you mean that there isn't a fixed price?'

'Certainly not! Why ever should there be? What are you writing in that notebook?'

'Notes.'

'So I see. What notes?'

'Private notes.'

'What about?'

'I said, *private* notes.'

'I heard you perfectly. But what are they about?'

'You.'

He was down, but not out. Rallying, he took the offensive:

'You smoke too much.'

It was the moment for the *coup de grâce*:

'You talk too much.'

Blessed silence! I looked at the ever-changing landscape, marvelling that Nature should still have a few untried pastels up her sleeve for tinting those cardboard mountains: that verdigris, for example; that russet, cinnamon and zinnia pink. But not a flower to be seen; nothing but the ubiquitous camel thorn, like greying tufts of hair. (What nonsense it is about the spring desert blossoming as the rose!) Yet there was colour enough and to spare without flowers. One mustn't be greedy.

I ate my sandwiches before we reached Qom, so that I should waste no precious minute of a brief halt there. It was towards midday that the golden dome that covers the last resting-place of Fatima, sister of the eighth Imam, and its accompanying battery of minarets, came into sight. To my surprise, the passengers greeted this Pisgah view of the second most sacred city in Iran with less display of emotion than a Women's Institute outing might accord a distant prospect of Salisbury spire. They were not pilgrims; most, I think, were travelling to Tehran on business.

We were allowed half an hour at Qom. I walked delicately in the direction of the mosque, knowing that the mere presence of Christians in this city is frowned upon by devout Moslems. Round the entrances to the court of the Mosque are clustered countless booths selling pious bric-à-brac as excruciatingly ugly as anything that Ste Thérèse has gathered round her bones at Lisieux—and that is saying a lot.

I had been warned not to attempt to enter the court, and today—as ill luck would have it—the twelfth Imam had attracted a large crowd. But through the gateways was visible an irresistibly tempting vignette. It would be so easy just to walk in. . . . At last I could bear exclusion no longer. They may drive me out, I thought, but surely they will not lynch me. Plucking up as much courage as is needed to dive into the Serpentine in January, I walked briskly through one of the entrances, turned sharp to the right and, flattening myself against a wall, made ready, if need be, to die with my back to it.

The brilliance of the scene surpassed even my expectations. Such colour, such glitter, such radiance, such flash of crystal mirrorwork and gilt! And round the fountained pool the thronging crowd of motley pilgrims, ebbing and flowing in the bright sunlight. It was dazzling, certainly; but was it not also vulgar? What would Robert Byron have thought? Was I not letting down the team? Was I not associating myself once more with that regrettable Omar Khayyam brigade? While I was still trying to decide whether I was merely the victim of my emotions,

I saw the tall figure of a *molla* bearing down upon me with horsewhips in his eyes.

The Mosque Militant! I fled.

Safely outside again, I found my knees trembling. I had not felt so frightened since that day, more than forty years ago now, when the headmaster of my preparatory school caught me smoking bracken cigarettes in the boot-room.

I had tried to find out in Isfahan at what time my bus was expected to reach Tehran; but such a question, being considered unlucky, is rarely answered, or at best receives a God-willing-by-nightfall reply which is as good as worthless. The Bishop, however, had told me I could count on about ten hours.

But the Bishop had not met our driver. The poor man appeared to be either ill or tired out. He mopped the sweat from his brow, and smoked incessantly to keep himself awake. Soon his head showed a tendency to flop on the driving wheel. Conscious of his condition, he slowed the bus to a snail's pace.

'Get on, old man!' cried a Persian who was sitting behind me.

'What has happened? Is he ill?' I asked him, in Persian.

'Maybe many things,' said the Persian, gladly airing his English. 'Maybe gentleman tired. Maybe Coompany tell him go slow. Maybe gentleman bad inside. Maybe autobus bad inside. . . .'

It was not until nearly six o'clock, after more than twelve hours on the road, that we crawled slowly—but none the less dangerously—into Tehran. As the bus drew up at the garage, the driver collapsed over the wheel and finally passed out.

*Beggar,
Vakilabad*

Garden Pavilion, Fin
(p. 177)

Harun-e-Vilaya Mosque, Isfahan
(p. 79)

Minaret of the College of the Mother of the Shah, Isfahan
(p. 35)

Minarets of the College of Hosain Baiqara, Herat
(p. 131)

(*Left*) *Bakery,*
Herat

(*Right*)
Gholamsardar
(p. 111)

7

Meshed

March 29th

'Fly to Meshed, now that there's a plane. It's two days by road—a road long as the entrails of Omar, through the dullest country imaginable.'

This was the universal advice, and I took it. But from the air, the view of that bleak lunar landscape was exciting enough; and doubtless, too, it was one long geology lesson for those who, in its lacerated and tormented rocks, could read the story of the cataclysms and convulsions that gave them being. The road, of course, clings mostly to the monotonous plain.

Shortly before reaching Meshed we struck a wall of cloud, whereupon old stagers began to moan that we would not be able to land. But at five hundred feet or so we broke loose from this white bondage; then came the swift flash of a golden dome, the click of my camera (dead failure!) and the long white runway stretching out to receive us.

Mr. Cassilly, the American consul, had kindly offered to put me up. Since he was not at the airport, I took a taxi to the Consulate.

'Shucks, I'm sorry!' he said. 'I thought you were coming tomorrow.'

For a moment I could not bring myself to answer, for the Consulate had jolted me into silence. From a cobbled, ruinous street, so narrow that a taxi can hardly pass along it, I had plunged through an unwelcoming arch and gloomy passage to find myself in a large garden, or rather orchard—an orchard 'wearing white for Eastertide.' From this, passing through unpromising swing doors, I had climbed a white, palace stairway to enter an immense drawing-room, treasure-house of lovely things. On the white walls, tall Korean *kakemonos* hung side by side with gay contemporary American oil-paintings. There were piles of all the right gramophone records (I mean the good ones, not the smart ones). There were Chinese pots and

Persian bowls and Japanese masks; there were books on Titian, Rembrandt and Picasso. The curtains and chair-covers were of exactly the right yellow.

'Shucks, oh shucks—I'm sorry!'

Now I have never been to the States. I know very few Americans, and those I had met in Iran had not led me to expect a citadel of art and culture in the wilds of Meshed. It was like entering a mud hut in Timbuktu and finding a Tintoretto on the walls.

But then, Tom Cassilly is an exceptional person, for in him are united the vitality of the New World and the inherited culture of the Old. He told me that his father's family was of Alsatian origin.

To have a room like that *and* be able to say 'shucks' in it . . . !

Meshed is the most holy city in Iran and almost as fanatical as its sister city, Qom.

It owed its foundation to the burial there of Harun er-Rashid, of Arabian Nights fame, who died in nearby Tus in 810 while on his way to suppress an insurrection in Transoxiana. It owes its glory to the bones of Reza, the eighth Imam, who also died (after eating certain grapes) at Tus a few years later and was buried in the same tomb-chamber. Good Shiahs, who believe that Harun's son Mamun was behind those grapes, still kick the tomb of the old Caliph as they pass.

The great agglomeration of buildings usually known as the 'Shrine' (though the term is sometimes limited to the actual tomb-chamber) consists of three large courts, two esplanades, the tomb-chamber crowned by its high golden dome, the Gauhar Shad Mosque, and a number of subsidiary mosques, *madrasehs* and the like. The Shrine area is now bounded by the broad circular avenue that Reza Shah cut ruthlessly through the old streets, and sacrilegiously through the cemetery to which for generations the bones of the pious had been carried from all over Iran.

For the artist or the architect, the miracle of the Shrine is the court of the Mosque of Gauhar Shad. This astonishing woman, the wife of Tamerlane's son Shah Rokh, was also responsible for what was probably the finest building in the whole Islamic world—the Mosalla at Herat.

Under Shah Rokh, at the beginning of the fifteenth century, a great renaissance of the arts was inaugurated in Herat—a renaissance in which Gauhar Shad, with the greater freedom permitted to Mongol women, played a conspicuous part. Ulugh Beg, their eldest son and an eminent astronomer, attracted scientists to Samarcand where he was Viceroy; the younger son, Baisanghor—aesthete, calligrapher and drunkard—lived with his parents at Herat where he collected round him a distinguished group of painters, scribes and musicians. This splendid period of artistic activity came to a close with the death, in 1447, of Shah Rokh. Robert Byron has described in detail the bloody family feuds which then broke out and which culminated in the assassination, a dozen years later, of the aged Queen.

It is to see—if it is humanly possible—the court of the Mosque of Gauhar Shad that I have come to Meshed; and my pilgrimage to Herat will be made principally in honour of the great but ruined Mosalla there.

Lunch over, Tom took me for a first view of the precincts of the Shrine. Passing the little Royal Mosque, to whose portal and minarets still precariously cling some of the bluest tiles in Persia, we came through the dark bazaar and out into the brightness of Reza Shah's great circular boulevard. Before us stood the graceful diapered minarets and turquoise-green dome of the Gauhar Shad Mosque. Yellow tendrils and bold black-and-white calligraphy relieve the broad surface of the swelling dome.

A verse inscribed somewhere within the Shrine states that 'in order to appreciate its full height and glory, the Heavens use the Sun and the Moon as binoculars.' I too could have done with a pair of field-glasses, for the jewelled loveliness of the tilework on the minarets was tantalizingly distant. God willing, I shall later get a closer view of it.

As we walked round the Shrine, other vistas opened before us. Soon the dome above the tomb-chamber, sheer gold upon a golden drum, became visible, with birds clustered as thickly about it as toadies round a millionaire. Then through forbidden gateways came the glint of Fath Ali Shah's portal—Midastouched also—with the flash of a fountain and the steadying velvet green of a group of pine trees. Gold too are the twin minarets of Shah Tahmasp. So much gold everywhere—and for foil the sapphire of the Iranian sky. Such were the prospects that spurred me on to seek a nearer view of the wonders of the Shrine.

Chains bar the approach to the two esplanades which lead to the Old Court. These esplanades are prolonged, across the circular boulevard, in the wide Bala Khiaban (Upper Avenue) and Pa'in Khiaban (Lower Avenue). The latter is the heart of the native city, and no less than an ethnological museum for the curious visitor. I wish I had the knowledge to place a man by the twist of his turban, the tilt of his eyes or the style of his robe. For here are gathered pilgrims from all parts of Iran and from beyond its frontiers. And here, unlike Tehran, native dress is the rule rather than the exception, though many an outworn European waistcoat or army coat has somehow or other found its way to Meshed to die.

By the side of the broad central *jub* is an open-air market where the pilgrims loiter over their endlessly protracted bargaining or subject themselves to the swift disfigurement of a religious head-shave. Here too one may be photographed *en pèlerin* against crudely painted backcloths of the Shrine. The Pa'in Khiaban is a spot to which the visitor to Meshed will return again and again. If only there were some equivalent to a café, where one could sit unmolested and observe the fantastic *va-et-vient*! One causes altogether too much of a sensation here.

Abandoning at last our weary feet, we entered the car that had been sent in search of us and drove down a splendid plane-bordered avenue until we reached an Italian provincial railway station fronted by a large pool, both lavishly ornamented with cheap and hideous statuary. This is Kuh Sangi, a pleasure resort instituted by Reza Shah with the prime object of enraging the *mollas*. The pavilion appeared to be shut; and someone having recently been drowned in the pool, bathing is now forbidden. A few mournful pilgrims loitered, staring bewildered at the silver demi-nudes. It was about as amusing as Glasgow on a Sunday evening when the whisky has run out.

Gayer far is the garden of Vakilabad, a remoter but preferred paradise whose gently sloping woodland and falling water attract the Meshedi in spring. I was lucky there in being able to photograph a Persian super-tramp.

We stopped on the way home at the shop of Meshed's leading painter. I beg your pardon—'gallery'; for whereas the artists of Isfahan exist in a certain Bohemian squalor, this Meshedi had a gallery of the Bond Street type. True, he had not yet acquired the full technique of certain London dealers : he could not pronounce the Persian equivalent of 'itreallyisratherprettyisntit?' as though it were all one word; he could not with the palm of the right hand manufacture those epicene, persuasive gestures that are worth a hundred guineas a time; he had not yet learned how to call down an imaginary staircase to an imaginary assistant, 'Mr. Greenbaum, are we still reserving No. 18 for the Duke?' He knew nothing of the hypnotic powers of red velvet and free sherry, and all the other tricks of the trade. He had not even managed to borrow an Old School tie. But he did give us tea and show us, with most embarrassing pride, twenty-two of the ugliest pictures in the world. No conceivable revolution of taste, no critics' advocacy or dealers' chicanery, could ever persuade a European to purchase a single one of his nightmare enlargements from nineteenth-century *salon* catalogues. Yet the Meshedi lap them up, and—so I am told—pay up too.

March 30th

The Consulate was built by, and for, a Russian, I learn— hence the immense stoves, the stately white staircase, the unfamiliar configuration of the rooms. I am becoming increasingly affected by the strangeness of this oasis of tolerance and culture in the fanatical heart of Iran.

The servant problem does not seem to exist here. Servants pop incessantly in and out. Clothes are carried away and washed, almost before one has time to take them off, by a Slavonic-looking woman who seems to have no other purpose in life. The food is delicious, the breakfasts a dream. That bread—how on earth do they do it?

Today being Friday, the Consulate is shut—out of respect for the Moslems. On Sundays it shuts for the Christians. If only, said somebody, there were more Jews and we could shut on Saturdays too—what a wonderful week-end.

'Tonight,' said Tom at that delicious breakfast, 'we are dining with Dr. Shadman at Malekabad. He is Governor of the Shrine;

he will probably be able to help you.' I imagined so too; I had a letter of introduction to him from Dr. Allevi.

There was obviously no need to ask what the Governor of the Holy Shrine of Meshed would be like; I could visualize him in every detail. His beard would be snow-white and piously long, his turban outsize, his glance alarming, his views fanatical. His wife—or rather wives: no doubt he had the full complement of four permitted by Islam—would be hidden away in some cupboard or other. We would, of course, eat on, and off, the floor and with our fingers, and my constitutional inability to give open expression to contented repletion would insult the hospitality of the host. Naturally the man would not speak a word of any European language, and I would be obliged to go through my customary linguistic hoops. It would be an interesting evening; but it would also be a difficult one. The prospect of it weighed heavily on me throughout the day.

In the morning, Dave Nalle, the American vice-consul, drove me (one puncture, one tyre-burst) to Tus, the precursor of Meshed and in its day one of the great cities of Iran.

Of the old town there remain the shell of a large domed mausoleum and the vast mound where once the citadel stood; the ancient bridge was washed away a year or two ago by the spring floods. The mound is a treasure-store of potsherds, which, since the city was finally reduced to ashes in 1389, cannot be of a later date. Among other attractive fragments I found a small piece of the finest Chinese celadon. I approached a peasant who was shovelling earth and asked him whether he had turned up anything of interest. 'Only this old bit of rubbish,' he seemed to say, producing from his pocket an exquisitely lustred blue lamp. We gave him about a shilling and he was delighted.

Tus is the birthplace of Ferdausi, author of the great national epic, *Shah Nameh,* or Book of Kings. In 1935, to celebrate the millennium of the poet's birth, a memorial was erected at Tus by order of Reza Shah. Robert Byron saw and praised it; Reza Shah, however, found it inadequate, and it was subsequently, I believe, modified or replaced. The building I saw, though a bit too Achaemenid for my liking, is certainly impressive, and stands agreeably among pools and cypresses.

'You ought to see the British Consulate,' said Tom.

Mr. Raj, the Indian caretaker of the Consulate (which has been unoccupied since Mossadeq days), gave us a sumptuous tea and did us the honours of the ruins—ruins less spectacular than those of Persepolis, but more poignant in that they still bear immediate witness of the happy life that so recently flowed there. In these crumbling rooms, glassless amateur water-colours of the English countryside and Medici prints in fly-blown frames hang skewly upon bulging walls from which Morris wallpaper is peeling. English arm-chairs and sofas lie half buried under the fallen ceilings. The dining-room has an English hatch, now warped beyond opening. Cyclostyled notices dealing with permits for visitors from Pakistan lie in a mildewed pile on the office table. In another room are toys where once children played. The house bears no witness of calculated evacuation; some sudden disaster—the fall of a bomb, perhaps—seems to have ended in a moment the ordered pattern of its daily life.

We climbed the staircase to the first floor landing, but it was impossible to venture farther. 'Look out!' cried Mr. Raj, stepping briskly aside as half a hundredweight of roof fell upon the farther end of the landing. He himself lives in the Lodge, keeping at bay with pit-props and tarpaulins the ravages of rain and snow. So well as he is able, he tends the garden, trims the privet hedges, sheds tears over the tennis court, and prunes the fruit trees—thankful to be somewhere where only the sky could fall on him, or the plane trees strong as steel.

'Tell them in Tehran,' he said. 'Tell them what it is like here. I have written many times. The reply is always the same : I am only to do "repairs that are absolutely essential." What is "absolutely essential"? Answer me that!'

I said I would tell them.

I am still haunted by that scene, and by the tearful eyes of Mr. Raj as he said goodbye to me with many proffered flowers and returned to the desolation that he must call his home.

'What is Malekabad?' I asked as we drove away towards our intimidating dinner.

It appeared that the house and its magnificent grounds had once belonged to a certain Mr. Malek. Unfortunately Reza Shah took a fancy to them :

'You have a beautiful garden, Mr. Malek.'

'Your Majesty is too kind.'

'A *very* beautiful garden, Mr. Malek. . . .'

There was an ominous pause : a royal command, however vaguely formulated, is not to be misunderstood. Mr. Malek did some quick thinking. 'Alas! Your Majesty, I have promised Malekabad to the Holy Shrine.' (A bore, this; but he would find some way to wriggle out of it.)

But he could not. And when, after the fall of Reza Shah, the properties that he had snatched were restored to their relatively rightful owners, Malekabad remained with the Shrine.

'Is the Shrine very rich?' I asked.

'Enormously. It's still the largest landowner in Iran. I forget the exact figures that I read somewhere, and anyhow they're now out of date—but I think there once used to be a thousand attendants and seven hundred doorkeepers. And that's without counting all the preachers and readers and prayer-writers and so on. Then there are the solicitors who fix up temporary marriages.'

I remembered reading about that extraordinary system of prostitution organized and blessed by Islam. *Sighehs* (temporary wives) can be legally married for any period from one day to ninety-nine years, and the prospect of combining religious duty with 'a good spree' (Lord Curzon's words and quotation marks) affords no small consolation to the pilgrim on his weary journey.

'Things are different now,' added Tom. 'The staff has been cut down. These temporary marriages still go on, I believe, but they no longer fix them up in the Shrine. And Islam has lost a lot of its power. Today the Governor of the Shrine is appointed by the Shah.'

I was going, after all, to ask him about Dr. Shadman, but there was no time. For we had entered the gates of Malekabad and were driving through a big orchard. On our left was a swimming-pool, and before us, surrounded by formal beds planted with the ubiquitous pansy, stood the low, white and unexpectedly small house of the Governor.

At the door stood a middle-aged man, spectacled, with a kindly smile. He was immaculately (but not over-) dressed in a dark grey lounge suit.

'How do you do? I'm delighted to meet you; I've heard so

much about you. Do come in!' he said in faultless English with
hardly the trace of an accent. 'This is my wife. My dear, this
is Mr. Blunt.'

I was so completely taken aback that I believe I said
'shucks!'

Except for the absence of alcohol, there was nothing about
the meal or the conversation to distinguish it from a London
dinner-party. Or rather, there was : it would be exceptional in
London to find a host and a hostess who combined such intelligence and culture with such kindness and charm.

'Didn't you like the Shadmans?' said Tom.

The question was rhetorical; I did not feel myself called upon
to answer it.

March 31st

If it were possible only to get into Westminster Abbey disguised as an Anglican bishop, I should probably spend a good
deal of my time at Wig Creations being metamorphosed for the
part; as it is, I always seem to sail by in a No. 39 bus on my
way to the Royal Horticultural Society's show in Vincent Square.
For the forbidden is always irresistible. To force an entry into
the Shrine here is no small undertaking.

There are two wholly different methods of attack—the orthodox and the unorthodox. First, the unorthodox—adopted by
Robert Byron and Christopher Sykes in 1934. For this you must
engage the services of a native accessory (no easy matter), mug
up your genuflexions, and go disguised. If you are discovered,
no one can save you. It is a risky affair, and one which, should
it miscarry, also brings trouble upon the Europeans or Americans who have sheltered and befriended you.

The orthodox method is to provide yourself with highest-level
introductions and hope for the best. They tell me here that there
is little doubt that the top officials are only too ready to do what
they can. But they fear the fanaticism of the pilgrims; they dare
not move too fast. There was a brief period in the late thirties
when Reza Shah called the bluff of the *mollas*, who were forced
to let the infidel in. Now, however, entry is harder than ever
before; though one or two people claim to have succeeded in
the post-war years, Tom is sceptical.

Partly through cowardice, partly because I could not imagine that all the make-up in Meshed could disguise my two metres of blue-eyed European self, and partly out of consideration for my host, I chose to proceed correctly. Mr. Taheri, the Administrator of the Mosque, has promised to take Tom and me tomorrow morning to see the tile manufactory on the roof of one of the Shrine buildings; from there it might, I understand, be possible to look down into the courtyard of the Mosque and . . . who knows?

Tom took me this morning to call on the Governor, and then delivered me into the kind hands of one of the Consulate servants, with whom I went off to the Pa'in Khiaban to take photographs.

In Iran, says Mr. Ebtehaj, 'no one is allowed to photograph in the public without having obtained a permit from the local police. . . . Two photographs'—presumably taken 'in the private' —'should accompany the application.' The photographing of fortresses, prostitutes and camels, he adds, is strictly prohibited. But, even if one eschews these forbidden subjects, photography, none too easy in western Iran, is here a nightmare. Twenty or thirty people follow me wherever I go. If I stop, fifty gather round. The sight of my exposure meter draws another fifty. Two hundred watch the camera leave its case. And as soon as I take aim, traffic is brought to a standstill and the police arrive to investigate. Hideous old men in Western clothes cry '*aks! aks!* (photo! photo!),' while women in fantastic tribal dresses, with faces like wonderful horses, bolt at the sight of a camera. *Mollas* are too holy to photograph, the descendants of the Prophet are too proud, beggars imagine that their poverty is being mocked; little girls burst into tears, and little boys go with the wind. There is no open hostility; but it requires a combination of luck, bluff and cunning to succeed. One does not like to hurt people's feelings; yet to ask permission is to ruin one's chances of catching a natural pose. What is needed (and I believe it exists) is a view-finder that points at right angles to the object that is being taken.

And still the crowd surges round me, staring, staring. . . . I know now what it must feel like to be a monarch, a film star or an aquarium fish.

Lunch in the garden, in shirt-sleeves and under the white cherry-blossom. It is as hot as an English June heat-wave.

The Shrine of Khajeh Rabi, erected by Shah Abbas on the site of an older building, lies four miles outside the town and is a popular holiday resort of the Meshedi. A picturesque gate-house and plane-shaded avenue lead to the tomb—a domed octagonal building with two storeys of open arcades. This is possibly the prototype of a design that was soon to become popular and which may have influenced the Taj Mahal.

The inside of the dome is prettily painted in blue with gold arabesques, in the manner of Jolfa Cathedral. But the charm of the place lies in its brilliant and varied (external) tilework, and its pastoral setting; it looked miraculously beautiful this afternoon in the spring sunshine. Repairs are in progress and, to judge from photographs taken twenty years ago, the contour of the dome has suffered in the process.

Outside the gatehouse I saw what appeared to be a drunken man—the first I have come across in Persia. Or maybe he was a little mad : drunkenness is rarer than lunacy here.

The Persian cinema sometimes shows native films, but I have not yet seen one; they are reputed to be both poor technically and dull. The usual fare is the American film, from which—either by accident or by design—a reel or two may be missing. Tom tells me that it is not unusual for the reels to be shown in the wrong sequence. There being no sub-titles, the film is inter-rupted from time to time for the projection on the screen of a lantern-slide giving a synopsis of the plot; this the literate chant in smug chorus for the benefit of the illiterate and their own greater glory. Tonight I saw *Helen of Troy* in a cinema whose roof seemed upon the point of collapse, and in a CinemaScope which overlapped the side walls. The seats were excruciatingly uncomfortable, and everyone ate melon pips.

April 1st. Easter Day

I woke to a white world and (for Tom rises early) the strains of the Schubert B♭ Trio : and only yesterday we were com-plaining of the heat !

Mr. Taheri received us in his office with tea and then con-ducted us along a series of dark passages which seemed to be leading in the direction of the Mosque. Imagining that we were being taken up to the roof, I looked—but in vain—for stairs. Then suddenly I understood : to our right, through a grille, was the prayer-chamber of the Gauhar Shad Mosque! On that bleak winter morning it was wholly deserted (seeing that inclement weather is the universal enemy of religious observance, it is odd that God has seen fit to be so lavish with it). Mr. Taheri hesi-tated a moment, then beckoned to us to follow him.

Though the *mehrab*—so far as it was visible in that gothic gloom—was obviously magnificent, and the inlaid wooden pulpit (recently admirably restored) a lovely and triumphant piece of craftsmanship, it is the court itself which is the crowning glory of the Mosque. We stood at the threshold of it, eagerly straining our eyes to catch some token, some faint echo of its beauty. It was still snowing—snowing so heavily that the far side of the court, robbed of all its glowing colour, was reduced to a wan silhouette that loomed in the half light. On four tall electric-light standards, of a design better suited to the Undercliff Drive at Bournemouth, orange globes glimmered, feebly illuminating the central pool where a little rising fountain fought the falling flakes and a handful of shivering ghosts were performing their melancholy ritual ablutions. Half a dozen officials mounted reluctant guard; and I realized how poor would be the infidel's chances of eluding their vigilance.

Emboldened perhaps by the sparseness of the congregation, or by the realization that we in our turn would also seem but ghosts to the few pale worshippers, Mr. Taheri led the way into the court. We buttoned our coat-collars and followed him, the snow-flakes whirling blindingly about our bare heads, and our Western rubber soles profaning with their jazzy imprints that soft and sacred Moslem snow. As the flakes on my head melted and trickled down my face and my neck there came into my mind a traditional saying of Mohammad's : 'In a mosque a believer is like a fish in water, but an unbeliever is like a cooped-up hen.' I felt much more like a fish.

To have had my first view of the Royal Mosque at Isfahan when half crippled by lumbago; and now to have, in a blizzard that reduced effective visibility to a few yards, what might well

be my only view of the finest surviving building in all Islam—
was almost more than I could bear. Yet, as a blind man may
sense the invisible forest through which he is passing, I too
sensed that which the eyes could barely apprehend—something
at any rate of the majesty and lustre of those towering walls and
portals. And by drawing close to a wall I could estimate, as in
imagination one can paper a room from a square foot of sample,
a measure at least of its grandeur.

I turned to Mr. Taheri and asked him if there was any hope
that I might come again. 'I think it will be possible,' he
answered.

Then I was happy.

When we had unshivered and grown a little dry again, Mr.
Taheri took us up to his tile factory on the roof. This is the
apple of his eye—and indeed he has every reason to be proud
of it. For the mosaic tiles are being cut with a precision that the
original craftsmen of the Mosque could not have surpassed, and
no praise is too high for the restoration that is being carried
out.

Having lavished such superlatives as we could muster upon
that apple of his other eye, the new Mosque lavatories, we were
conducted to the Museum. This is an admirably designed building in pale-coloured marbles, within the precincts of the Shrine;
it contains, among other treasures, some six-foot-high pages of a
gigantic *Koran*, a few wonderful carpets, and a twelfth-century
manuscript of Dioscorides of which there is a facsimile in the
Library of the Society of Herbalists in London.

In the Library of the Mosque is a large collection of manu-
scripts and printed books ranging from commentaries on the
Koran to a complete set of Proust (presented, needless to say, by
Dr. Shadman).

Dinner party at the Consulate: Dr. Assadi, Dr. and Mrs.
Shadman, Mr. Taheri, Mr. Ghauri (the Pakistani consul), the
Jespersons, and Dave Nalle (fresh from a ping-pong tournament
at the Reza Shah School).

Mr. Ghauri is discussing traffic problems:

'Do you know that three hundred years ago there were no
motor-cars?'

I do. But now there are, and he has one; and he has kindly offered to take Tom, Dave and myself to Nishapur tomorrow, Tom's car being indisposed and thus unequal to Persian country roads in their present state. Tomorrow is *sizdah*, the thirteenth day of the Persian New Year—a holiday when all the world goes out into the country, to some shrine or garden, to picnic. We should see Nishapur at its gayest—if only the weather will behave.

April 2nd

Yesterday was mid-winter; today, radiant and cloudless, might be June. Yet there is a briskness, an exhilaration in the air that even Switzerland hardly knows. Seven inches of snow have almost vanished at the miraculous touch of the hot sun; only shadows still are white.

We left at ten o'clock in Mr. Ghauri's chauffeur-driven Chevrolet. Nishapur, as the crow flies, is fifty miles due west of Meshed; by road it is double that distance, for the long south-east-thrusting tongue of the Nishapur mountains intrudes.

A blue-domed shrine: but we cannot stop. The eleventh-century mausoleum of Sangbast, a mile off the road: but having slithered in slime we turn back, forced to content ourselves with the distant view of its crumbling dome and minaret. A steeply banked river to ford: we hit a submerged boulder, which has to be dug out by our long-suffering, wading chauffeur.

The caravanserai of Sangbast, however, lies on the road—a huge, derelict building where once the Meshed pilgrims halted. We halted also. While the American vice-consul was snowballing the American consul, and the Pakistani consul was losing a galosh in the squelching mud, I took photographs of the high arched entrance and spacious courtyard.

About half-way between Meshed and Nishapur is Qadam Gah, 'the place of the step,' a shrine commemorating a stopping-place of Imam Reza on his way to Tus. It stands well above the road—a pretty, octagonal, seventeenth-century building with open galleries and a strongly patterned bulging dome —among groves of stately pines and plane trees. Like Khajeh Rabi, it too claims to be the prototype of the Taj Mahal. A happy little stream drops, terrace by terrace, from the steep nearby mountainside. These terraces were crowded with picnickers, who at our approach looked up from their bubbling kettles to greet us with surprised, friendly smiles of welcome. The youths gathered amiably round us, staring as though we were Martians. Europeans must be rare birds in these parts.

Shedding our shoes (always carry a shoe-horn in Persia) we entered without gainsay the shrine—a dullish, dark little chamber containing the size 12 footprints of the Imam sunk in black stone. They seemed appreciably larger, but notably less convincing, than the concrete imprints of Michael Redgrave's feet outside the Granada Cinema in Slough. Odd, as Curzon remarks, how saints always have outsize feet—though the Imam's shrink to insignificance in comparison with Mohammad's at Jerusalem or Buddha's on the summit of Adam's Peak in Ceylon.

Qadam Gah is a charming spot, and Ebtehaj would seem to show a certain lack of sensibility, and indeed of patriotism, in writing of it, 'the garden and building are both shabby.'

Another mosque, it seemed, grew visible to the right of the road. In fact it was the railway station of Nishapur, built fifteen years ago and still awaiting the coming of the line—an event which is confidently expected to take place this very August.

As we drew nearer to Nishapur, the country grew more welcoming and more fertile. The Emamzadeh of Mohammad Mahruq, in whose green garden old Omar lies buried, stands before the town, a little aside from the road. Here, too, the swift advent of spring had brought its flood of pilgrims and holidaymakers. We joined these guests star-scatter'd on the grass, and in our joyous errand reaching the spot where He made One, uncorked a bottle of claret beside the poet's crudely phallic flowerless tomb, drank to his immortal memory—and turned down an empty glass.

Little remains visible of the great past of Nishapur, for, as Curzon says, 'it has certainly been destroyed and rebuilt more than any other city in the world.' Tom's sense of duty, which is very highly developed, made him call upon the Governor. Unfortunately the man was at home, but on the point of leaving to visit a certain Mr. Ezatollah Ganji, a rich merchant who lived 'just outside the town.' He insisted upon our accompanying him upon what proved to be a twenty-mile journey each way, through mud and flood and pot-holes.

Mr. Ganji was out; but we drank tea in his rambling green garden and were shown his great treasure, Kamal-ol-Molk's oil-painting of 'The Birdsellers of Arles.' This is considered to be the *magnum opus* of Iran's greatest artist of recent times, and indeed it was largely on my account that we had been tricked into making this lengthy excursion from Nishapur. Mr. Ganji is reported to have said that he would not part with the 'Birdsellers' for two hundred thousand *tomans* (£10,000). At Sotheby's it would fetch less—perhaps about three guineas; but it may well be an object of value in Iran. Kamal-ol-Molk studied in Paris in, I dare say, the nineties of the last century, and no doubt this vast painting, in the French academic manner, reached in its day the walls of the Salon. We stood rapt before it, as though in the presence of a great Rembrandt.

Sunset was painting the wall of snow mountains to our north as we set out again for Nishapur. It was nearly midnight by the time we reached Meshed, where Dave restored us with welcome hot soup and whisky before we finally took leave of our kind and cultured Pakistani host.

April 3rd

The Shah is expected to arrive in Meshed this morning. Workmen have been labouring overtime filling in the more outrageous cavities in the Avenue Pahlavi. Triumphal arches have been erected—cardboard modernistic eyesores against which, rising in tiers like a Victorian conservatory, are riots of pot-plants, electric-light bulbs, and portraits of His Majesty tinted to the life. Stuffed lions with Iranian flags in their front paws and dust sheets over their backs mount guard; each has an electric-light bulb in its mouth, another attached to the tail, and a flower-pot on its head.

At eight-forty-five the telephone rings: the Shah is arriving at the airport at nine o'clock. Tom screams for his morning coat and is just about to leave the house when the telephone rings once more: the Shah will not be arriving after all.

Here is yet another example of the difficulty of arriving at *facts* in Iran. I have been successively told that:

There is no bus at present to Herat : the road is in ruins and nothing has come through for five days.

There is a bus about to leave for Herat, but it is not expected to arrive there.

A bus is leaving for Herat at one o'clock, or perhaps three o'clock, but it is full.

The bus is not full. There is still one place.

And this place is to be mine !

I examined the seat allotted to me : it was fair accommodation for a child of six. The driver offered to change it for me if I made it worth his while, and I readily agreed. But he still urges me to wait a few days, until the floods have subsided. I will not wait. I went home to pack, and to collect my passport which is said to have arrived by the morning plane from Tehran, where I had left it for the Persian exit visa. The passport was handed to me : it proved to be, not mine, but that of an unknown American.

The next bus cannot leave before Saturday. I went upstairs and miserably unpacked.

After dinner I went to see Mr. Rodgers—an American who is doing something important out here that I cannot quite remember—and a friend of his with whom he has just returned from Herat. They spoke gloomily of the state of the roads. After endless delays, they finally got away in a truck piled sky-high with crates of glass that fell off at intervals. They were carried pick-a-back across the rivers. Among their trophies from Afghanistan were a dazzling waistcoat, and a pair of yellow shoes that looked like slices of melon.

They too spoke of the incredible end-of-the-world feeling, the sense of utter remoteness, that comes upon the traveller after he crosses the Afghan frontier.

April 4th

Eton breaks up today; how far away it all seems !

Eight-fifteen. The Shah is arriving this morning, and Tom has just left in his splendour for the airport. The Scouts are all lined up, the little Girl Guides are clutching their bouquets; carpets have been spread, the Diplomatic Corps and the ministers are waiting. . . .

The Shah is not arriving after all. The diplomats, the ministers, the Scouts, the Guides disperse; but no one tells the crowd (including myself), which continues to line the streets.

Waiting for the Shah is like waiting for Godot.

In the evening, workmen begin to dismantle the triumphal arches.

I have been looking into one or two fairly recent Middle East travelogues—they shall be nameless—and was interested to observe how an author's enthusiasm for veracity tends to vary indirectly with his distance from London or New York. No good writing that the dome of St. Peter's is seven hundred feet high and made of solid gold; too many people know that it is not. By the time he reaches Asiatic Turkey he is feeling his way to better things. In Persia he gets nicely into his stride, yet is still a shade cramped by Curzon's restrained and accurate descriptions of the country. R., for example, took 'a matter of hours' to reach, from the Shapur valley, the fallen statue of King Shapur and 'gaze into six foot of blue-blooded Aryan face'; Curzon makes the climb forty-five minutes, and Flandin measures the head as three feet three inches. Fortunately for the writers of such travelogues, Curzon and Flandin are unlikely to come the way of the general reader.

In Afghanistan, of course, one can get away with murder. Doubtless I shall soon be doing so.

April 5th

My friends Sacheverell and Georgia Sitwell are arriving this morning with Lady Alexandra Metcalfe, Lord Curzon's daughter; so my enforced delay in Meshed has its compensations. The Sitwells are always the most charming of companions. Conversation with Sachie has something of the excitement of a lucky dip—one never knows what new and delicious treasure one will fish from his inexhaustible *tutti frutti* of information.

But I am a shade under the stomachic weather. It happens to everyone here, sooner or later, I gather.

After tea, Mr. Taheri took us all to the Library and the Museum, where I was glad of the opportunity to review various objects, especially the manuscripts and miniatures. From the

Museum, we passed to the nearby store of a turquoise merchant, where the ladies of the party wallowed semi-preciously for a glorious hour—trying on interminable bangles and ear-rings and necklaces; effecting no purchase, yet somehow conveying the impression that they would come back tomorrow and buy up the shop. The turquoises, which come from mines near Nishapur, are the finest in the world, though Mr. Ebtehaj will commit himself no further than 'Its turquoise quarries operated since twenty centuries are well reputed.'

But the principal object in visiting the jeweller was to ingratiate ourselves on to his roof for a better view of the Shrine at sunset. A barrage of telegraph wires made photography difficult. Lady Alexandra, with remarkable agility and assisted by Tom, swarmed on to a superstructure which commanded an unimpeded prospect. Being no alpinist, I remained below and photographed the wires.

Then, as the last rays of the sun tired of gilding the lily dome, a shrill consort of trumpets sounded its pre-Islamic, customary serenade from the roof-top of the Shrine, and night and Lady Alexandra descended.

Lady Alexandra travelled extensively after dinner through Asia, Africa, America, etc., carrying us joyfully with her. We had an ugly moment in Algeria when a captive leopard broke its chain just as she was photographing it. I played the only trump card that a male traveller can play against a female: Mount Athos. But Lady Alexandra had often sailed up and down the coast observing monkish behaviour through binoculars, and clearly knew the set-up far better than I did.

And so, outwitted, to bed.

April 6th

The Shah is arriving today. Workmen are busy re-erecting the triumphal arches.

The Shah is not arriving after all.

(I heard later that the Shah did get to Meshed in the end.

A gigantic thunderstorm broke at the precise instant his plane touched down. But not for nothing is the Shah his father's son. He passed unhurriedly along the line of wretched, dripping delegates and members of the Diplomatic Corps drawn up to welcome him, pausing here and there to say a friendly word of greeting or to comment unfavourably upon the climate of Khorasan; he took a damp salute from the miserable troop of Boy Scouts, and accepted a wet, wilted bouquet from a sopping little Girl Guide. Then, while the diplomats and the more securely established delegates made an unedifying bolt for cover, he walked slowly towards the airport buildings, closely attended by a small group of those whose reappointment is in doubt and who were ready to drown rather than forgo this welcome moment of access to the royal ear.)

Sachie has discovered an old woman who, for the sake of economy—or maybe from mere whimsy—lives in a dog-kennel in a street near the Consulate. The *mise-en-scène* struck his fancy, and Lady Alexandra has promised to photograph it for him. But the old woman will not play, and slams her kennel door. Her son is no more enthusiastic; he plants himself in front of the kennel and assumes a threatening attitude. A crowd collects and assumes more threatening attitudes. The project has to be abandoned. But only temporarily : Lady Alexandra will try again tomorrow.

Is this, I wonder, her Waterloo? . . .

Mr. Ghauri had invited us all to lunch at half past twelve.
We found him knee-deep in trays of pink and yellow sweets, in a room hermetically shuttered, curtained and sealed. I thought for a moment that lunch was to be preceded by a lantern lecture on the beauties of Pakistan; but it was just an old Pakistani custom. I gave Lady Alexandra five minutes to get something open; she did it in four.

'Forgive my turning my back on you, Mr. Ghauri.'
'There is neither back nor front to a flower.'
Ta'arof again! Botanically unsound, but a pretty conceit.

At half past two, the pink and yellow sweets gave place to more serious food—much to the relief of Lady Alexandra, who was champing at losing valuable daylight for her photography. As we left, soon after four, to visit Khajeh Rabi, rain set in.

The Sitwells went on to tea at the British Consulate, from which Sachie returned almost in tears.

In the evening Tom gave a dinner-party for Lady Alexandra and the Sitwells: sixteen persons, seated at four small tables. I kept company with two speechless women, and the Afghan consul who wore an English polo-sweater and after dinner puffed at an English pipe. Yet never can Afghan consul have looked more like an Afghan—nor, incidentally, less like a consul. How magnificent he would appear in native dress, on horseback, surrounded by roaring lions!

'You will persuade Mr. and Mrs. Sitwell to visit Herat?'

I said that they were too pressed for time. But, truth to tell, I doubted whether they would have considered the beauties of Herat sufficient reward for the discomforts of the journey.

'You will write some nice articles about Afghanistan?'

'*Ensha'allah* (God willing).'

April 7th

A stag party, from which even Lady Alexandra was excluded, to see the tile factory on the roof of the Shrine. From here, Sachie and I were allowed to climb one of the minarets for a God's-eye view of the court of the Gauhar Shad Mosque. But the sun had drawn too many worshippers there, and we were not able to enter the Mosque itself or the court.

It was almost impossible to believe that the dazzling court below us was the very same that, only six days earlier, I had seen in snow and misery. Now it shone like a garden of summer flowers, richer and more resplendent than anything that I had found in Isfahan. Before us rose the whole unbroken glory of the golden dome and twin golden minarets; and the crowding pilgrims were as ants at our feet. But there was no more time than to capture a general impression of turquoise, green and a darker blue; of black, white and crocus yellow; of great calligraphic friezes, and purple shadows under the tall portals—and a gesture summoned us to abandon our preview of paradise.

So Byron was right after all!

8

Meshed to Herat

SACHIE said goodbye to me as though I were going to certain death. Perhaps I am.

The bus stood there, empty still but now piled so high with luggage that it was as tall as a double-decker. On the pavement, passively resigned to their fate, squatted my fellow-travellers—wild tribesmen in white turbans, striped pyjama trousers and flapping shirt-tails; veiled women with infants in their arms; a bumptious youth in an American wind-jacket, looking like an international crook; and an obese man who appeared to be the owner of the bus.

I too squatted on the pavement; but my exotic appearance soon drew so great a crowd that the loading of the bus was impeded, and I was hauled into the office. There I sat, gloomily surveying my tickets (for greater comfort I had taken two seats) and trying to discover whether the curious legend that they bore on the reverse, presumably for the enlightenment of European travellers, was intended to be in English :

ooay mq Addes

feleke junubj jenb

Muze

Te' Address

KHAWAR TOR

The loading now in progress consisted of filling the gangway of the bus with large sacks (how shrewd of the Romans to call luggage 'impedimenta'!) When access to the seats had been rendered virtually impossible, the proprietor began to call the roll and the passengers were pushed and pulled into their appointed places. My seats being beside the door, I climbed in last. At this moment an elderly man appeared with his bed and entire household property tied together in one vast clanking bundle. Room was eventually made for him by forcibly ejecting another passenger, and the baggage wedged upon the sacks in the gangway and on one of my two seats.

We were less than three hours late in starting. Immediately behind me sat two women, with a pair of green-faced infants who were suffering from whooping-cough or its Afghan equivalent, and who were to claw the back of my neck intermittently for the next twenty hours. Very grimy the children were, and one had a pustule as well. Beside the solid driver were the owner and the bumptious youth in the wind-jacket. The two men who had seen to the loading of the bus now accompanied it in the capacity of odd-job men and sat at, when not on, my feet. Behind us, packed in indescribable confusion, came the rabble of pilgrims, who, having paid for only one seat apiece, had no special claim on the management's compassion. Five more were on the roof.

It was only too obvious that the bus was already more than full, yet a couple of extra passengers were picked up before we reached the edge of the town; they carried spades, and were soon deposited to play their small part in the much-needed repair of the road.

As far as Sangbast, we followed the already familiar way to Nishapur. At the little blue-domed *emamzadeh,* which again I could not stop to see, a funeral was taking place. All went well until we reached the first river-bed, the place where our car had got into difficulties five days before. On the brink of the precipice, the bus, like a caterpillar reaching the edge of a table, stopped to take measure of the danger ahead.

'Cry *"Yallah!"* '[1] ordered the bumptious youth.

'*Yallah!*' wailed the pilgrims in chorus as the bus plunged down the steep incline, ploughed its way through the water and safely mounted the far bank.

These invocations, always conducted by the bumptious youth, constituted the regular ritual at every subsequent water-jump. Often the danger appeared to be so slight as hardly to warrant disturbing the Deity: a 'Hold tight!' would really have met the case. But doubtless the recognition of perils encountered added virtue to the pilgrimage.

The way now lay straight across a broad plain. Blue, snow-capped mountains, not very high, barred the horizon; by the roadside were scattered little yellow irises, and scarlet tulips that

[1] 'O God!'

the evening sun painted bright as medieval glass. Then something went wrong with one of the front wheels of the bus, and while it was being repaired I was able to get out and collect a few flowers, among them some wan little tulips no bigger than daisies. Meanwhile the bus had collected another mother and child, who were also dumped on the floor at my feet. The child —it was incredibly tiny—moaned pathetically, and the mother, still carefully veiling her face, bared her breast to suckle it.

Having made a big detour to avoid floods, we arrived, just as the sun was setting, in sight of Fareman. At this point the bus ran out of petrol, which had to be fetched from the village. Unfortunately it was too dark to see more of Fareman than the two ludicrous plaster lions that guard its approach. Here, twenty-one years ago, Reza Shah planned to set up a model rural community. Schools, factories and private houses were built. There was a fire-control tower, an Hotel Splendide, and the usual consignment of plaster figures to add a touch of Western civilization. Everything sprang up overnight in obedience to the royal command. Then came the war and the end of Reza Shah. Equipment decayed or was looted; the neat Teutonic cottages collapsed or were torn down and used as firewood; the population deserted *en masse*. A vast silence descended upon Reza Shah's Utopian settlement.

The Imperial Villa still stands—no doubt because it was not built of materials suitable for the household fire. A friend who has seen it described it to me as being 'approached by way of a circular piazza surrounded by a plaster colonnade apparently designed by someone who may have passed by St. Peter's once in a closed car. In the centre is a huge fountain composed of cupids (painted silver) gushing into oversize shells. Inside the Villa grounds there is only one occupant—one in no way connected with the royal family : a donkey.'

Such was, and is, Fareman—an enterprise doomed from the start. Now the present Shah has inaugurated a more modest, more realistic scheme of land development, which stands a better chance of success.

We stopped at Fareman for 'supper' in what looked like a brigands' den. I managed to get a couple of boiled eggs and a glass of tea; the bread was virtually inedible. While we were eating, the police arrived to examine my passport. They were favourably impressed by the seals on my letters of recommendation; the letters themselves they seemed unable to read.

On now into the night. At one stream the bus lurched dangerously. '*Yallah, yallah!*' cried the pilgrims under the direction of their regular conductor. I tried to comfort myself with the recollection of a picture of a London bus tipped at forty degrees, at the same time trying to forget that this was *not* a London bus. We backed to make a second attempt—with the same result. There was a murmur in the bus which sounded like 'throw the Christian overboard.' We backed again.

'Now one great big *yallah* from everyone,' said the bumptious youth, looking straight at me.

I ostentatiously join in. Allah hears us, and we are safe.

At last, towards midnight, the welcome lights of Torbat-e-Jam. On reaching the little town the bus drove into a courtyard, where it deposited us in pitch darkness and a foot of squelching mud. Fortunately I had a torch. The pilgrims vanished into the night, and I was led through the mire to a room deep in filth. It contained three 'thrones of sleep,' all unspeakably dirty. The first collapsed at a touch. I took the second and discarded the bedding, to find that time or deliberate malice had transformed the springs into a bed of spikes fit to test the piety of a fakir. I spread my sleeping-bag on it; in five minutes I was asleep.

April 8th

'Did you sleep well?'
'Yes.'
'They say you are writing a book.'
'Yes.'
'You will say in your book that Torbat is a very nice place?'
'*Ensha'allah.*'

We were off at seven and there was no time to see the Shrine. The green children looked better, but no cleaner, and were whooping less; I stuffed them with sweets, and one was promptly sick. But the bus seemed to have aged during the night. Had it been human, one would have diagnosed a sharp attack of bronchitis. I had the impression that it was determined (and perhaps this very day) to die in harness, and that its owner had accompanied us in order to witness its end.

A rival prayer-leader now announced himself from the back of the bus. His natural tremolo exaggerated by the vibration and accompanied by the wheezings of the engine, he began to intone an endless litany which seriously interfered with the effectiveness of the *yallah* campaign in the front. There was little else to enliven the journey across a flat, flooded plain : only a few red and yellow tulips, the skeleton of a dead camel or two, and far away the first black tents of the nomads.

Soon, however, we reached a formidable river. Here the passengers alighted—all but a few women with children, who preferred to risk death in the bus—and were carried across pick-a-back by one of the odd-job men. When my turn came he shouldered me reluctantly, daunted by my weight and perhaps also by the thought that I might well be a *nasnas*. Meanwhile the other odd-job man and one or two co-operative passengers were prodding the river-bed with shovels, adjusting the contours of the banks, and generally facilitating a crossing. Then the 'all clear' was given. The bus bounded down the hill, breasted the waters manfully and joined us on the farther bank.

At Yusefabad, the Persian frontier village, the bus, which may go no farther, deposited its bedraggled pilgrims. I was conducted to the military, who obligingly offered to escort me in a jeep to the Afghan frontier station, Eslam Qaleh.

Immediately outside the village was a fearful river with precipitous banks. A tattered shoe trod hard on the accelerator.

'A nasty spot,' I cried, clutching grimly.

'Odd you should say that,' said the driver imperturbably; 'only the other day a jeep with four Americans in it overturned at this very place. They were all killed.'

(I mildly embroider what I understood, namely : 'recently . . . motor . . . four *Amerikani* . . . dead,' accompanied by an upside-down gesture with a hand that had been better on the steering-wheel.)

The precipice safely behind us, we drove at hair-raising speed, over a plain bright with giant yellow umbelliferous plants[1] and

---

[1] Dr. Amsel (see footnote on p. 149) gives an illustration of this plant, which he identifies as a species of Ferula (giant fennel). 'The size of the inflorescence—we cut one and found that it weighed about 20 lbs. and that the stem was four inches thick—gave one the impression of walking through a forest of umbelifers. . . . The plant flowers after from five to seven years, and then dies.'

a-flutter with cranes, till we reached the frontier—marked by an
unguarded pole across the track, and a signboard. At the sight
of the bold-lettered AFGHANISTAN my heart sang; at the
sight, a few minutes later, of Eslam Qaleh, my heart stopped
singing.

'When will there be a bus to Herat?'

'God is the Most-Knowing.'

April 9th

Eslam Qaleh consists of five solidly built houses set in mud-
walled compounds: the Customs, the Telegraph, the Barracks,
the Road Repairs and the guest house. Except for a few out-
buildings and a handful of stunted pine trees, this is all. Upwards
of a hundred and fifty persons are said to live here, but so far
I have failed to discover a dozen. The Telegraph is out of
action: telegrams from Meshed to Herat take four days and are
sent (I was told) via London. The Road Repairs is, or are, shut.
Within the Barracks compound sits one seedy-looking soldier
endlessly cleaning a rusty rifle. The Customs seems dead except
for a man who stands all day long on the roof, staring vacuously.
In the guest house, where I am the only guest, there appear to
be the proprietor, his brother Gholamsardar—a boy of seventeen,
and a menial. Gholamsardar (if I got the name correctly—and
this, since he cannot write, is uncertain) means 'the general's
servant.'

The guest house is reasonably clean. The large rooms are airy
and permanently full of swallows. On the floors are rugs that
would not disgrace a palace. It was erected, a dozen or so years
ago, to impress Iranian visitors with the high degree of civilization
of Afghanistan—hence that remarkable phenomenon, a bath!
Superfluous to add that this never has been and never could
be used. It stands there, plugless and pipeless, white and forlorn,
a symbol of Progress. The food might, I suppose, be worse,
though the bread looks, and tastes, like the lid of an old pigskin
suitcase, and the purple limbs of an ancient hen appear at every
meal. But with eggs, rice and excellent yoghourt, and tea that
tastes better than one has any right to expect after seeing the
green water from which it is made, one does not starve.

There is little at Eslam Qaleh to tempt the traveller to a prolonged stay. There is no wine; there are no women; and for

song, not even the bright laughter of children : only the plaintive
throbbing of Gholamsardar's *dotar* (two-stringed guitar), the
amorous croaking of frogs in the marshes, and the gusty, obscene
chortlings (like that of City men enjoying a Stock Exchange
joke) of jackals that disturb my sleep. It is impossible to buy
cigarettes or matches, and I am running short of both. For walks,
you may go north, south, east or west across a waterlogged
malarial plain until you are weary, and except for a few tulips,
an infinity of tortoises, and ants so large that I was tempted to
photograph them, the reward is slight. A good mile away—it
looks but a few hundred yards in this clear air—is a crumbling
mud-walled castle which, to judge from potsherds visible on the
surface, might be worth excavating. And there is one black tent
in which I found two brothers—lads of perhaps nineteen and
sixteen—gentle, sad-eyed, malarious, surrounded by sheep. They
said the tent was warm enough in winter, when a couple of feet
of snow is not unusual. It was hard to believe.

Such are the attractions of Eslam Qaleh, and not even the
radiant spring sunshine can make much of them. In winter, the
place must be a nightmare.

I walked out early this morning in search of flowers. As I
seem likely to remain here long enough to compile a flora of
north-western Afghanistan, I might as well begin work now. But
by ten o'clock it was so hot that I came in again. Gholamsardar
was sitting on the hotel steps looking dejected and complaining
of a headache. I gave him a couple of Disprins and received in
return a box of Russian matches—splendid stout matches that
actually light. We were both content with the bargain. I spent
an hour talking with him. Since his English is limited to the
single word 'OK,' this meant talking Persian, and I was agreeably surprised to find how far I could get.

We compared monarchs. The King of Afghanistan, he said,
was young and good and handsome, every inch a king. Not to
be outdone, I told him that we were ruled by a young, good
Lady-King of astonishing beauty, called Elizabeth.

'Elebzeth?'

'Well, roughly.'

'Why has she no man?'

'She has a man, and two beautiful children.'

'Then why is her man not King?'

'Because our Lady-King is the daughter of our dead Gentle-man-King—I mean our dead King—who had no sons.'

He could not understand, and I could not explain any better.

He told me about the wonders of Herat. Since it is the only town that he has ever seen, it seems to him a miracle of modernity. The cars: there are so many of them that—believe it or not—sometimes you can actually see two in the same street at the same moment. Then there are policemen controlling the traffic; there are marvellous modern buildings, some of them as much as three storeys high; and there are no less than *two* cinemas!

And how about the Mosalla of Gauhar Shad, I asked? He did not know; but on reflection he thought that he did faintly remember having seen two or three minarets in a pine grove on the fringes of the town. 'But they are nothing,' he added. 'They are a ruin.'

Would I like to learn Pashto, he inquired.

Pashto is the language of Afghanistan, though fortunately for me Persian is universally spoken in the north-west, which is culturally a part of Iran. For the moment I have my hands full with Persian, but the boy was so eager to display his know-ledge that it would have been churlish to refuse. No doubt there will be time enough to learn both before I leave, and perhaps even to read the great Pashto epic *De Sal Wzham* (which means, of course, 'The Breeze of the Desert').

At all events, my Disprins had worked a miraculous cure. Was I a doctor? No, a teacher. Just so—a teacher of medicine. The rumour soon spread that I was a famous doctor. After lunch, an old man arrived for a consultation, prodding his stomach and howling with pain. Probably I ought to have oper-ated. I gave him a couple of Disprins too, and prayed he might live through the night. These are the wild places where every 'Frank' is a doctor.

Towards sunset, when it was cool enough to go out again, I decided to visit the castle. I asked Gholamsardar if he would come too.

'Is it necessary?' (He is idle. His shoes are terrible.)

'Not necessary, but good.'

Actually I rather thought it *was* necessary, for I hadn't much cared for the look of certain Afghan sheepdogs that I had seen during my morning walk, and he would know how to deal with them.

It was on the top of the castle mound, the endless green and golden plain wide-spread below us, that we watched the tortoises courting : the butting match between the rival males, the neck-biting, the sudden—surprisingly sudden—dorsal attacks. Meanwhile the coveted female, larger than the male, and singularly lacking in sex-appeal, placidly observed the outcome of the encounter till, seeing that no blood was being shed, she became bored and waddled away in search of a more valiant cavalier.

I like Gholamsardar. He is so proud of his country, proud of his King, proud to be an Afghan, proud to be a Sunni (though even he is ashamed of the state of the roads). His manners, too, are impeccable. He looks like a school prefect dressed up to play Hassan. He is mad about *buzkashi*, the Afghan national game. In better boots he would, I am sure, make a magnificent 'three-quarter.'

April 10th

Taking my lead from Queen Isabella, I have vowed not to change my shirt until Herat has fallen.

'Sister Anne, sister Anne, do you see anything coming?'

Yes—a JEEP! It belongs, they say, to the Telegraph and has come from Yusefabad. It will go back to Yusefabad again this morning, will return with cigarettes for me at lunch-time, and might even carry me to Herat in the evening.

Six men are now visible in the Telegraph Office. The soldier has stopped cleaning his rifle. Gholamsardar has borrowed a razor-blade from me and effected a notable improvement in his appearance. On my now empty State Express cigarette tin I have been trying, with a red Biro, to change DELICIOUS SMOKING into RELIGIOUS SMOKING—an operation made the easier by the curious shape of the letter 'D.' Such are the epoch-making events of the morning. In other words, I am indescribably bored.

After lunch my cigarettes did indeed arrive. But the jeep was full : five passengers already. Tomorrow, *ensha'allah*, there will be a bus. . . .

I shall believe it when I see it.

6 p.m. A speck on the horizon. . . .

'The Bus!'

Not the 'Thalassa' of Xenophon's soldiers was cry more heartfelt.

It staggered into the courtyard, panting, quivering, jangling, to disgorge its unhappy, motley band of pilgrims. Striped red, green and yellow, its windows unglazed, its form sprawling, it looked like some gigantic beetle wearing club colours. At some stage in its career—thirty years ago, maybe—most of the back had fallen off and been replaced by portions of an Indian tea-chest upon which the word 'Allah' stood inscribed in bright blue. Had the bus been 'painted all over with roses,' I would have supposed it the very one in which Byron had made the same journey more than twenty years before.

I got out my camera to photograph the scene. There was an instant cry of dismay, and I was ordered to put it away. The evil eye, no doubt.

So tomorrow, *ensha'allah*, I shall leave for **Herat**.

'Not tomorrow.'

'Why not tomorrow?'

'The road is a ruin. The day after tomorrow, *ensha'allah*.'

'But will the road be better the day after tomorrow?'

'*Ensha'allah*.'

But at all events there is life here now. I take pleasure in contemplating the Mongol, exquisite features of a young boy in a green-and-gold turban, pretty as a flower. There are men, with splendid savage faces and flashing white teeth. And women? They crouch on the ground, forgotten and neglected, veiled from head to foot, hardly to be distinguished from the bales of merchandise that are being dumped beside them. That is as much as a foreigner ever sees of the women of Afghanistan.

Night falls. There is laughter now in the guest house. On the steps, by the light of an oil lamp, the men are scooping up great handfuls of rice. The kettle boils; a hubble-bubble is gurgling. Gholamsardar has brought out his *dotar* and is singing a strange, plaintive song.

'What is the song about?' I ask.

'Love.'

April 11th

Four cut-throats burst into my bedroom at 6.30 a.m. to ask the equivalent of 100 rupees in *afghanis*—a pleasant start to the day. Then Gholamsardar came in with a bunch of buttercups— real *English* buttercups; I had not seen any on my walks. Soon the Eton meadows will be golden with them. . . .

The bus has gone off to Yusefabad and will return, *ensha'allah*, tomorrow. I took again the shadeless walk to the castle, but the heat, and three savage dogs, soon drove me indoors. Meanwhile my room had been once more invaded—this time by ants : not, mercifully, the giant ants of the field, but little harmless creatures no bigger than our own.

Startling developments! Three German entomologists, on their way to Herat, suddenly arrive at the guest house. Their specially designed *Volkswagen*, labelled in bold letters 'Deutsche-Afghanistan Expedition,' is very blue and very splendid, but packed to the last cubic inch with tents and equipment. So I must wait for the bus. Gholamsardar sniffed scornfully at the *Volkswagen* and proclaimed that it could never get through five feet of water to reach Herat. I would back it any day against the bus. *Nous verrons.*

The Germans—one of them is hardly more than a boy— stopped for lunch, for which they were charged about three times the proper amount. They recommend me to pass myself off as a German while here, since the English are, they allege, so hated in the Middle East, especially in Afghanistan. Everywhere except in Iraq, they said.

'I found nothing but kindness in Iran.'

'Then you were lucky. It isn't difficult for an Englishman— especially an Englishman travelling *alone*—to *vanish* in Afghanistan!'

And with this heartening thought they drove away, leaving me to wonder how much I shall fetch in the slave markets of Balkh.

But I must not be too ungrateful : for they have lent me two books on Afghanistan, which better suit my mood than Mrs.

Herati boys

Afghan boy on the bus to Herat
(p. 119)

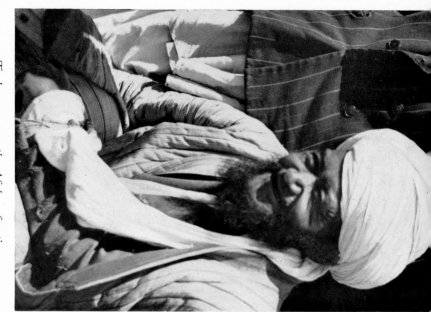

Turkoman near the Afghan frontier

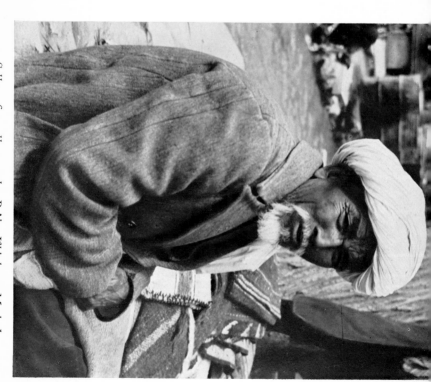

Seller of woollen goods, Pā'in Khiabān, Meshed
(p. 88)

(*Above*) *The Volkswagen in difficulties*
(p. 152)

(*Below*) *Punctured. The Afghan bus*
(p. 120)

Herati boy

Dotar seller, Herat

Woodham-Smith's *Florence Nightingale*, the only light reading I have with me. One of these is Mohammed Ali, M.A.'s *A New Guide to Afghanistan*, with a map and thirty-three illustrations; Kabul, 1955. I shall have more to say of this book in due course; for the moment, here are one or two snippets that caught my eye:

'Wolves are said to go ahead of their victim, and with their hind legs throw up snow on his face and body, and when they see that his hands and feet are benumbed by the effect of the snow, they fall upon him and tear him to pieces. . . . The villagers use various methods to defend themselves. When one of them is pursued by a wolf, he, having no fire-arms to frighten him off, generally employs the following method to get rid of his enemy. Tying one of his shoes at the end of his turban, and holding the other end in his hand, he lets the shoe trail after him. The wolf coming near his victim is attracted by the shoe and tries to catch it, but finding it moving forward leaps aside. So this goes on for a long time: the shoe keeps him busy. In the meanwhile, the poor villager reaches his destination, where the wolf, finding his life in danger, makes for the neighbouring hill.

'There is a kind of beautiful cat known by the name of Baraqi, which has long brilliant hair.

'The yak prefers a temperature below zero. If the snow on the elevated flats lie too deep for him to crop the herbags [*sic*] he rolls himself down the slopes and eats his way up again.'

Mohammed Ali also has a good account of *buzkashi*, which has been described by an English writer as making polo seem by comparison like vicarage tennis and—I would suggest—the Westminster pancake affray as innocuous as spillikins. '*Buzkashi* is a very dangerous sport. A goat is beheaded and the dead body thrown into a ditch. Hundreds of competitors, all riding swift-footed horses, take part in it. Every one tries to get the goat and take it to the goal. In this hard struggle many receive serious injuries, and some even lose their lives, being thrown off their horses and trampled upon by other riders.' (Hence the expression, 'he gets my goat'?) Spectators, Gholamsardar tells me, also sometimes get killed. *Buzkashi* must be 'sport' in the fullest sense of the word, and should obviously be introduced into England.

5—PS

Six o'clock. The bus returns from Yusefabad; it will leave tomorrow morning at eight, and we shall be in Herat in good time for lunch—*ensha'allah*.

The bus will leave at five o'clock.

The bus will leave at four o'clock.

For a three- or four-hour journey this hardly makes sense. They really do make life unnecessarily uncomfortable.

April 12th

We got away soon after five. As a European, I was courteously given a front seat.

Our clientele had changed, some of our original party having remained at Yusefabad. But there were still a few familiar faces, and the two green children and one pustule were ever with us; the bumptious youth, however, had vanished, and oh what a joy it was to be free of his despondent *yallah*ings!

We proceeded in agreeable silence along a road which, but for a few excruciating stretches, was better than the Persian. Soon, however, there was minor trouble with the engine, and we were obliged to stop. It was then that I noticed, and pointed out to the driver, that the left front tyre was ripped to pieces. 'The road is a ruin,' he answered.

To pass the time, and with little hope of gaining accurate information, I asked him on which days of the week the bus went from Yusefabad to Meshed. He prided himself on knowing some English, but his reply, though three times repeated, remained quite unintelligible. He was hurt, and insisted upon writing it down :

'The day in the ane wek today the bas is given from Usufabad.'

I said I still couldn't quite understand, and would he mind telling me in Persian. He was mortally offended.

We were about midway on our journey when there was an explosion. The bus lurched violently, righted itself, and finally came to rest in the middle of the road.

'Here we sleep,' said the driver in impeccable English, drawing out his Russian cigarette-case and lighting a cigarette.

The passengers descended without any signs of emotion and wandered away across the plain to pray or to relieve nature, as the spirit moved them. I examined the tyre; even to my inexpert eye it was obvious that it was beyond repair. I asked the driver where the spare wheel was; he replied that there was none. Then, taking a rug, he spread it in the shade of the bus, lay down upon it and immediately fell asleep.

For mile upon mile we had driven across flat, desolate, lifeless plain; it was better luck than we deserved, that precisely here the land to our north was pleasantly undulating and bright with scarlet poppies, and that barely a couple of miles away lay a small village where it should be possible to buy food. For, over-optimistically, most of the passengers had, like myself, counted upon lunching in Herat and had brought nothing. While two men went off in search of provisions, someone produced a kettle and proceeded to convert the local ditchwater, fetched in an old petrol tin, into passable and very welcome tea with which I, as a foreigner, was the first to be served. Yet another climbed a telegraph post and, using some apparatus that the bus carried against such contingencies, tapped a message informing Herat of our plight. I gratefully noted this unexpected efficiency.

Our common fate soon broke down all barriers. When I tentatively pulled out my camera there was no cry of horror; indeed there was a rush to be photographed, and those who were left out felt slighted. I was thus obliged to waste some film on several very unphotogenic models. All the while I was taking photographs, the green children, no longer having access to my neck, clawed at my knees. And it was then that I discovered the source of a curious tinkling noise that had accompanied us the whole way from Meshed: these children wore ringlets of bells on their ankles.

To pass the time and mitigate the boredom, I invented simple games such as seeing how many pebbles could be piled on top of one another without falling. Almost everyone joined in—even the driver, who woke with a start, set to work as though it were a matter of life and death, and was almost reduced to tears when repeatedly defeated by a small Afghan boy of about fourteen. (This boy was something of a wonder where delicacy of touch was involved.) To restore the driver to good humour, I changed the game to one of throwing stones at a distant petrol tin. This time he won.

The foraging party returned at last with bread, yoghourt and some eggs. Of the latter there were not nearly enough to go round, but once again I, as a guest, was served first. And, needless to say, I was not allowed to pay. I found these little gestures of courtesy and hospitality deeply affecting; for the others were as hungry as I, and far less affluent.

A pleasant breeze had been blowing, but towards midday the wind dropped and it became uncomfortably hot (it was 95 degrees that day at Herat). As the sun rose higher in the sky there was not enough shade to go round, and most of us were obliged to lie in serried discomfort under the bus. It was then that I made the discovery that the body of the bus was held together with string.

At two o'clock a jeep arrived with a spare wheel, and after the exchange had been effected I was offered a lift to Herat. I gladly accepted.

'Afghanistan,' says Mr. Ali, 'is extremely rich in water-power.' Long stretches of our road now confirmed the absolute truth of his statement. For difficulty, they surpassed even the worst we had encountered between Meshed and the frontier. Though feeling far from secure in the jeep, I was profoundly thankful to be out of the bus; indeed, as we pitched and tossed upon the rough river-beds, drenched by the spray that broke above our heads, I found myself more than once wondering how on earth that dilapidated vehicle could ever hope to get through.

For mile upon mile there was no sign of human habitation beyond an occasional crumbling wall and the distant black tents of the nomads. But now and again we came upon tents not far from the road, and fierce, enormous dogs that sprang alarmingly against the canvas bodywork of our machine; Greek sheepdogs, which I hadn't much cared for at the time, seemed by comparison harmless as Pekinese. These were the only moments when I had rather been in the bus.

After some two hours, the hills to the north drew closer to us and the country began to grow greener. Soon there were signs of cultivation, then meadows and orchards. Finally, six tall factory chimneys pierced the distant horizon: the minarets of Herat!

9

Herat

THE jeep put me down at the bus office, where I was held prisoner until the bus should arrive with my luggage. But the ever-changing pattern of the street-life—the camels and donkeys, the endlessly varied twist of a turban, the rich colours of the *abas*, the splendour of beards and wild-glinting eyes—made me forget that I had hardly eaten anything since dawn. There was barely a woman to be seen : the few who passed were completely enveloped in *chadors* unbroken but for a little grille over the eyes.

The bus limped in at six, and we were taken with our luggage to the customs house, near the Friday Mosque. Outside the Mosque, perched upon a kind of bandstand and looking as self-important as a mayor and corporation waiting to receive royalty, stood the religious elders of Herat, scanning the primrose sky for the slim crescent of the moon that was to announce the beginning of the holy month of *Ramazan*. Suddenly there was a confused murmur of voices, and a flutter of hands—a signal that was transmitted to waiting gunners; then, as the gun resounded, all the dogs of Herat began barking, and a great shout of praise to Allah, a pulsating pillar of sound, rose above the walls of the mud-built city.

Tonight I would like, better than anything else in the world, to be dining at a certain house not much more than three thousand miles away. I see the soft light of candles and the glitter of silver; the port is circulating, and twenty feet of passage cannot dumb the laughter that awaits us when we can bring ourselves to add again the charm of our hostess to the kindness of our host. In short, I am feeling rather homesick—or rather, Eton-sick. This is as it should be : it is part of the cure.

April 13th
  Parc Hotel, Herat—of which more anon.
  Seduced by the beauty of the morning I rose early, put on a

green shirt (is it wise here? Green is the colour sacred to the Prophet), and demanded breakfast.

'It is *Ramazan*,' said the waiter reproachfully. 'We do not eat between sunrise and sunset.'

'But I am not a Moslem. I do.'

Grudgingly he brought some dry bread and a pot of tea to my room. In a glass-fronted showcase in the corridor I had noticed a number of tins, including one that contained Oxford marmalade; it looked as though it had been buried for fifty years, but I bought it and found it an excellent addition to the hotel's simple fare.

Then I set off towards the town.

There are parts of Meshed that the West has not yet ruined; but in the old town of Herat the Orient reigns triumphant. You may see a European herringbone waistcoat, but it will be worn with such Asiatic *abandon* that one forgets its origin; there may be petrol tins, but they will have been flattened out and used to decorate a wedding chest. Even the rare cars have so woebegone an appearance as to seem a different breed from those we know at home. Two wide streets have been driven through the bazaar, and at their junction, under a tin mushroom, stands a Ruritanian policeman who with operatic gestures and shrill blasts upon a penny whistle urges forward a haughty camel or bars the advance of a child of five on a donkey. When he grows bored with this futile occupation he coils himself up in his stand and takes a nap. The Herati are intensely proud of him, and are reluctant to believe that we have anything so up to date in Europe.

A characteristic feature of the sparse traffic is the *gadi*—a jingling little dogcart that plies for hire and announces its presence by two bells a diminished third apart. Horse and cart are usually genuine antiques; the driver may be anything from a mere boy to a centenarian. The back seat of the *gadi*, which a single passenger must use for the sake of balance, is precarious in the extreme.

Below the towering citadel is a square, laid out in the Western style, linking the old city with the new. Here stands another policeman, and helpful notices such as STOPT PLACE and

BE CAREFULY would aid the motions of the European motorist if he existed.

The new town is approached by—or rather, consists of—several avenues planted with pine trees beneath which roses (not, alas, in full flower yet) grow in great profusion—for it is Herat, not Shiraz, that is now the city of roses. (Though a Herati will pluck a rose to wear in his mouth, he is not yet Westernized enough to behave like those English hooligans who root up wayside trees). Beside these avenues are meadows incomparably green, strewn with poppies, cornflowers, wild mustard, purple larkspurs (no doubt Byron's 'purple monkshood') and a white, lacy plant that fulfils the functions of our cow-parsley. The beauty of the place, after the wild deserts, is amazing.

The Parc Hotel, Herat—the best of a small group of national hotels built by the Government some fifteen years ago—is an institution sufficiently curious to deserve a detailed description. Large, white and imposing, set in a charming and well-tended garden with green lawns, pools, shady pines, roses and flowering fruit-trees, it makes at first sight a most favourable impression. There are two solaria, a lounge, a bar decorated with a vast mural showing Omar Khayyam and his lady drinking underneath the inevitable bough, a dining-room, and a spacious entrance hall with reception desk. There are (for I have counted them) more than a hundred and twenty comfortable chairs and sofas, a couple of dozen tables—some of them topped with big slabs of rare marbles, a number of superb rugs, and a grand piano; and three soldiers mount guard all night to see that property is not stolen. The beds are fairly clean. There is electric light, a bath, and three water-closets. What more could one want?

The real trouble is the management. There is no visible manager, the hotel being directed by a man who calls himself the hotel clerk and who lives in the town. He is thirty-five, and assures me he does not look his age: I should have put it at forty-two. That perpetually puzzled look on his face reminds me of Sherlock Holmes when the case is going wrong. In many ways he is a remarkable man, with an intelligence well above the average. This he knows, and so aspires to a job more suited to his abilities; and I hope he will find it. He wears European dress, has taught himself a surprising amount of English and would like to become a translator. He is interested in everything under the sun, and is a magpie accumulator of information of every kind; thus, though he does not realize it, his questions are often pointed and embarrassing. At the moment he is busy translating *Cox and Box* into Persian—dangerous pabulum for an hotel clerk.

With a wholly absentee manager and a partly absentee clerk, the running of the hotel is chiefly in the hands of servants who are not familiar with the European way of life. My room was never swept, my bed rarely made at all and never in the Western sense of the word. Shoes cannot be cleaned in the hotel, but have to be sent away—presumably into the town, which is a mile off. Every mouthful of food has to be specially ordered from the town. The doors of the bathroom and lavatories cannot be shut, still less locked, and the state of these rooms (one of which, through some caprice of the architect, opens into the solarium) is not agreeable. Many of the bedrooms are protected against theft only by a bolt on the *outside* of the door, and I could not make any servant understand that this was an unusual and indeed an unsatisfactory arrangement. (It also means that any one of the nine Arab children who are staying in the hotel could lock me in.) I asked for two hooks to be fitted, and went off to the bazaar to buy a padlock. I returned to find that the hooks had been fixed to the floor and the bottom of the door, so that I have to grovel to lock and unlock it.

The dining-room is not allowed to be used—perhaps because it is *Ramazan*—and meals must be taken in the bedrooms. (Eventually I revolted against this and had them served on the veranda.) The normal entrance to the hotel is through the scullery. The bar, needless to say, is a mere bottleless, glassless, boozeless shell. The electric light is as temperamental as the water system. The notes of the piano still play in the right order, but they do not seem to suggest that there is a resident piano-tuner in Herat.

I was expecting to live the simple life in Afghanistan; but I was not expecting to live it in the sort of hotel that one might find on Lake Como. It was like being asked to dine at Buckingham Palace and only getting fried fish and chips. How I would love to let Lady Alexandra loose for a week here; it would be a challenge worthy of her powers.

I went to see Dr. and Frau Pfisterer, who are the only resident Europeans here in a population of a hundred thousand. The Doctor's first wife was killed a couple of years ago on the Afghan Airways, and he has recently remarried in Germany. The German entomologists who passed through Eslam Qaleh—Dr. Amsel and his son Benjamin, and Dr. Wilke—are his guests.

Pfisterer told me that he came to Afghanistan after the war, because the medical profession at home was overcrowded. He said that life was becoming increasingly difficult and dangerous for foreigners here; he hopes to return to Germany in a year's time.[1] His wife is pregnant, and he intends to drive her to Meshed for her confinement; he would have a spare place in the car, and could give me a lift.

The entomologists have spread themselves and their endless equipment over half the ground floor of the house. Dr. Wilke showed me some of the moths that they had caught; to the layman they looked as regrettably similar to one another as do English medieval coins, but to the expert they were obviously thrilling.

Frau Pfisterer made me stay to a delicious lunch, during which there was much political talk—chiefly anti-French. As always when politics are under discussion, I remained for the most part silent.

The comte de T. has arrived here from Kandahar. He is a good-looking young man of twenty-eight, with china-blue eyes, fair hair, and a complexion that many a woman would envy; one is almost tempted to use the epithet 'pretty.' But for the cut of his clothes, which is unmistakably French, he could pass for an Englishman; and, oddly enough, but for the war he would have been educated at Eton. He is a journalist by profession, and has been travelling for seventeen months in the Far and Middle East.

He arrived at Herat at two o'clock this morning, and might well not have reached the hotel until daybreak had not a kindly Afghan befriended him; and had he not allowed that kindly Afghan to spend the rest of the night on the floor of his room he might never . . . But I must not anticipate.

[1] He never did. He was murdered shortly after I left Herat.

The Count says that the roads of Afghanistan are by far the worst he has yet encountered. He has had an unspeakable journey—nine days to cover four hundred miles—from Kandahar here. Four or five of the rivers being too deep for the bus to pass, the passengers and their luggage had to be put down and precariously transported on camels to the far bank, where, eventually, another bus carried them on to the next obstacle. At one stage an unscheduled ten-foot-deep chasm in the road put a halt to the bus.

'What do we do?' asked the Count.

'Get out and walk.'

'How far is it?'

'Nine kilometres.'

'How can I carry my baggage nine kilometres?'

The driver said something which obviously meant, 'I couldn't care less.'

Now the Count is an omnivorous collector, and his luggage must weigh a hundredweight. Aided by the aforementioned kindly Afghan, he struggled on for a kilometre or so, then sat down in a ditch to die. From a fate no worse than death, he was rescued at last by a camel caravan which carried him as far as the next river and, ultimately, the next bus.

He added that where the road was very bad the passengers had been turned out and made to repair it. The bus stopped at fixed times for prayer. While the men were praying, the women, who remained in the bus, lifted their *chadors* and smoked a cigarette.

As I sat writing on the terrace, suddenly the sunset gun broke the tense silence. Then once more the dogs began to bark and the fanatical cry, chilling to Christian ears, rose from the distant town. Waiting hands lit cigarettes; water already boiling was poured into waiting teapots: the long, noisy, sleepless night of *Ramazan* had begun.

What is the result of this turning of night into day? That the Moslem does no work by day, and the Christian gets no sleep by night. This mortification of the flesh, which makes everyone ill-tempered and more inefficient than usual, is difficult for me to understand. Allah is the Most-Knowing!

The Count asked one of the servants whether it was possible

to buy a bottle of arak in Herat. The man turned whiter than a Parc Hotel sheet and drew a knife-hand across his throat. I remembered that Mr. Ali had written : 'Drinking wine, prostitution and gambling are strictly forbidden throughout the country, and defaulters are very severely punished.' Personally, I shall stick to tea; in any case, there is nothing else to stick to.

I daren't even smoke in the streets.

April 14th

The Count is anxious for me to introduce him to the Pfisterers. Knowing their views on the French, it was with some trepidation that I took him round to their house after breakfast this morning. They have, however, invited us to go with them this afternoon by car to see the Mosalla, and a celebrated garden, the Takht-e-Safar, that lies outside the town.

The hotel clerk having some business to transact in Herat, the Count and I offered him a lift there. The clerk rejected the first two *gadis* that presented themselves—one because the cab was falling to bits, the other because the horse was lame. I told him that my rule-of-thumb test was never to engage a vehicle where the collective ages of man, beast and cab appeared to be more than a hundred and twenty, and he applauded my sagacity.

I sat in front with the driver, the Count and the clerk in the back.

'How many children have you?' I heard the clerk asking the Count, in English. (The Count's English is bad, but the clerk knows only a word or two of French.)

'I'm not married.'

'Why are you not married?'

'Oh, I don't know. . . .'

'What do you do?'

'I live with my mother.'

'I mean, about your life of sex?'

'Oh, there are lots of nice girls, you know,' said the Count breezily.

'So you fornicate, *Monsieur*?'

To avoid becoming involved in this embarrassing catechism,

I plied the driver with my now rather worn record about the beauties of Herat in spring. . . .

We dismissed the *gadi* near the bazaar and watched, not without a certain feeling of relief, the disappearing figure of the clerk.

The Count has a theory that everything in Afghanistan tastes or smells of sheep. As we plunged into the crowded bazaar he snuffed the air and said, 'Am I not right? *Ça sent le mouton.*'

'I smell nothing—except a general oriental smell of spices, and perhaps camels—but certainly not sheep. If you'll forgive my saying it, there is far less smell in an Afghan crowd than in a Paris *métro*.'

He didn't like it. '*Non, mon ami, vous vous trompez. Ça sent le mouton.*'

The Count, so he assures me, is a past-master of the oriental art of bargaining. I wanted to buy one or two coins for my brother, and he insisted upon helping me. In the bazaar is a long row of goldsmiths' shops, and in one of these I found what seemed a desirable coin.

'How much?' I asked.

'One hundred *afghanis*.' (An *afghani* is about twopence.)

'Offer him one *afghani*.'

'But surely . . .'

'One *afghani*,' said the Count.

The shopkeeper snorted with contempt, snatched away the coin and returned to his interrupted labours at a small forge.

'Two *afghanis*,' I said.

The shopkeeper might have been deaf.

'Come back in a week's time and you'll get it for three *afghanis*,' said the Count. '*Vous remarquez? Il sent le mouton!*'

'But I shan't be here in a week's time, and anyhow I shall never be able to find this stall again—they all look exactly alike. And I want that coin. . . .'

'You can't have it. It's robbery.' And he dragged me away.

This performance was several times repeated, with the result that I returned to the hotel empty-handed. It was only after the Count's departure that I ventured to go back to the bazaar and purchase three coins, at prices that would have horrified him but which were none the less considerably below the true value.

As we were walking back through the town, I noticed, through an arched entrance, a garden with rows of chairs obviously set out for some kind of open-air performance. At the gate, where a small crowd had gathered, a man was selling tickets.

'A cinema,' I said. 'Why don't we go tonight?'

Ignoring for the moment the blandishments of the box office, we went into the garden to investigate. A small and extremely primitive stage showed that we had stumbled upon a native theatre.

'This will be *most* remarkable,' said the Count; 'on no account must we miss it.'

'*Khanom, khanom!* (women, women!),' cried the ticket-seller. 'Come tonight and see the women!'

'But this is tremendous! At last we are going to see a real live Afghan woman. Let's get tickets at once.'

True to his promise, Pfisterer came round in the afternoon with the Amsels, to take us to the Mosalla and the Takht-e-Safar.

The road from Eslam Qaleh enters Herat by way of the Mosalla; I had therefore already had a close though fleeting view of the minarets, and the blue melon-ribbed dome of the Mausoleum of Gauhar Shad. After Byron's ecstasies I must confess to an initial shock of disappointment. One knows only too well the temptation to over-praise little-known and little-accessible objects. Six blue chimneys and a tomb-chamber: why all the fuss?

The remains are of three distinct buildings: the Mosalla (mosque, or place of prayer) of Gauhar Shad; her Madraseh (college), one corner of which constitutes her Mausoleum; and the College of Hosain Baiqara. (As at Meshed, some confusion arises from the fact that the name of one building—here the Mosalla—is often used to describe the whole group.) Until eighty years ago, all these were still in part standing, though in various stages of decay and dissolution. It was then that, under the threat of a Russian advance from the north, all buildings likely to afford cover to the enemy were demolished, on the advice, if not under direct orders, of the British. So perished, but for its minarets, the Mosalla, by general consent the finest building of the Moslem world.

Of the four minarets of the Mosalla, two were destroyed by an earthquake in 1932, and a third fell about three years ago; there now remains (and for how long will it survive?) a single yardstick by which the glory of the whole building can be measured. Of the College of Gauhar Shad, a double-balconied minaret and the Mausoleum are still fairly intact. Four minarets, tottering and mutilated, shedding their tiles like autumn leaves, mark the corners of the College of Hosain Baiqara.

Two schools have been built relatively recently: one adjoins, and may help to support, the last minaret of the Mosalla; the other stands at the north-east corner of Gauhar Shad's College. Gauhar Shad's two buildings are now enveloped in a grove of young fir trees and roses, criss-crossed by shady paths; but the minarets of Hosain Baiqara's College rise severely from the buff, rubble-strewn plain.

Magnificent as is Gauhar Shad's Mosque in Meshed, there can be no doubt that Byron is right in his assertion that the Mosalla at Herat must, in its day, have far excelled it in brilliance and splendour. The Mosalla minaret emerges from a polygonal base as intricately ornamented as the finest carpet. The circular drum is decorated with bands of white lettering and lozenge-shaped patterns; it culminates in the honeycombing that once supported the balcony, and finally a diapered net of white faience. The overall colour of the decoration is a softly glittering pale blue, relieved by a deeper blue, pure yellow, Indian red, a gentle green, and white. The quality is as subtle as that of a piece of rare porcelain. Gauhar Shad's minarets at Meshed seem, by comparison, no more than the rough sketches for the masterpiece of Herat, and no doubt the rest of the mosque was also proportionately more miraculous. It was natural that this should be so: Meshed was the early work of the Shirazi architect, Qavam ad-Din; the Mosalla was the achievement of his maturity.

'*Sehr schön, nicht wahr?*' said Dr. Pfisterer, with little conviction.

'*Sehr schön!*' echoed the entomologists with still less, leaving '*Fort joli!*' for the use of the Count.

For I fear they were one and all disappointed that the real goal of my pilgrimage was nothing more than a single minaret so precariously balanced that we might well have arrived to find it prostrate. And I too perhaps was a little shaken; not by the *quality* of the sample, but by the magnitude of the mental effort necessary to reconstruct—as must the palaeozoologist an extinct mammal from one stray fibula—the glory of that transcendent building from so fragmentary a relic.

The Mausoleum is a little turquoise-capped building, exciting chiefly for the corrugated dome which links it to a splendid monument that I shall never see—the Mausoleum of Timur at Samarcand. The tilework, though gay enough, is not of the highest quality. Gauhar Shad's tomb, and five other of the nine that once stood within the building, have vanished, leaving three black anonymous stones, ornamented with stylized flowers.

The two-storey minaret of Gauhar Shad's College may be climbed—indeed, Benjamin climbed it. I did not; I doubted if it would stand my weight, and I felt that the English had done enough damage to the Mosalla already. It is pretty enough and, with its lozenges of coloured tiles set in unglazed brick, not unlike the minarets of the Royal Mosque at Meshed.

The Eslam Qaleh road passes directly through the centre of the College of Hosain Baiqara, whose drunkenly lurching minarets must surely one day fall upon it. These minarets, though they do not stand comparison with that of the Mosalla, are prettily netted with white faience and inlaid with turquoise and other colours of the Persian palette. Hosain Baiqara, with his passion for poetry, sport, swordsmanship, drink and debauchery, was a typical Timurid; he ruled in Herat from 1469 to 1506.

From the Mosalla we drove out towards sunset to Takht-e-Safar, or 'Traveller's Throne,' a pleasure garden clinging to the hillside a mile or so from the town. This 'paradise' was laid out by Hosain Baiqara and built by forced labour. Each gate once bore the legend: 'All who have been indulging sinfully in the pleasures of wine and beauty must, by command of Soltan Hosain, add a stone to the Takht-e-Safar.' To judge from earlier descriptions of the place, there can have been no shortage of sinners. Now there is only an ugly modern pavilion, and a large tank from which water trickles half-heartedly, terrace by terrace, into the plain. But the view is what Baedeker would term '*sehr lohnend*,' and the neglected lawns and the meadows blue as an

English bluebell wood with a pretty lilaceous flower—*Ixiolirion montanum*, I think—that I have seen everywhere in north Persia but never in such abundance as here.

For Dr. Amsel, however, the Takht-e-Safar will remain memorable chiefly for its moths. As he leaped and floundered through the meadow grasses, dabbing his net wildly among the blue lilies, I recalled some lines of John Gay :

> *Philosophers more grave than wise*
> *Hunt science down in Butterflies;*
> *Or fondly poring on a Spider,*
> *Stretch human contemplation wider.*

Why 'grave'? Whoever could find the antics of the entomologist anything but comic? But why is the pursuit of butterflies (by adults) generally agreed to be a rather ludicrous spectacle, whereas the stalking of deer (for example), though it involves as much inelegant posturing, wastes more time, and stretches human contemplation not a whit the wider, is not considered a fit subject for mirth?

We arrived at the theatre about twice as late as one would in France, to find ourselves still twice too early. The curtain was up, and a stage hand was busy arranging the set—an interior with a few chairs, a table upon which stood a bunch of flowers in an old jam tin, and some photographs of film stars pinned upon the red curtains that served for the walls of the room. Another stage hand was picking large boughs of greenery in the garden, no doubt for use in some subsequent scene.

We were given seats of honour in the middle of the front row, next to the only opulent-looking and well-dressed Herati I had yet seen.

'Perhaps he can tell us what the play is called,' I said. '*Pardon, Monsieur. Est-ce que vous parlez français. . . ?* English. . . ? *Deutsch. . . ?*'

But it was no good. Of his Persian reply I could only gather that the play was about a wedding.

It began with a prologue—wholly incomprehensible to us—in front of the curtains, which were then drawn back to disclose a single figure, dressed as a woman but most obviously masculine, seated in an arm-chair. 'She' was clearly in pain—mental, I thought, rather than physical, though some physical discomfort may also have resulted from the biscuit tin that was doing service for her bust. For a good ten minutes she muttered inaudibly to herself; then the curtains fell in silence—or rather, failed to fall and had to be pulled into position by stage hands.

The second Act, which had the same setting as the first, showed our gloomy male heroine, now dressed perhaps as a bride, receiving one or two of her near relations. Among these there seemed to be a villain, who, after the guests had left, returned and frightened the poor girl out of her wits.

The setting of Act 3 must have been intended to represent a wood—by night, unless it was that the lights had fused—for although the photographs of film stars remained upon the walls, the chairs had been replaced by greenery. The bride, except that she was now standing, behaved exactly as in Act 1. Suddenly the ghost of the villain appeared, floodlit, behind some mosquito netting, scared her a bit more, and faded out. Then a man (her fiancé?) came in and cheered her up again.

Act 4 was an exact repetition of Act 1, but rather longer.

After the final curtain, there was clapping no louder than that of duchesses at a charity matinée. Except for a few laughs scored by a comic relation in the second Act, this was the only audible evidence of the existence of spectators.

In conclusion, an actor appeared in front of the curtains to make the only remark of the evening that I understood—namely that the play was over and he wished us all a very good night.

'*Very* remarkable!' said the Count as our prancing *gadi* carried us back in the chill starlight, down the long, pine-edged avenues, to the Parc Hotel. '*Very* remarkable indeed!'

I hear that several rich Herati have installed one or more W.C.s in their houses, the town's leading citizen having no less than three. They are not, of course, for use; but favoured guests are shown them, and sometimes even allowed to pull the plug. Our neighbour at the theatre looked at least a two-closet man.

April 15th

This morning, as I was standing shivering in my cold bath (how I hate it!), the door of the bathroom was suddenly flung open, and the gardener, clutching a large goatskin, burst in. Without so much as a word of greeting, he proceeded to sluice the floor, the lavatory seat, my pyjamas and myself with coldest water. Then, as abruptly as he had come, he departed. This is called 'cleaning the bathroom'; in fact, it merely shifts the dirt on the floor from one end of the room to the other and makes the lavatory unusable for a couple of hours.

But the gardener is a good fellow. He may not be interested in bathrooms, but he tends his plants lovingly, and is one of the few men about the place who really works. He knows the name of one flower only—*gol-e-shabbu* (night-scented flower, i.e., stock), and this he applies to almost every plant in the garden. Incidentally, I have discovered—but not, of course, from him—that those blue lilies are here called *shirdushak*(?); this is said to mean, 'he-who-eats-it-his-mother's-milk-will-dry-up'—which is as whimsical as 'pick-your-mother's-eyes-out' or any other of the local English plant names that Mr. Geoffrey Grigson lists in his *The Englishman's Flora*.

I set out early for the Mosalla, hoping to study the building in the morning coolness and without interruption. But I found the pine-grove already fluttering with students, who immediately attached themselves tenaciously to me. They are all learning English, and several of them speak it well enough to make themselves understood.

'We speak badly because we have a bad teacher,' said one—a precocious, unattractive boy, he seemed: one knows the type.

'You speak it very well. What are you going to do when you leave school?'

'We will be a very good judge. And you—you are a pilgrim?'

At this point the teacher appeared. The precocious boy, to whom I had given my card, introduced me as '*Aqa-ye*-Bloont, my very dearest friend'—a relationship that could hardly, I felt, have been established after only three minutes' conversation.

The schoolmaster was a melancholy individual who must have had many pen-boxes thrown at him in his time. His pupils obviously despised him. He might be a poor teacher, but his own English was far from bad; out of loyalty to the profession, I praised it heartily and congratulated the students on their good fortune in being taught by someone who was practically bilingual.

But he was not to be comforted. Life had got him down. He hated boys. He hated Afghanistan. He wanted to go to England, to America. Nor was he sound on matters of religion : 'This *Ramazan*,' he said gloomily, 'it is terrible ! All day long we may not eat, we may not drink, we may not smoke, we may not copulate. . . . And in England, do you also fast ?'

'Not to that extent.'

I was not altogether sorry when, at ten o'clock, he carried off his much-protesting pupil to his classroom, leaving me to pursue my studies in peace.

Or rather, in relative peace. For cohorts of knee-high infants soon replaced their elders (but not, I thought, betters). Fortunately I like small children. And these were poppets : no bother, all turbans and smiles, gazing honey-cheeked and black-eyed up at me like Americans taking their first view of the Eiffel Tower. I patted a few turbans, acknowledged a few smiles, distributed a few sweets, and drove them off in search of bits of tile. They returned in due course with enough to build a mosque.

Wanting to change a film near the Mosalla, I made use of a little recess in the wall of one of the schools. Immediately an outraged *molla* rushed up and drove me away : the niche was a *mehrab*, prayer-pointed towards Mecca. How could I have known ? There was no decoration of any kind to suggest its function. So might a Moslem, unversed in the local ritual, mistake the font for a tank in which to wash on entering a Christian church. One has to be very careful here not to drop religious bricks.

I noticed on my way home that the first opium poppies are in flower—bold white blooms, innocent-looking as choirboys.

'In English, do you say, *a* country or *the* country ?' asked the clerk, who sat hungrily watching me trying to extract some depressing hunks of goat from a mountain of rice.

'It all depends what you mean. You say "Afghanistan is *a* country," but "Afghanistan is *the* country in which I live." '

'Could I say, "I live in *a* country"?'

'I suppose so.'

'But I do not; I live in a town.'

'Well, then, obviously you couldn't. In any case, if you didn't live in a town you would live in *the* country.'

'Why?'

And so on, in this vein, for twenty minutes. Really, his thirst for knowledge is insatiable. Among other things he has asked me to explain are the mechanism of the Tower Bridge, Parliamentary elections and procedure, the construction of the atom bomb, and the meaning of several obscure metaphysical poems that he has found in an English anthology left behind by a last year's visitor. My answers have been so unsatisfactory that he is beginning to form a very low opinion of my intelligence.

To turn the tables upon him, I asked him whether the Afghans, like the French, use the second person singular when addressing relations and intimate friends.

'Never!' he said.

'Then what is the use of having a second person singular at all?'

'Perhaps,' he said, 'a man may so address his woman, but no woman could speak so to her man.'

'Not a sister to a brother?'

'Never!'

For a few moments he sat wrapped in thought. 'It is possible,' he said, 'that a man might speak so to his very, very dear friend. Not to his dear friend; not to his very dear friend. Only to his very, very dear friend. . . .'

This evening, so far as the Parc Hotel's temperamental electric-light plant allowed, I have been reading more about Afghanistan in the books that I borrowed from the Germans.

Afghanistan has been described (by an Afghan)[1] as 'the Switzerland of Asia.' 'To those who . . . want rest and recreation in a lovely country with a pleasant climate and abundance of delicious fruit, Afghanistan would, undoubtedly, prove one of the best health resorts in the world. . . . Here are towns where one may sleep or dine in comfort. . . . It is totally unsophisticated and unspoiled. Those who have felt its refreshing and

---

[1] Mohammed Ali, *op. cit.*

invigorating climate . . . fear no degeneration of any kind.' If I add that a room in the best hotel in Afghanistan costs two shillings a night, and that meat is sevenpence a pound, then why, you will ask, is not the country overrun by tourists?

I will tell you.

First, there is that 'pleasant climate,' with temperatures ranging from 22 degrees below zero Fahrenheit to 120 degrees above. Even Mr. Ali admits that in the plain of Jalelabad 'the air is so hot as to often cause the death of persons exposed to it,' and that in Seistan the heat is 'more deadly than the sword of a human enemy.' Spring? Ah yes; Mr. Ali is moved to poetry at the mere thought of it :

> *And here's that glorious life in bloom*
> *Gone are the blankets too,*
> *As Nature starts to paint again,*
> *And man comes out to view.*

But fail to catch those three or four weeks of spring, those five or six weeks of autumn, and you stand the chance of being frozen alive or roasted to death.

Now transport. 'The plan for the reconstruction of the roads of Afghanistan is nearing completion,' I have somewhere seen it stated. Unless the plan was limited to a stretch of a dozen or so miles of road round Kabul, this is untrue. In winter the roads are mostly blocked by snow, which melts in spring and washes them away. Mild repairs may perhaps be undertaken in the summer, making them usable in places in the autumn until once more they are buried in snow and again left in ruins. I can speak at first hand of one road only; that, however, is not merely the main road but, I am informed, the only road linking Iran and Afghanistan. The road from Herat to Kandahar is undoubtedly worse. There is not a yard of railway in the country, and only the most rudimentary air service.

That Afghanistan is the Switzerland of Asia is true in so far as both countries are mountainous and land-locked. No one, however, would be tempted to call the Afghans a nation of hotel-keepers. If the hotel at Herat is—as I have been told—the best in the country, then some of the others must be very odd indeed.

Although I saw only one small corner of the country, I am certain, from everything I heard, that it is no use pretending that

Afghanistan as a whole has made more than the most elementary and superficial progress in modernization in the Western sense of the word. The present Moslem year is 1375 A.H.; A.D. 1375 would be a fair equivalent. And that is one of the reasons why I have come to Afghanistan; had I found it like Grindelwald I should have been disappointed. None the less, I am sorry that Mr. Ali has seen fit to paint a picture of Western comfort. One day, no doubt, the country will be opened up to tourism; and then it will lose its innocence and its charm. Its friendly people will become as rapacious as Neapolitans, as importunate as Egyptians.

Then you may look for me in the Gobi Desert.

An inscrutable Russian has arrived on the scene. He plays records of Russian folk music in his room, hums the *Volga Boatmen* in the passages, but will talk to nobody. He looks so exactly like a spy that he probably isn't one. Or is it double bluff : is he a spy disguised as a business man looking too like a spy to be true?

Tonight's great thought : 'The political climate of Afghanistan is healthier for the delicate plant of democracy than anywhere else in the East' (Mr. Ali).

April 16th

I noticed this morning, through the glass, that the shelf of the locked store-cupboard in the passage is lined with the front page of an English newspaper. A tin of peaches obscures the name (though I think I can guess it); a tin of sardines lies upon the date, and various other obstacles affect the continuity of the text. The main headline reads TENSION GROWS IN T . . . Where can it be? TWICKENHAM? TIMBUKTU? or simply THE FAR EAST? Tension is always growing everywhere. Other information concerns the fate of a missing typist, a divorced actress, and a liner that had unadvisedly hit a whale, and a rise in the cost of practically everything : in short, the usual nonsense upon which we waste (why?) twopence and an hour every day. And then the twins. Joint finalists they were, in a beauty competition—blonde Diana, and Rachel the brunette; and heaven alone and the bottom of a two-pound tin of strawberry jam know which of the pair was victorious. I favour Diana; I can hardly wait to discover the verdict of the judges.

While the Count and I were lunching together—off goat, I thought, but the Count alleged it was mutton—I happened to say how much I disliked carrying a lot of money round on me, but that the labour and difficulty of changing travellers' cheques in Iran made it almost inevitable. 'Can you change them at an hotel in Afghanistan,' I asked, 'or only at the State banks?'

'Mine can be changed anywhere,' said the Count, 'and here they don't even have to be countersigned in the presence of the payer.'

'All very well until you lose them!'

The Count smiled a superior smile. He thrust his hand into his breast pocket, groped about a bit, withdrew it, turned very pale, then feverishly searched his other pockets. 'My God!' he said. 'They've gone!'

'They're probably in one of your suitcases.'

'I never—or practically never—put them there.' None the less, he leaped up and ran to his room. Three minutes later he was back again, and his white face forestalled my question.

'Eighty thousand francs! Of course I've got the numbers. I shall get it back. I can wire for more money in Tehran, but the trouble is that I don't know if I've got enough to get me there.'

'I expect I can lend you something. I don't want to seem depressing,' I added, 'but if the cheques can be countersigned in the way you said, surely any thief can cash them. If that happens, will the bank refund you? I just don't know how these things work.'

Nor did he. While he frantically emptied the contents of his pockets over the table, we discussed and rediscussed every possible aspect of the case.

'I'm sure it's those servants,' he said; 'I never trusted them. That hen: you remember?'

(He was referring to an old hen of which we had consumed the half one day at lunch, asking for the remainder to be served cold for supper. In the meanwhile it had been eaten by the servants.)

'It's far more likely to be the Afghan who spent the night in your room. Do you know for certain when you last had the cheques?'

'It couldn't possibly be the Afghan; he was so kind and helpful. Now there's that Russian. . . .'

'But why on earth should it be the Russian? You'll be saying it's me next.'

At last the clerk appeared on the scene; and in due course the mythical hotel manager and two yawning senior police officers looking like generals were gathered from the town. All the afternoon we sat in the *salon* while the servants were brought in one by one and cross-examined. It was a slow process, made still slower by the complications of interpretation, in which the clerk and I played our part; neither the police officers nor the manager could of course speak a word of anything but Persian. The clerk presided, and demonstrated that his likeness to Holmes was more than skin-deep.

Strongly against my advice, the Count said nothing about the Afghan, thus unjustly strengthening the suspicion against the servants; fortunately, however, one of the latter had seen the Afghan leaving the hotel, and I was delighted when the Count was forced to come out into the open. The Afghan was duly tracked down and arrested, but nothing to his discredit was discovered. When the Count came to leave Herat the mystery still remained unsolved, and I have never heard the outcome of the affair.

To cheer the Count up, I suggested after tea that we should go to Gozar Gah, a shrine that stands on the first foothills of the Paropamisus, about two miles to the north-east of the town. The clerk, overhearing the words 'Gozar Gah,' immediately invited himself too.

The clerk picked the *gadi*, but with less skill than before. The horse responded not at all to coaxing, and little to treatment that would have distressed the R.S.P.C.A.; more than once I thought we must overturn. Partly from fright, partly (I hope) from compassion, I walked much of the way.

Everyone from Babur to Byron visited Gozar Gah, which remains the most delectable pleasance in the neighbourhood of Herat. Khajeh Abdollah Ansari, who lies buried there, died in the year 1088, but the shrine, in its present form, dates from the time of Shah Rokh. The visitor comes first to an informal garden shaded by pine trees beneath which are beds gaily planted with stocks. An elegant white polygonal pavilion for the use of picnickers, but shut against us, stands among the trees. Gardeners were watering the flowers, and the bright spring evening had drawn a few Herati—pilgrims and mere idlers—to the enjoyment of the cool and scented retreat.

A second enclosure, pretty as an English village churchyard, contains a rectangular pool, scattered pines and rose bushes, and a handful of tombstones standing in the long green grass. Passing through a high-arched portal, and a vestibule whose ceiling is decorated with curious still-life paintings, one enters the principal court. This is tightly packed with graves. At the far end of the court, in front of an eighty-foot wall pierced by a lofty portal, is the tomb of the Khajeh, enclosed in an elaborate cage and formerly shaded by a great ilex of which the stump alone remains. Byron gives a racy description of this old bore, who was finally, at the age of eighty-four, stoned to death by some boys. (Where did he find his material? There is not a word of it in the *Dictionary of Islam*.) He also adds an illustration of the portal with its curiously Chinese stylized lettering.

But of Gozar Gah I shall chiefly cherish the memory of the soft evening sunlight falling upon the little white pavilion, and of the golden way home, descending as from Fiesole by happy paths into an expectant valley.

In spite of all my efforts, the Count is still depressed.

April 17th

There are two beds in my room. The one I was occupying having disintegrated under me, I moved last night into the other. I woke to find that a part of the ceiling had fallen upon the one in which I had previously been sleeping.

The inscrutable Russian has gone fishing. That is to say, he has left the hotel carrying a rod and a basket. But he carries them without pride or conviction; he walks without eagerness, and furtively. I would give a lot to see the inside of that basket.

There is a village near the hotel, and the Count and I set out to explore it. It is, of course, utterly untouched by the West.

The Count began to smell his accustomed sheep everywhere. I thought I did too, but was disinclined to encourage him in his obsession. 'Nonsense!' I said. At that instant the prettiest child in the world came round the corner with a flock of fifty undoubted sheep.

'*Voilà—vous voyez . . . ?*' said the Count triumphantly.

After lunch and much bargaining, the Count purchased a *chador*. Having failed, in spite of repeated efforts, to photograph a genuine Afghan woman, I asked him if he would put it on and pose for me. Since it envelops the wearer from head to foot, it could hardly, I thought, matter what human being was concealed beneath it, and it seemed a safer proposition than risking the knives and horsewhips of an irate Afghan husband.

We have often been warned that the camera cannot lie. Later, when the film came to be developed and printed, it revealed what was quite obviously no Afghan woman, but a French Count dressed up as one. The gauzy garment clung to him as though he had been freshly fished out of the Seine or were on his way to a fancy dress ball as Epstein's 'Lazarus.' The Count also took a photograph of me (minus the feet, for the *chador* was too short); I should like to see the result.

The Count is leaving this evening—or so he thinks; I am still hoping for a lift from the Pfisterers. Four days of Herat, he says, are more than enough. Had I been travelling at that dizzy speed for seventeen months I should by this time either have archaeological indigestion or be dead.

He had been successively told that the bus would leave at eleven, twelve, one, two and finally at seven-thirty. At two o'clock he was instructed to ring up the office again at seven to verify. He did, and it was shut. There is, I learn without surprise, no word in Persian for 'efficiency.'

I asked the hotel clerk why the bus company cannot make up its mind when its buses are going.

'They are like so,' he says, 'because they have too little work.'

'Might it not be that they have too little work because they are like so?'

But the subtlety of this is beyond him. No doubt *Ramazan* has made matters worse.

The Count left the hotel at eight o'clock, and by ten o'clock had not returned; perhaps he has really got off after all.

April 18th

I ought to have mentioned that four Afghans have arrived at the hotel: a wool merchant, a sanitary inspector, a man who is trying to buy two buses for Aryana Airways, and a philosopher. The philosopher has actually been seen with an open book in his hand (though he was asleep at the time), and is therefore by Afghan standards something of a phenomenon; he is gentle, pensive and taciturn, but as he does not speak a word of English I have not been able to get very far with him. The wool merchant also has no English. He looks like a very sunburnt Hitler without the moustache; upon the slightest or no provocation he collapses into uncontrollable laughter. The sanitary inspector has black curly hair and flashing teeth and would look well beside an ice-cream cart. Both he and the busman, who is urbane and amiable, speak a certain amount of English, and it is through them that I have some sort of a picture of the set-up of this incongruous party.

All, except the philosopher, spend most of the morning in bed, and play cards or chess or strum the piano with clenched fists for the rest of the day and a large part of the night; they show no inclination to buy buses or sell wool or inspect drains. Chess is played at the rate of one move a second, and every form of cheating is allowed; a game is over in less than a couple of minutes. They wear European dress, and are the first Afghans I have seen eating (though only furtively) between sunrise and sunset. What is more, they have secured some arak from a Herati Jew and smuggled it into the hotel—a criminal offence. Today they invited me to join them at lunch in their bedroom, where behind barricaded doors the bottle was stealthily produced from under a bed. There seemed to be something on their minds; when healths had been drunk, the busman, acting it appeared as spokesman for the party, turned to me and said:
'You are the Emperor of the world; why do you hate us?'
I wondered what my claim to the title could be, and how I

had offended them. But it appeared that the charge was national rather than personal: why did the British, who (once?) ruled the world, dislike the Afghans?

I had no idea that we did. I knew, of course, that we fought them at regular intervals throughout the nineteenth century; but only in a playful, imperialistic sort of way that should have offended no one. I knew that we were largely responsible for the destruction of the great Mosalla; but then, soldiers will be soldiers and must have their bit of fun. I knew that they had been angry when we appropriated Baluchistan in 1876 and so rendered them truly land-locked; but that was surely done to make them feel that they were really the 'Switzerland of Asia.' And I knew that they had not much cared for the way our troops, during the first Afghan War, had invaded the harems and raped their women, who failed to appreciate (as someone said of that regrettable episode) that Necessity, the mother of Invention, is also the father of the Eurasian. But in any case, these could only be reasons for their disliking us; why on earth should they imagine that we disliked them?

I had no intention, however, of being dragged into a political discussion. I told them that I had found the Afghans friendly and hospitable, and that, speaking for myself, I liked them very much. As for politics—it was not my *métier*. They seemed disappointed, and went off together to hit the piano. The little Arab children clustered round, beguiled by the sweet music.

The busman breaks away at last from the piano and asks me if I will photograph him. I agree, and he goes off to shave and clean his teeth.

April 19th

Unable any longer to bear the suspense, I bought this morning the tin of strawberry jam. Diana did indeed win!

The Iranian consul demanded three photographs of myself before he would give me the Persian re-entry visa. What does he do with them all?

At the police headquarters, where I went for the exit visa, there were endless difficulties. A policeman with a pain in his stomach asked my advice and started undressing; my inability to help him (which he took as deliberate unfriendliness) involved me in further delays. Finally my passport was returned to me, and I wandered off to review the Friday Mosque. Just as I was looting a fine piece of tile from a rubbish dump, two policemen rushed in. But they had only come to tell me that my passport had never been stamped. I thought at first how clever it was of them to find me; probably, however, I was being shadowed all the time I was in Herat. At all events it was fortunate for me that I was discovered; had I not been, I would doubtless have been turned back at the Afghan frontier.

The clerk has been given, by his brother, an English letter to translate into Persian, and asks me if I will explain one or two words that he doesn't quite understand. Of course I will.

The letter begins :

> Dear Sir,
>   We thank you for your inquiry of the 28th ult. re our heavy capacity precision engraving, copying and reducing model GM 2 to 3 . . .

'What machine is this? What is it for?'
'It would appear to be for engraving, copying and reducing.'
'What does it copy?'
'Well, it doesn't say exactly—something heavy, I gather.'
'What does it look like?'
'I haven't the least idea, I'm afraid.'
'What is "ult."?'
'I don't know. They always put it in business letters. It's just —just a way of being friendly, I think.'
'You do not help me. My brother will think that I do not understand English.'
'You can tell him that I don't, either.'

The Malan bridge, which is at least a thousand years old though it has been repeatedly rebuilt, lies about three miles from the town. For centuries it has carried traffic to and from India across the Hari Rud. This evening I drove out in a *gadi* with the clerk and the sanitary inspector to see it. At Malan the Hari Rud is as broad as the Thames at London Bridge, and the spring floods were in full spate; they are said to be the worst for fifteen years. The sanitary inspector gazed thoughtfully at the roaring torrent :

'By God, a fine water-closet !'

'*Bha, bha*; very good !' said the clerk, slapping him on the back.

The sanitary inspector remained pensive, then said suddenly, 'Don't talk to me of women; it brings my water to the mouth.' He has, it seems, fallen in love with the eldest of the Arab girls.

'What do you think,' he said, turning to me, 'of Afghan women?'

'How can I tell when they remain invisible?'

'*Bha, bha!* What he says, it is very true ! But in the house they are very good.'

The clerk was not to be left out when so fruitful a topic as women was under discussion. He mentioned his wife, and, thus encouraged, I ventured to ask a question that I was not sure ought to be put to a Moslem : 'Did you see your wife before your marriage?'

'No, I did not,' he answered sadly, 'and now I am sorry.'

When I had taken one or two photographs, we crossed the bridge and turned down a side road 'to see the ruin.'

'What ruin?' I asked.

'You will know,' said the sanitary inspector.

Soon the road ended abruptly, the swirling waters of the Hari Rud having carried a good two miles of it away.

'Is it not a ruin?'

'It is a ruin.'

'Now there must be more pictures,' announced the clerk, who was busy throwing stones at a snake that was being swept away in the flood water.

So the driver, the sanitary inspector, the clerk and I photographed each other in every possible combination and permutation until the film ran out. I admired the way in which the sanitary inspector—grinning dazzlingly, and looking more than ever like a successful ice-cream merchant—invariably stole any scene in which he appeared.

Towards sunset we started back for the town, our jingling *gadi* scattering to right and left the peasants who were returning in the bright evening to their villages. The driver flicked his whip playfully at those who were slow to take cover, and deftly tickled the rumps of the mules; he was an amiable fellow. The sanitary inspector sat with me in the back and enlarged his mind. 'Are there,' he inquired, 'many good schools in England for training sanitary inspectors?'

The 'Délégation Archéologique Française en Afghanistan' arrived here late this evening (in the dark, because the electric-light system is again 'a ruin'). It consists of a Frenchman and his wife. They are leaving at dawn tomorrow, so we shall see nothing of each other.

April 20th

I have been fraternizing with the Arabs. They live, all eleven of them, in a single room and at the cost of the municipality, and the clerk does not much care for them. The father and the eldest son are hoping to fly to Kabul to try to get an interview with the King; I cannot imagine why they should succeed. The mother never leaves her room, and is known to me only as a black bundle occasionally glimpsed through the open doorway. The eldest daughter—a pretty girl of about twenty—is becoming more friendly and more careless with her veil; this morning she went so far as to smile and say '*bonjour*' when she passed me. The second son, who is not quite right in the head, divides his time between letting off home-made fireworks and making melancholy noises with one fist on the piano. On Ibrahim, a staid youth of fourteen, now falls a heavy burden of responsibility. And he bears it admirably. For it can be no small undertaking to control Mohammad—a pickle of four who is permanently up to mischief, that apparently mild little girl of five who becomes a hell-cat when opposed, and the tiny infant who seems, and not inappropriately, to answer to the name of Howlah.

My favourite is the eight-year-old Khorshid (which means 'Sun')—a radiant, black-eyed, curly-haired boy, intensely vital, intensely animal. I sail paper boats with him in the pond in the hotel garden, for the mere pleasure of hearing him laugh. The sounds that he emits to register surprise, indignation, joy or pain resemble those made by English children about as little as the roaring acceleration of a modern sports car resembles the gentlemanly purring of my pre-war Lanchester; I only wish I had a tape recorder with me.

The sanitary inspector heard the Arab girl speak to me, and is very much put out. The ice-cream smile fades from his face.
'What did she say to you?'
'She said "good morning." '
'I do not think so.'
'She said it in French.'
'Why did she say it in French?'
'I don't know.'
'If you do not know, who knows?'
'Perhaps *she* does. Why don't you ask her?'

The Pfisterers are not going to Meshed yet, so I shall have to take the bus tomorrow. The prospect of another night in that pigsty at Torbat is far from inviting. Poor Dr. Wilke is ill and must return to Germany; if only there were a spare place in the *Volkswagen*!

April 21st

An aeroplane arrived this morning from Kabul—the first that has come through for six weeks. At the unfamiliar sight and sound, everyone in Herat stopped doing nothing and looked up.

With it has arrived an Indian. He has come, he says, 'the hard way' from Bombay; but because the Kabul-Kandahar road is impassable he has been forced to make use of the soft, perilous and expensive aeroplane from Kabul. He hints that he is therefore rather short of money. He is an ingenuous young man, very small, all mahogany and spectacles. Within less than a minute, he produced an article about himself from a Calcutta newspaper. He has spent five years in England with a firm of electrical engineers, and speaks English passably. The job he has recently had in India turned out to be mere office work and he has thrown it up in disgust. Returning to England with him, and for the same reason, is an Irishman who is reading Trollope. They are as curiously assorted a couple as one could hope to find crossing half the world together.

At tea-time—the moment when prayers are happening all over the garden—the entomologists come round to say that

Market scene at Herat

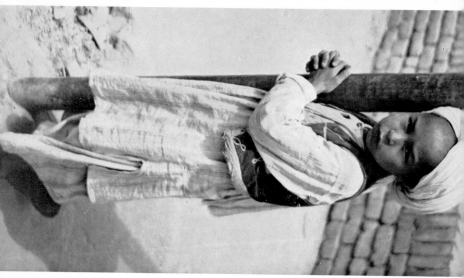

Herati children

Qadam Gah
(p. 98)

Shrine of Shahzadeh Hosain, Qazvin
(p. 162)

(*Left*) *Herati boy on a windy day*

(*Right*) *Basket seller near the White River* (p. 162)

Benjamin is to drive Dr. Wilke back to Meshed as soon as their papers are in order. Dr. Amsel will remain in Herat; there will therefore be a place for me in the car. This is splendid news.

Dr. Amsel does not a bit want to stay in Herat; he has made up his mind that Eslam Qaleh is a treasure-store of rarest moths, and would like to be deposited there while Benjamin goes on to Meshed. Had he got his way, there would have been no room for me. But fortunately there is no moon, and Benjamin has also made up his very strong mind that it would be madness for his father to wander about the Afghan frontier flashing torches all night. He enlists my only too willing support.[1]

April 22nd

A sultry day, idly spent in the garden.

While Khorshid teaches me how to draw palm trees, his barmy brother is perfecting a method of exploding gunpowder in the tube of an old bicycle pump. (Surely he is the person to explain the workings of the atom bomb to the clerk?)

There is a sudden bang—but not louder than that made by an eighteenpenny firework. We shake the dust from our hair.

[1] Dr. Amsel has published an account of his expedition in *Beiträge zur naturkundlichen Forschung in Südwestdeutschland*, Band XVI, Heft I, 1957. Dr. Amsel was taken ill at Sarobi with intermittent fever and oriental jaundice, and was obliged, after some weeks in hospital, to fly back from Kabul to Germany. His son performed the magnificent feat of driving the *Volkswagen* alone, in exceptionally difficult conditions (the Indus had risen forty feet above normal) over the Khyber Pass to Karachi, where it was shipped to Hamburg.

10

Herat to Tehran

April 23rd

A grey morning with a few drops of rain—not enough even to lay the dust.

It was sad to leave Herat just as the roses were beginning to get into their stride. Benjamin, his mind on higher things such as carburettors and differentials, drove unseeing down the flowery avenues, past the shining Mosalla, and out into the wide plain.

The *Volkswagen* took the wild roads well and ploughed its way pluckily through floods and stony river-beds. When we stopped to rescue a lesser vehicle caught in mid-stream, Benjamin glowed with the pride of knight-errantry. The spot where my bus had broken down on the outward journey we found still marked by a burst of red poppies. We lunched at the hotel at Eslam Qaleh and were charged a formidable sum for it; but black thunderclouds were rolling up from the west, and there was no time to waste upon argument over a few *tomans*—nor, alas, to collect the tall lavender irises (*Iris songarica*) that were now everywhere in flower.

The Persian-Afghan frontier is, as I have already said, marked by a dilapidated wooden barrier and a small signpost. There was not a soul in sight. Without slowing down, Benjamin swerved into the desert and rejoined the road beyond the barrier. At this moment there appeared from nowhere a pair of ferocious soldiers, armed to the eyebrows, who planted themselves aggressively in the middle of the road and gesticulated wildly to us to stop. Benjamin (I half thought he wouldn't) drew up, and we both sprang out and advanced to meet the two men. They were gibbering with rage, and had unslung their rifles.

The rule with fierce dogs is, I knew, never to appear frightened; I therefore tried to look a lot braver than I felt. Benjamin behaved magnificently. He strode forward as though he had chanced upon a couple of old school chums in the desert, slapped the nearer soldier warmly on the back, and said

breezily in German, '*Herr Gott noch einmal!* What on earth
is all this fuss about? It's really too absurd. You ought to have
been at your post. I shall report you to the commandant.' Then,
turning to me : 'Cigarettes, quickly !'

The soldiers were dumbfounded. One even dropped his rifle.
Then they snatched at the cigarettes like starving men snatching
bread. And first the one, then the other, saluted.

Big raindrops were now beginning to fall, and soon the
heavens opened. Thunder crashed all around us, and the light-
ning seemed almost continuous. The windscreen wiper was as
good as useless and we were obliged to stop.

'It's bad enough now,' I said, 'but tomorrow, when the
water has come down from the mountains, we shall be
completely stuck.'

Benjamin's military victory had, I suppose, gone to his head.
'*Quatsch!* (bosh !)' he said.

The Commandant of Yusefabad, to whom we both had
letters of introduction, was again away, but a kindly French-
speaking colonel took charge of us. 'If you can go on tonight,'
he said, 'you will be wise to do so. By tomorrow the rivers will
have risen.'

I translated.

'*Quatsch!*' said Benjamin.

'Really, I feel too tired . . .' said Dr. Wilke.

So we spent the night in our sleeping-bags on the floor of the
upper room of the customs house.

April 24th

A sparkling, repentant morning after the rain. We got away
at half past seven.

The first river did not look very formidable, but in mid-
stream the car stuck fast on a submerged mudbank. We spent
an hour wading almost knee-deep in icy water, collecting stones
which we embedded in the mud to support the jack, and more
to place under the wheels. The car was then backed—into, as
it proved, another mudbank, and the performance had to be
started all over again. We had lost three full hours before we
finally gained the farther bank.

The second river was a broad, raging torrent, obviously impassable. The water, however, was falling rapidly; in four or five hours it might be low enough to attempt a crossing. The doctor and I went off in search of lepidoptera and flowers, leaving Benjamin by the car.

Suddenly there was a cry from the doctor, and I saw him leaping like a stag across the countryside, now flinging his hat on the ground, now retrieving it and springing into the air. His performance would have done credit to an Olympic gymnast; I could hardly believe my eyes. Then came the final swift plunge and the shout of triumph : the flying beetle—a beetle new to science—was his !

Leaving the hat weighted with stones, the doctor ran back to the car to fetch a box. I stared at the hat for a minute or two. The beetle, knowing that it had met its master, gave no sign of life; I therefore left it to its own devices and continued my search for flowers. It was a fatal error : the doctor returned to find that the bird had flown. Thus through my carelessness the world of science was robbed of a brand-new beetle.

A few minutes later I heard another cry from the doctor : not this time a shout of triumph, but a shriek of anguish :

'*Ach, du lieber Herr Gott!* Look ! No—don't look. It's better not to look.' And he pressed his hands to his eyes.

Of course I had to look. The doctor had just cause for alarm : Benjamin, with the impetuosity of youth, had decided to attempt the crossing. The car was bounding down the bank. It struck the water, which broke in a great wave over the roof, plunged forward a dozen yards or so, then came to rest with its back wheels in several feet of swirling torrent. For a few moments there was silence. Then we could hear Benjamin trying, unsuccessfully, to restart the engine.

The doctor sat down on a stone and wept. '*O du lieber Gott! Und wir sassen so schön!* [1] The water has got into the engine. Now we will be here all night. All our things are in the car. If the river rises again, then the car will be washed away. *O du lieber, lieber Herr Gott!* Youth, youth, when will it learn that it does not know everything !' He rose, seized me by the arm and began walking rapidly from the scene of the catastrophe. 'Come

---

[1] 'O dear God ! And we were sitting so pretty !'

away! He has brought this on himself; he must ladle out his
own soup (or, as we should say, "stew in his own juice").'

I looked back. Benjamin was wading towards the bank. The
soup was up to his knees and the current very strong; I began
to wonder if he would make it. But in any case we were too far
off to attempt a rescue.

Though the plain had seemed empty for miles around, at this
juncture three natives—one of them with a bicycle—appeared
miraculously on the scene. Benjamin, who had reached the
bank, returned with them to the car and the now hopeless
operation of jacks and stones was begun all over again.

Two hours later we were rescued. The colonel, fearful for
our safety, had set out in a truck to see if we were still alive;
with his help, the car was hauled back to the bank. We found
that the water had damaged only the electrical part of the
engine, and Benjamin soon put this right again.

'The next river is worse,' said the colonel. 'You are coming
back to lunch with me at Yusefabad.'

We needed no persuading. When we again reached the first
river, which only a few hours before had been a sizable stream,
we found it completely dry—so quickly do the flood waters of
Iran come and go.

The colonel lived in a pretty house with a courtyard full of
flowers. He gave us a wonderful meal—a meal that had
obviously been prepared in advance; clearly he knew that we
could not hope to get through.

Benjamin was fretting at the delay, but the colonel became
military and refused to let us go until four o'clock. Even then,
he insisted upon seeing us across the first three streams. It was
as well that he did: twice more we stuck in the swirling waters
and had to be towed by the truck.

The colonel also came to the rescue of a sugar merchant
whose jeep had become marooned in mid-stream. This man
immediately promised that we should dine with friends of his
at Torbat, and that he would arrange for our lodging. Remembering my previous experience there, I was deeply grateful.

The sugar merchant's friend made us welcome, and produced
his son—a remarkable young man to find in these wilds. The

youth spoke good English. He was mad about T. S. Eliot. He liked the music of Beethoven and Tchaikovsky 'because it was so abstract.' He painted abstract pictures (which I did not see). He wanted to be an artist, but his father thought that a business career was safer. He hated business. Would I persuade his father to let him take up art? Would I assure his father that painting was far more lucrative than trade?

I would not.

For the four hours, from six till ten, that we melon-pipped until supper was ready, the young man culture-vultured at me till my head reeled. The doctor went to sleep. Benjamin, sobered by his recent experiences, was agreeably docile. White doves flew round the room. I noticed that the pictures—cheap colour-reproductions of sentimental landscapes and still life—were hung in identical pairs above the mantelpiece and on each side of the doors, for perfect symmetry.

Our dinner-host having no spare room, we spent the night— in real beds—at the house of a friend of a friend of the sugar merchant.

April 25th

Again there was no time to see the Mosque at Torbat, but I took comfort in the remembrance that Byron had found it disappointing.

The next stage of our journey was memorable for a fine blaze of giant red tulips,[1] whose bulbs were so deeply buried that I failed in my attempt to dig one or two up. Though the waters had subsided, we were again more than once in trouble. At Sangbast, where several lorries and a bus had broken down, a rescue squad that had been sent out from Meshed towed us up the almost vertical bank.

We reached Meshed at half past one. Its streets, that on my arrival from Tehran had seemed so oriental, now looked to me almost Western. I found Tom lunching in his shirt-sleeves in the Consulate garden, under a cherry tree hung with blossom.

A private performance this evening of the *Rubaiyat* of Omar Khayyam and Matthew Arnold's *Sohrab and Rustam*,

[1] *Tulipa Greigii, T. Eichleri* or *T. Fosteriana*? I wish I had looked at them more carefully.

declaimed, on gramophone records, in broad American. This was succeeded by a cultural party for the intelligentsia of Meshed: Ravel and an act of *Julius Caesar*, on the radiogram also. Mrs. Shadman's translation of *Julius Caesar* was read first. We sat in silent piety, as if in church.

April 26th

By air to Tehran.

Being unwilling to impose myself so soon again upon the Embassy, I had intended going to the Hotel Ferdausi. But Dr. Wilke would not hear of it. On his outward journey he had struck up acquaintance with a certain Dr. H., a Persian chemist who lived at Shemran; 'No point in wasting money at an hotel,' he said to me. 'I'll get him to put us both up. He's rolling in cash. He enjoys having people. I'll give him a ring at his office.'

The chemist would, of course, be only too delighted. . . . I had my doubts (which were soon confirmed). Moreover, though it would be interesting to stay with Persians again, I did not much care for the cool admission that we were merely saving an hotel bill.

It turned out that we could hardly have chosen a more unfortunate moment. The chemist and his brother lived in adjoining identically hideous houses in the summer suburb of Tehran; the brother's house was being redecorated, and both families were for the moment occupying the same building. To make matters worse, we arrived to find a party in progress: a party of women, none of whom spoke a word of English.

When that great conjuror Reza Shah lifted the veils of the women of Iran he revealed, as good conjurors often do, that there was very little underneath. This act of forcible emancipation had merely transferred the tittle-tattle of the harem to the drawing-room—but not by way of the schoolroom; it is the next generation who will reap the reward of improved education for girls. I have in my time been forced to listen to a dozen Frenchwomen with nothing to say, saying it; for sheer ear-splitting din, half a dozen Persian women can give them points. Almost impossible to believe that the human larynx is capable of producing such parrot sounds. My head began to ache, the doctor's head began to ache, as we sat on hard chairs, totally ignored, left to our own thoughts (for speech was virtually impossible) and a bowl of suspect lettuce, for three intolerable hours. And all night long, as I lay on the drawing-room floor, the aviary seemed still to echo with the cries of the birds that had flown.

April 27th

The doctor, who had been prostrated by last night's experiences, rallied at breakfast and began to run the house. He expressed so much surprise at the absence of yoghourt that the maid was sent out to buy some; he touched so repeatedly upon the convenience of cars as a method of transport that the chemist was obliged to devote the whole morning of his one free day to taking us to Tehran on a shopping expedition. I looked in at the Embassy to collect letters, and found that Tim had left word that I was to use his house in his absence. This is typical of his kindness. I shall move in tomorrow morning.

A thunderstorm was being arranged for the mid-afternoon. The chemist, to whom I had mentioned an interest in wild flowers, asked me after lunch whether I would like to go to the foothills of the Elburz to a spot where there was a splendid purple wild iris. Would I not! The storm was about to break, but by the time the car reached the mountains it might well be over.

'Then let us start,' said the chemist.

It was not until we had left the house, and were irrevocably committed to our botanizing, that I discovered that we were to go *on foot*!

Of all forms of exercise undertaken by the eccentric in the pursuit of health, that of walking uphill in the rain touches, I have for long known, the nadir. The four of us (for the chemist had brought with him his eleven-year-old son, Mohammad) started up the broad avenue, bordered by the ugly summer houses of the rich Tehrani, that leads to the mountains. It was bucketing.

How far was it to those irises? God is the Most-Knowing.

The chemist adored his son, and was determined to make a prodigy out of him. Not a moment must be wasted. Today's lesson, which neither the rain nor the steepening gradient could an instant abate, was devoted to arithmetic—in French, which the chemist spoke well (but the doctor not at all).

'If twenty tubes of toothpaste cost twenty-five *tomans*,' said the father, 'what would a hundred and twenty tubes cost?'

The child beat me to it: 'A hundred and fifty *tomans*, father.'

'Very good, Mohammad. Suppose I buy six cakes of soap at one *toman* each, and sell them at twenty per cent. profit, how much shall I gain?'

He loved his son; it was almost inevitable that he should spoil him.

'I want an ice, please, father.'

'I want a glass of carrot-water, father.'

'I want another ice, please, father.'

No request was ever refused. And at first I was grateful, for we were thus from time to time afforded a moment's respite from the storm. But soon we had reached saturation point; the rain could hurt us no more.

'Is it much farther?' I asked at last; and a burst of thunder drowned my question. I repeated it, but the chemist was not listening: '*Si cinquante flacons de parfum coûtent soixante tomans . . .*' he was saying.

We never reached those irises—if, indeed, they really existed. Ignominious though it was to be defeated by a child of eleven, the moment came when the doctor and I could bear it no longer. Even worms will turn. We turned.

'We think that perhaps we will be going back. But of course if you and Mohammad want to go on . . .'

Of course not. The whole expedition had been arranged for our pleasure. He and his son could come up there any time. He merely thought that as I was so keen on irises . . .

When we were nearly half-way home, the rain stopped and a penitent sun flooded the distant valley with light. I looked at the chemist, and thought that I detected a mischievous glint in his eye.

Had this expedition been his little revenge? I shall never know: Orientals, as we are incessantly reminded, are 'inscrutable.' Next morning, when I came to take leave of him, he implored me not to go. Would I not stay just one more night —just one?

April 28th

Maria Wiggin, the wife of one of the Secretaries at the Embassy, drove me this afternoon to Varamin, about thirty-five miles south-east of Tehran, to see the ruined fourteenth-century Mosque and the yet earlier fluted grave-tower there.

The Mosque stands on the flowerless plain, a little apart from the village, and is defended by a typically Persian enclosure: that is to say, there is a padlocked gate in the front and a large hole in the wall round the corner. The building must once have been very splendid, and its buff-coloured dome, which stands upon an octagonal drum, still has dignity. There is just enough Eton-and-Harrow blue tilework and stucco decoration remaining to make it possible to form a picture of the building as it had been in its prime. It is a foretaste of the greater mosque at Soltaniyyeh, which I hope soon to see also.

Varamin is utterly neglected; a few more years, and there will be nothing left of the Mosque. You walk now beneath its crumbling walls at the risk of getting half a ton of Kufic frieze on your head.

I engaged some children to find fragments of tile for me; they came back with a handful, for which I rewarded them, and with an older boy. 'You must give this boy some money,' said one of the children. 'His father looks after this Mosque.'

That was really too much!

Two exquisite turquoise-coloured rollers were flying about the dome. The beastly son of the guardian of the Mosque produced a catapult and began tormenting them. I was more than ever glad that I had given him nothing.

We stopped a moment on the way home to see the grave-tower at Rai. It is monumental, but much restored and now wholly lacking in charm; that at Varamin has at least a certain elegance. But since I have no hope now of getting to Gonbad-e-Qabus, the masterpiece of this art, I am glad to have seen at least these two lesser examples.

April 29th

A leisurely drive and picnic with Charles and Maria Wiggin in the Lashkarek valley of the Elburz Mountains. Beside the mountain streams the poplars are green now, and peach, plum and Judas trees are in flower. The gaunt cliffs are fantastically coloured as in the Persian miniatures. In places the rocks are lit with the flame of red or yellow tulips; I collected a few bulbs, and one small iris which I would like to believe is my long-sought *Iris persica*.

April 30th

I called this morning on Mme Moghadam at the National Museum. She has invited me to tea. A Dutch portraitist, Mme Dr. Lily Eversdyk Smulders, came in while I was with her, and I was carried off to her very native hotel to see her drawings. She has been all over the Far and Middle East, and her studies of oriental types make an interesting ethnographical record. But does not the camera work better, and quicker, where accurate representation is the main object?

Mme Moghadam lives in a fine Qajar house with a white *loggia* and the first Persian garden that I have seen which contains any plants interesting to the horticulturist. The house has an underground room whose walls are patterned with fragments of rare Persian pottery. Three French archaeologists from Susa were also at tea; they discussed the latest progress of their dig, and made me feel ashamed of having failed to visit it. There simply is not time to see everything.

May 1st

Mr. Roberts, who is attached to the British Council, has invited me to go with him tomorrow by car to the Caspian and thence to Soltaniyyeh. This is most kind of him; there is no greater pleasure than motoring through beautiful country at someone else's expense. At Soltaniyyeh we are to meet Maria, who will come direct from Tehran. She is anxious to see something of north-west Persia before she leaves for Washington in July, and Charles, who is too busy to come, has asked me to take her with me to Tabriz.

II

North-West Iran

May 2nd

The Chalus road across the Elburz, constructed by order of
Reza Shah, is one of the most remarkable in the world.

On leaving Tehran, we followed at first the Tabriz road
across featureless plain; then, turning northwards, we engaged
the barren foothills of the Elburz. Soon the way began to climb
steeply among rugged, desolate rocks, winding up valleys whose
streams gave life to narrow strips of herbage and ranks of slim,
greening poplars. So clear was the air that the red and tortured
mountain walls seemed cut out of cardboard.

After some two hours we came upon a rest house constructed
for the use of the late Shah. Like the road, it was sadly in need
of repair. Big, infelicitous urns, crudely smeared with cheap
silver paint, gave it the familiar Reza Shah touch.

Now the snow-line came down to meet us. At about eight
thousand feet a tunnel has been cut through the mountain; the
pass being still closed at this season, we plunged into the cold,
dark rock, to emerge into the blinding snows that crowd the
northern summits of the Elburz.

As we began to descend, the air grew heavier and a faint
bloom of green veiled the mountains. The road was fringed now
with violets and cowslips, with scarlet poppies no bigger than
a shilling, and bushes of flowering blackthorn. Soon came moss
and ferns; then small beeches, sycamores, poplars and wild
crabs. For a mile or more the hillside was covered with wild
roses (*Rosa foetida?*), still in tight bud. The air was lazy, the
mountains shrouded.

Still lower came forest trees, dressing the slopes as lushly green
as Cliveden Reach in June. We motored on through leafy
Bucks, descending at last to the coastal plain where the orange
trees were hung with fruit, and thatched cottages stood among
rice fields and tea plantations. There were groves of eucalyptus,

and bananas thrusting out their tattered leaves. In half an hour
we had exchanged Buckinghamshire for Japan.

The extraordinary progress from the arid Persian plateau,
over snow-bound mountains to the sub-tropical southern shores
of the Caspian has been described by many wondering writers.
No words, however, can convey the sensation of thus traversing,
in a mere five or six hours, such an astonishing variety of scenery
and vegetation.

Chalus had little to detain us. Turning our car towards the
west, we skirted the grey sea's flower-starred beaches, past herds
of humpbacked cows, past scattered Hänsel and Gretel mud-
and-thatch cottages where white irises grew, till we reached
Ramsar.

Ramsar—a luxury hotel and casino on the shores of the
Caspian—is one of Reza Shah's unhappiest attempts to impose
Western civilization on his reluctant and impoverished subjects.
To give the long white building an air of splendour and culture,
a double ration of plaster maidens, cupids, griffins, lions, bulls,
vultures and Sasanian warriors had been doled out from the
royal repository, and enough bronze and silver paint to treble
their natural ugliness. A mile-long avenue leads from the hotel
down to the sea and the casino (which is closed, and likely to
remain so). Our tea cost us six shillings a head. We are not
staying the night at Ramsar.

We did not reach the port of Pahlavi till ten o'clock, and
therefore counted ourselves lucky in finding rooms. Pahlavi has
a pleasant, shoddy, down-at-heel look that is typically Russian.
There is much coarse white concrete round the harbour, and
blue paint appears to be cheap. The 'promenade' is slipping
into the sea; the houses, which look as though they had been
run up by their owners from fragments of other ruins, are
slipping into the promenade. The iron cores of broken balusters
and statues are visible everywhere. A White City, improvised
for an ephemeral exhibition and then left to disintegrate.

May 3rd

Having spent half a damp grey English morning discovering
that there was nothing to discover at Pahlavi, we set out for
Qazvin.

Beyond Rasht the road strikes inland, following the broad and gentle valley of the Safid Rud (White River). Here and there we came upon groves of old olives that added a touch of Italy to a Devonshire landscape; of flowers, however, there were few and but dull. The picturesque dresses of the peasant women ('to see a group of these rose-coloured women working in the fields makes a pretty picture' says Ebtehaj) tempted me to try to get some photographs, but irate husbands brandishing sticks soon drove me post-haste back to the car; the women could hardly have made more commotion had they been being raped. Some basket-sellers, however, enticed by the sight of my money, paused just long enough for me to take a couple of photographs before they bolted for cover.

We lunched surprisingly well in a very little village. Our host had been in Baghdad and spoke some English. His cottage was roofed with bamboos covered with branches of fir and a foot of rolled earth. A violent wind was blowing; he told us that it blew without intermission all the year round.

Then, gradually, the green faded from the hillsides, though not even near Qazvin did we return to the cruel deserts of central Iran. Qazvin—like Isfahan, Shiraz, Tehran, Suleimanieh, Ardabil, Nishapur and Meshed—was in its day (in the sixteenth century) the capital of Persia. Towards setting sun, we saw all too rapidly its mosques and palaces: the Friday Mosque, dating from the twelfth century but much renovated, where waving grass grew upon the blue-tiled dome: the Haideriyyeh, now a school, with remains of Mongol plasterwork; the Shrine of Shahzadeh Hosain, with its sparkling mirror-mosaic porch, where my camera did a sterling job; and an Ali Qapu and Chehel Sotun of the early sixteenth century (now the police headquarters) which must have served as models for their counterparts at Isfahan. The jaunty little tomb of Hamdollah Mostaufi, also of the sixteenth century, is decorated with an ultramarine band of script and crowned with a turquoise cone. So charming that they seduced me to rise next morning before breakfast to photograph them are the jutting wooden balconies of the houses, infinitely varied in design, which are a characteristic feature of Qazvin.

We spent the night at an hotel such as one might find

in a small French provincial town, except that alcohol could only be consumed in the bedrooms.

May 4th

On the map, it looked so easy to get from Qazvin to Soltaniyyeh. As the crow flies it is only sixty-five miles. The road goes there. The railway goes there. Three hours, perhaps? In fact it took us nearly seven. And had we travelled by train we would never have reached our goal at all, for ten kilometres of alternating dike and desert separate the great Mongol Mausoleum from a station yard that does not know the meaning of the word 'transport.'

A slow, sunny journey, uneventful but for the collecting of a handsome brown iris, brought us at last to Soltaniyyeh station. Our road, which for miles had commanded a tempting prospect, to our left, of the Mausoleum, appeared still to forge relentlessly ahead. Where, we asked the stationmaster, was the road to the town?

'Five kilometres back you should have taken the turning to the left.'

'But there was no road.'

'It is not a good road. It is a ruin.'

A soldier who was asleep on a packing-case in the station yard was roused and detailed to be our guide. It seemed doubtful whether he had ever before been so far as the town; at all events, his tentatively chosen way appeared to involve us in an unnecessary quantity of bogs and ditches. At last, still a couple of miles from the little town, we drew up, beside Maria's car, before a dike that would have daunted a jeep.

Accompanied by our guide, who was slowly recovering from the shock of seeing two cars on the same day, we set out on foot towards the long row line of mud hovels, and the vast Mausoleum—a roc's egg in a great octagonal egg-cup—that dominated them as the Roman amphitheatre of El Djem dominates its sprawling mud village. *Splendeurs et misères!*

The Mausoleum of Soltaniyyeh was built by the Mongol prince, Uljaitu, in the opening years of the fourteenth century, to house—could he secure them—the bones of Ali and Hosain; it served, in the event, only to receive his own. Even in decay, the magnitude and simple dignity of the architecture are over-whelmingly impressive. Lapis lazuli and turquoise tiles still cling here and there to the base of the rosy-buff dome—the largest in Iran—like colour-notes on a sepia sketch. The eight minarets are now little more than roughed in. The whole is a skeleton whose bones the imagination must clothe again with the blue robes of their vanished splendour.

And all around, what misery! Impossible to believe that Soltaniyyeh was once a large and thriving capital; that only three centuries ago travellers praised its numerous palaces and mosques; that even in the early nineteenth century Fath Ali Shah, his court and his army could pass the summer heats there in royal state.

How could we have missed Maria and her party in little Soltaniyyeh? Hide-and-seek, perhaps, round the Mausoleum. When, in despair, we were compelled to leave without them, we saw her cavalcade ahead of us, on foot and donkey-back, making slowly towards the cars. On donkey-back, because Mrs. F. had broken her ankle; we therefore put her at once in the car for Tehran, leaving the other free to take Maria and myself to the station.

The railway, which aspires one day to reach out to Tabriz, now dies at Mianeh. The train was German, comfortable, slow; the track seemed good. A golden evening journey, through fertile country with emerald cornfields and groves of poplars serving as a foil to rose and lavender mountains, carried us to Mianeh, where we were obliged to spend the night. A Turki-speaking taximan herded us into an already overcrowded car and deposited us at what in Mianeh does service for an hotel— a drear little building busy trying to better itself by the lavish application of paint and the addition of frills. In the dining-room hung two big gilt mirrors with the prices still attached, a poster showing a priggish little girl assiduously watering a wire-less set with coins, and a picture of a houri orientalized a long way after Boucher. But the hotel had one virtue: we were able to buy a bottle of wine and, what is more, drink it in public.

Mianeh has only one claim to fame—or rather, to infamy: its notorious bug, the *gharibgaz* or 'stranger-biter'—so called because it is said to spare natives. This grey, red-spotted little brute, apparently common enough in the nineteenth century, causes serious illness and sometimes death. Persian doctors are said to recommend a variety of treatments. A homoeopathic precaution is the swallowing of a bug wrapped in bread. Those already bitten are served with a bowl of sour milk and then rotated until they vomit. Hardly more attractive is the enclosing of the bitten limb in the skin of a newly killed bullock. Recent travellers in Mianeh have little to relate about the exploits of the stranger-biter. Maybe DDT has exterminated it. The smell of paint would in any case have driven it headlong from the Hotel Derakhshan, and I cannot therefore report at first hand on its enormities.

Reza Shah has given even little Mianeh the Western touch. The main street now terminates in a superfluous roundabout, glorified with a statue of R. S. freshly refurbished with mud-coloured paint left over from the hotel redecoration.

May 5th

They had told us that the bus for Tabriz would go at eight o'clock; at six-forty-five there was a cry that it was leaving immediately. Horrified at the thought of having to spend another twenty-four hours in Mianeh, we rushed out, half dressed and quarter breakfasted, to tumble into front seats courteously vacated for Europeans.

Rolling hills, another child with whooping-cough, splendid snow-clad Mount Sahand, cries of *Yallah* followed by a precipitous, perilous drop into the valley—and Tabriz lay before us, big, sprawling, walled by raspberry-pink mountains that the sunset turns to potted shrimp. It seemed at first sight a characterless town; but two buildings, both ruinous, reward the weary traveller—the Ark and the Blue Mosque. And from Tabriz it is possible to visit Maragheh and—given the time—Ardabil.

Ghazan Khan, the Great Il-Khan, on ascending the throne in 1295 embraced Islam and erected in Tabriz what may perhaps have been the most remarkable building ever raised by the hand of man—his own mausoleum. Wars and earthquakes have destroyed all that he accomplished; but the ruins of a lesser building erected shortly after his death—the Mosque of Ali Shah, generally known as the Ark—give at least a clue to the pomp that has vanished.

The Ark is colossal. The great brick vault, now fallen, once spanned a space of one hundred feet (Gerona Cathedral, the largest brick vault in Europe, spans only seventy-five). All that remains of the Ark is a gaunt façade, one hundred and twenty feet high, built of exquisitely laid buff-coloured bricks. Tilework, marble and gold have vanished without a trace. We can only stand astonished before these towering walls and ask ourselves what the Mausoleum of Ghazan Khan must have been like in the days of its glory.

The Ark has suffered many vicissitudes. One hundred and fifty years ago it was converted into an arsenal. From its summit adulteresses used to be thrown to their death; but—according to Curzon—the practice was discontinued after one of these ladies, sustained by her voluminous petticoats, parachuted safely to earth. It was in the courtyard of the Ark that, in 1850, the Bab met his death.

You cannot miss the Ark; the Blue Mosque, however, shyly conceals its charms. We took a taxi from our comfortable Hotel Metropol and told the driver to take us there.

'The Blue Mosque? I don't know it.'

(The fault was partly mine; I found out later that I had not selected the right one of the four words for 'blue.')

'The *old* Mosque?'

'No.'

'The *big* Mosque?'

'No.'

'The *famous* Mosque?'

'Never heard of it.'

'The *ruined* Mosque?'

Everything was in ruins. Ah yes—he thought perhaps he knew it. And he drove us to the Ark.

But eventually we found it, tucked away in a shoddy corner, the wreck of the stupendous building that Texier described as having once been the '*chef d'œuvre* of Persian and, perhaps, of all Oriental architecture.' It was built, in the fifteenth century, by Jehan Shah (not to be confused with Shah Jehan), last sovereign of the Black Sheep dynasty. Earthquakes have shattered its walls and destroyed its nine domes; but enough tiling remains to stir the imagination. Much of it is of the deep lapis lazuli blue which has given the Mosque its name. The pink mountains, caught and framed by that exquisite blue, are indescribably lovely.

Having studied, and most unsuccessfully photographed, the towering portal, which now leads no farther than to a small prayer-room, we won—largely by force of my visiting card—admission by way of a schoolyard into the Mosque itself. Round the yard were classrooms packed to bursting-point with unprepossessing, convict-cropped urchins in black Norfolk jackets and drainpipe trousers.

The headmaster (I think) showed us round, and urged us to help ourselves freely from the tempting heaps of fallen tiles, some of which were prettily picked out in gold. For year by year the tiles continue to fall like autumn leaves, though an attempt has been made to arrest the collapse of the walls. Brushing aside all thought of the wicked charges for excess air luggage, we stuffed our pockets and reticules.

May 6th

To Maragheh by car—a little Russian one that held the rough roads bravely.

It was a fresh morning full of scudding clouds—one that enhanced the natural beauty of the fertile plain and the rolling foothills of Mount Sahand. At our feet, smooth and glittering as a silver salver, lay Lake Reza'iyeh. A large detour round the skirts of the twelve-thousand foot peak added nearly forty more miles to what a very high-flying crow could do in forty-six. The journey took us four hours.

Maragheh, now little more than a large village, was in the thirteenth century a place of considerable importance—the capital of the Mongol prince Hulagu Khan, brother of Kublai Khan, and the centre of a distinguished band of philosophers and scientists. The remains of Seljuq and Mongol architecture in Maragheh, though mostly on a small scale, are to my mind as perfect as anything in Iran.

Of the five principal buildings, the most striking is undoubtedly the so-called 'Tomb of the Mother of Hulagu'—a terracotta-coloured polygonal brick tower, originally domed, with walls netted like a melon and relieved with tiles of the purest turquoise imaginable. (Byron describes the brick as 'plum-red'; possibly some unripe plums assume, for a brief moment, this particular shade.) Round the inside of the building an ornate Kufic frieze runs and pigeons fly. Below the tomb there is a vaulted crypt. The tomb has no connection with Hulagu's mother, who was in fact a Christian; it is Seljuq work, and dated 1196-7.

Dogs, a high wall and lack of time prevented our getting a proper view of the Gonbad-e-Surkh ('red dome'), earliest of Maragheh's monuments. Near the river is the Mongol Gonbad-e-Ghaffariyyeh—a handsome square brick building, Tudor red with blue-tiled decoration.

We thought Maragheh a pleasant place, and found its inhabitants amiable. A *molla* whom I asked to pose agreed readily, but with feminine vanity craved a moment's grace to set his turban straight and dust his little donkey. The little tea-house gave us a good but expensive meal.

Maria had set her mind upon seeing Hulagu's observatory. No one, however, seemed to know where it might be, beyond vaguely supposing that it lay outside the town. This we already knew. The Chief of Police, who had been amusing himself for an hour with our passports, came to our rescue and offered to go with us.

The day had changed its mind. Heavy rain-clouds now obscured the sky. As we drew up in a morass at the foot of a steep hill about a mile from the town, the heavens opened. The Chief of Police was in his shirt-sleeves and had a very nasty cough; the rest of us were rather better, but still inadequately, protected.

'That,' said the Chief of Police, pointing to a black dot high up the hillside—'that is the cave.'

I would most readily have said, 'Splendid! Most interesting! Some other time, perhaps. . . .' But Maria seemed suddenly to become possessed by an almost religious frenzy. Springing from the car into the squelching mud, she set off with great Diana-of-the-Uplands strides up the slippery slopes.

What's Hulagu to her, I wondered, or she to Hulagu?

And what could gentlemen do? The Chief of Police splashed out; I splashed out; and together we advanced in dripping pursuit.

I suppose that the ascent took us about twelve minutes, though it seemed longer. It was entirely unpleasant, and the rewards were slight : a dank cave; two altars—if such they were; and two tunnels leading into and beyond two small inner chambers. Above, on the top of the hill, are said to be certain orientated paths connected with Hulagu's astronomical calculations. Even the Hulaguphile was now prepared to take these on trust.

Then, in the wild-lashing rain, we slithered down again to the car and, back in Maragheh, took a tender farewell of that kind, coughing, unshaven policeman to whom we had probably given pneumonia.

Is there, do you suppose, in all England a Chief of Police who would thus have sacrificed himself for a couple of mad foreigners?

Very much I doubt it.

May 7th

A morning in the bazaar, where Maria was determined to find some blue donkey-beads. With the help of the kindest man in the world she at last succeeded. He then demanded about a pound for what was possibly worth fivepence; so dazed with shock was she that she forgot to refuse to pay what he asked. Not to be outdone, I bought the loudest waistcoat in Persia.

Then, after a notable lunch (to the accompaniment of Strauss' *Alpine Symphony*) at the American Consulate, we boarded a beautiful new orange Chevrolet bus for Mianeh.

May 8th

Hotel Derakhshan again. *Derakhshan* means 'shining' : 'Hotel Splendide,' therefore.

Sleep was made difficult by various nocturnal noises. First came a raucous-voiced muezzin, who might have been perched on my window-ledge, so loudly did his invocations reverberate round my room; it was worse than an Etonian fagmaster calling 'boy.' His *aubade* was succeeded by that of other and remoter religious crooners and, soon after dawn, by the hammerings and blastings of certain workmen who are 'improving' the hotel by demolishing most of the back of it. Good luck to them! But I could gladly have dispensed, as I washed in a bucket in the courtyard, with the clouds of dust that their labours generated.

They said the train went at eight o'clock. It went at seven-forty-five, and we caught it by a miracle.

With us in the carriage was a very handsome young Iranian with a Maclean-your-teeth smile and a family estate of 200,000 square miles—or so he said. This is almost exactly the area of France : perhaps he meant feet; but he refused to reduce his estimate by even a square perch. He had about as much English as I have Persian, the most curious feature of his English conversation being the determined way in which he persisted with a wrong word—a tendency I had already noticed in other students.

'You are proudly human,' he said to me.

Mystified, I asked him to tell me in Persian.

'*Khosh be hale shoma.*'

'But the English for that is, "You are very lucky." '

He was far from convinced.

Very lucky? Yes—because I was travelling with Maria. He just could not take his eyes off her. Might he write to her? Might he send her a present? Might he visit her in Tehran? He had horses; would she come and stay with him, ride with him? When the train stopped in open country, he scrambled down and picked her bunches of eremurus and purple gladioli; when it reached a station, he bought her bunches of wild asparagus (and, almost, a live turkey). He shared his lunch with us—butter from home, cheese from home, eggs from home. He tried to pay for our tea. He tried to pay for everything.

But the odd part of the story is the denouement. Though furnished with the necessary name, address and encouragement, he was never heard of again. Perhaps the word 'Embassy' intimidated him.

At four o'clock the train stopped for half an hour at Zenjan, though whether to rest the engine or to allow the passengers to perform afternoon prayer on the lawn I do not know. Zenjan station (I hope I am not betraying military secrets) is a little, rectangular, buff-coloured building, identical with others up and down the line. Having soon drunk our fill of its architectural beauties, Maria and I walked the length of the platform, studying our fellow travellers. An old peasant was doing a brisk trade in wild asparagus. I took out my camera and was about to photograph him when I felt a firm hand laid on my shoulder.

In the guardroom, a pompous little captain attempted, in halting French, to explain the nature of my crime. I must surely realize, he said, that all stations were objects of vital military importance.

'But not, surely, sellers of—of *asperges sauvages*?'

A seller of wild asparagus plying his trade on a station platform, said the captain, became *ipso facto*, a military object.

At this point Maria unfortunately got the giggles.

'*Je vois que pour vous c'est un spectacle, Madame,*' he said severely. 'You will both remain here until I give you permission to leave.'

'But our luggage is in the train!' (And so, fortunately, was our friend Jalil.)

'*Ça m'est égal.*'

The cat had found a mouse—the first, no doubt, for many weeks. It was not until the whistle had gone, and the engine was panting impatiently, that he finally set us free.

It was nearly ten o'clock by the time we reached the Embassy. Tim's non-resident housekeeper had not expected me, and I was obliged to break in. I had no idea how difficult it was to smash a pane of glass in cold blood.

May 9th

This is the kind of thing that stretches one's Iranian patience to breaking-point :

Having made up my mind to go from here to Kashan— which, as the map shows, should not be a very major operation; moreover it lies on the railway—I went to a travel bureau to buy my ticket. I am informed that there are only two trains a week to Kashan, though a daily one to Qom—the half-way house.

'Then I will go to Qom on Friday, spend the night there, and go on to Kashan the next day.'

'You cannot stay the night at Qom, sir. Qom is a holy city. It is not allowed.'

'Then I will go to Qom by train on Friday and take a bus from there to Kashan. Please give me a ticket to Qom.'

A large notice states, RAILWAY TICKETS SOLD HERE; but it appears that they do not sell tickets to Qom—only to Ahwaz and the Persian Gulf. I must go to the station. Further, I must buy the ticket in advance.

From force of habit, as I leave I say, 'Thank you.'

'O.K., that's my duty,' answers the imperturbable young man.

The station is right at the other end of the town. At the ticket office I am told that if I buy the ticket *two* days in advance I must pay a supplement of six shillings; it should be bought the day before leaving.

And yet they announce these absurdities with such radiant smiles, with such gracious gestures of hand upon heart, with such proffering of cigarettes, with such solicitude for one's welfare, happiness and longevity, that it is impossible to be really angry.

None the less, I am through with the railway. I shall go to Kashan by bus.

May 10th

I have managed to book a place in a bus for Kashan on Saturday.

Walking back from the bus office by way of the bazaar, I was approached by a student who for an hour clung tenaciously to me. His motive was pure kindness. He had a holiday; he had nothing to do.

I said something to him in Persian. He corrected it and observed that my accent was deplorable. 'If you accent your words thus, people will think that you are not Iranian.'

He said he would like to spend all tomorrow with me. He had another holiday; he had nothing to do.

Lunch with Charles and Maria. The Ambassador and Ambassadress were there too, and there was much talk about preparations for the visit they are paying to the south, including Yazd where I shall hope to meet them.

Maria said, 'Now what are the really important things not to forget?'

'Whisky,' said the Ambassador.

'Lavatory paper,' said the Ambassadress.

May 11th

I had often wondered why the roof of the Martens' greenhouse should be decorated with a row of exotic antlers and skulls. They form part of the bag of a Polish big-game hunter, Count X, who has arrived here today. Elegant, grey-haired, fascinating, the Count may well attract his victims to within gunshot range by sheer charm. He has been romping with bear-cubs and held up by bandits, but he has failed in his ambition to secure Marco Polo's sheep *(Ovis poli)* on the Pamir plateau. He now wants four new tyres for his Land Rover. But tyres are so expensive. . . . He has only to smile that wonderful smile in the right quarters, talk that wonderful broken English, and tyres will come rolling in.

12

Tehran to Isfahan

May 12th

He was so very small, so very wasp-waisted, so very dapper, so very kind, that young Persian lieutenant who sat beside me in the blue-and-red bus of the Transport Nau Company that was carrying me, on this gallant morning, from Tehran via Qom to Kashan.

He was returning to Kashan, his home town, for the wedding of his sister. Having spent six months in the States, he spoke some English—an English that showed surprisingly little trace of an American accent. Needless to say, he offered me the seat next the window, and was most reluctant to allow my refusal; he tried, but failed, to pay for my tea when we made a mid-morning halt at a tea-house; he unfortunately succeeded in paying for my lunch; he invited me to stay at his house; he invited me to the wedding; he offered to show me the sights of Kashan; he promised me a letter of introduction to a friend at Ardistan; he offered me the use of a horse and a gun, and the prospect of unlimited gazelles.

And at Qom—God bless his little heart!—he saved me from arrest. How could I have known that photographing the Mosque from the street was forbidden? How could I have seen, occupied as I was with domes and minarets, that the Qom Chief of Police filled half the foreground of the picture? Then it was that the little lieutenant rushed to my aid, pacified the indignant officer, claimed me for a friend of long standing and impeccable respectability, and so snatched me from the menacing arms of the Law.

The lieutenant led me into the courtyard of the Mosque; with such escort, pygmy though it was, I had nothing to fear. Gay and glittering in the blinding sunlight, thronged with worshippers, the spacious court now seemed perfectly adapted to its purpose, and all suspicion of vulgarity was forgotten. But once again, time pressing (for our halt was occasioned only by minor repairs to the bus), I had to leave before my eye could catch and retain more than a vague impression of brilliance and light : of the golden dome and the Qajar mirrorwork, of plashing fountains and polychrome tilework, and of the infinitely varied dresses of the pilgrims. I do not think that even the little lieutenant could have saved me from the fury of the mob if I had tried to reinforce my memory with the camera's aid; nor do I think that any black-and-white photograph would have been able to give the faintest impression of the glory of it all.

The Persian landscape was now bleaker and more arid than it had been a month before, the road to Kashan more neglected than that to Isfahan. Sometimes the driver, bored by its monotony, wandered off the track and picked his way at random across the desert stones; sometimes we stopped to admire a distant gazelle; sometimes we just stopped. The young bus-mechanic, impervious to the charm even of gazelles, ate melon pips and read Hafez.

Lunch we took idyllically on the terrace of a wayside tea-house. An old woman was smoking a hookah; hens pecked at our feet; dogs dozed in the sun, and our blue-and-red bus in the shade. As we left, the proprietor conjured up out of the desert and distributed red roses all round, and the lieutenant ('You are the guest of Iran') paid, as I have said, the bill.

How many ways one can wear a rose! I put mine in my buttonhole; the lieutenant clutched his resolutely, as though he were presenting arms with it; the young mechanic stuck the flower in his turban, and wrapped himself up once more in Hafez and melon pips. The driver, rose in mouth, drove grimly on and on across the desert in the drowsy noontide heat.

The bus slept.

A sap-green and a magenta jeep—you can take your choice —ply as taxis in Kashan; the lieutenant selected the magenta one and drove me to his house.

We alighted in a mud-walled alley, dived into a mud tunnel, passed through a little mud-coloured courtyard, and emerged in a larger courtyard trellised with roses, honeysuckle and vines. Through a gate to the left was visible an orchard of flaming pomegranates. The house looked dazzlingly white and clean;

how, I wondered, could anything so enchanting rise from mud.

Mr. R., Hesam's father, came out to welcome us. He was as small as his son; his kind little black eyes surveyed the monster before him. 'My son's friends are my friends,' he said simply. 'Your slave's humble dwelling is yours.'

'You may tread on my eyes,' I said, hoping that he would not.

I took off my shoes and followed my luggage into the drawing-room—a white, vaulted room whose six french windows opened on to the courtyard and the orchard. In small niches in the walls were a picture of the Prophet and photographs of Hesam and his father.

'You will like to change your clothes,' said Hesam.

To show willingness, I changed—*en plein salon*—my shirt. Hesam disappeared, to return a few minutes later in immaculate turquoise pyjamas; he seemed surprised to find me still fully dressed.

One of three black-veiled, 'year-eaten' women who were huddling together in the courtyard like *Macbeth* witches—perhaps she was Hesam's mother, who, of course, I could never meet—came to the threshold, deposited two immense iced lemonades, and silently vanished. Never was drink more welcome—or perhaps more rash, for I had not much cared for the look of that pool in the garden.

At five o'clock, Hesam suggested we should go out. He went off again to change, this time into a new full-dress uniform calculated to stagger the Kashani: he had, I found, an almost feminine passion for dress. It was still fantastically hot, and I was thankful when we plunged into the labyrinth of the covered bazaars; it was, however, a holiday, and most of the shops were shut. Hesam proudly showed me the sights of the town: the Maidan Mosque[1] and its pretty, honeycombed entrance; the new, inevitable roundabout with its statue of Reza Shah that Princess Shams had unveiled that very yesterday; the remains of the leaning minaret, which had recently lost its head by leaning a little too far. Returning home, we climbed up to the roof of

[1] The *mehrab* of this Mosque found its way to an antique shop in Wigmore Street, and is now in the Berlin Museum.

the house to watch the fiendish sun plunge behind purple mountains. And suddenly it was cool, as if a gas fire a foot away had been turned off.

Mr. R. was on the floor of the drawing-room, inscribing wedding invitations in his neat little hand; Hesam joined him there. It was the moment when in an English house a tinkling tray would have announced itself, and a dulcet voice would have been heard saying, 'A little sherry, or would you rather have gin?' In Kashan, one must expect to do as the Kashani; for three hungry, thirsty hours I comforted myself as best I could with a basinful of dried melon pips.

Supper was at ten, on the floor. Then, surrounded by empty yoghourt bowls, Mr. R. said his picturesque prayers (what a fine sense of theatre the Prophet had!). Hesam did not; I have the impression that the younger generation in Iran is not much interested in religious observance.

In Persia, supper is immediately followed by bed. I was not sorry. For an hour or more I lay wakeful, listening to the crying of the jackals, watching the moonlight playing upon the scarlet flowers of the pomegranates, and wondering whether the infamous scorpions of Kashan would pay me a visit. The scent of the honeysuckle was almost overpowering.

May 13th

My bedroom again became, all too soon after sunrise, the drawing-room, and there seemed general surprise that I was still embedded at that late hour. I shaved in the pool among the goldfish, dressed in a corner of the drawing-room while Mr. R. and a friend discussed matrimonial matters, and then breakfasted off a couple of boiled eggs, cheese, and fresh, sweetened milk that tasted faintly of cinnamon. This milk comes from one of the farms that Mr. R. owns.

Four miles from Kashan, at the foot of the mountains, is the famous royal garden of Fin—a favourite summer retreat of Fath Ali Shah. At seven o'clock, while it was still—allegedly—cool (say not much over 90 degrees), we took the magenta jeep there. Here at last was a garden that lived up to the Persian legend: tall, Villa d'Este cypresses and groves of pomegranates; long, shaded tanks trimmed with flowers; pleasant, airy pavilions cooled by blue-tiled runnels. Garden-boys were paddling in the tank and watering the flowers. Peace and silence reigned. Transport the garden to Tivoli, and it would be like any other; in the heat of this scorching desert it seemed a paradise.

In the garden is the bath-house where, in 1852, Nasr-ed-Din brought about the death of his first great minister, Mirza Taki Khan. It has now been almost entirely stripped of the yellow Yazd marble that once covered the walls and floors. On the hillside above is a large tank where I would gladly have joined the handful of happy bathers; but there was no time, no wherewithal.

Hesam was sure that the Governor of Kashan would like to see me. I felt fairly sure that he would not—not in those dusty and travel-stained clothes; but I had to submit. The Governor spoke English and was very amiable. I praised the kindness of the Kashani in general, and of Hesam in particular. A peculiarly unfriendly colonel, Member of Parliament for Kashan, happened also to be present; he stared reprovingly at my shoes. We drank much tea.

Hesam was certain that I would like to meet the Director of Education for Kashan. I felt fairly certain that I would not—not in that heat; but I was beginning to understand that the young lieutenant was, in some mysterious way, gaining prestige by parading me about the town, so of course I had to submit. We found the Director of Education sitting in a small office with fifteen other large men, all doing nothing in particular. There was some vapid conversation in a sort of French, much amiability all round, and more tea.

I was then displayed in the bazaar—where, incidentally, I must pause to put on record the exquisite manners of the small children of Kashan, who might well have smiled, if not indeed jeered, at the comic conjunction of the little lieutenant and myself. But, one and all, they laid hands on hearts, salaamed, and angelically wished us the Persian top of the morning: it could not have been more prettily done. Hesam, of course, knew everyone. It was tea here, and tea there, and finally a great godsent goblet of iced lemonade (sheer madness) with the barber, who asked for my photograph to hang alongside his picture of the Prophet, and offered me a free haircut.

Back, parboiled, to the house at midday, where there was more reckless iced lemonade into which, unobserved, I managed to pour the last driblet of whisky from my pocket flask. Whisky is said to be a prophylactic.

Hesam announces that it is *beginning* to get warm.

Mr. R. was again on the floor and still surrounded by piles of invitations. He seems to be a man of utter integrity and infinite kindliness. Charming to see him with his son, who is obviously devoted to him; there are six more sons somewhere, and at least one daughter, but I suspect Hesam of being his favourite. He shows me the family photograph album. Though he does not smoke, Mr. R. keeps a box of special Kurdish pipe tobacco for his guests. He has also given me several pieces of Kashan pottery to take home with me; they are not, however, as he supposes, four hundred years old, but quite modern.

Lunch also was on the floor, followed by a terrestrial siesta. Troublesome as were the hornets, I could easily have slept standing up. For four hours I could dream of nothing but iced lager, a drink that I normally detest. I saw it in tall, frosted, foaming glasses—dozens and dozens of them. I imagined myself drinking a whole row of glasses, one after the other. Thirty years ago, glued all day for a week to the back of a camel in the northern Sahara, I had similar hallucinations.

A note—while I think of it—on smoking in Persia.

Mr. R.'s Kurdish tobacco is the only good pipe tobacco I have come across; the ordinary shop brands make a just passable smoke when mixed with an equal quantity of real tobacco. I have not sampled the *qalian* (hubble-bubble), for which one should buy one's own mouthpiece. *Oshnu* cigarettes are three a penny and not unlike the French *gauloises*; they seem to be despised by the Persians, who prefer a slim, effeminate kind called *homa*. Persian matches are very bad. With practice, a skilful smoker can probably learn to strike one in four; of the remainder, two will fail to ignite, while the last will explode in his face.

'A Frank once stayed in this house,' said Mr. R. 'He was writing a book about old buildings. I forget his name.'

'Was it Godard, by any chance?'

He thought it was. I liked to feel that I was following in the steps of the Frenchman who had done so much towards preserving the ancient monuments of Iran.

Then Hesam began to teach me the military commands in Persian. It is hard to think ill of an army that cries '*Pish—'fang!*' when it wants to 'Present—arms!'

May 14th

The household was astir as usual at a quarter to six, and again I was caught napping.

I am determined to get, by hook or by crook, to Natanz today; for I have imposed myself for long enough on these kind people, and my continued presence must be a burden to them at this busy moment. The trouble is that *ta'arof* compels Hesam to create every possible obstacle to my leaving, yet without his help I can hardly hope to get away: I am the prisoner of his kindness. The garages in the town, where we made some inquiries yesterday, were unutterably vague: 'Nothing for Natanz at the moment; tomorrow, *ensha'allah* . . .'

Hesam realizes that I am now in earnest, and, since the buses still will not play, arranges the hire of a jeep—alas, the sap-green one; the magenta is bespoke. Weighed down with pottery and affection, I said farewell to my charming and hospitable hosts. May Allah bless them! May their shadows never grow even less!

Natanz first discloses itself from the summit of a little pass. It lies below in a saucer-shaped valley, cradled in green and defended by low hills from the uttermost heat of the Great Salt Desert.

A friend of Hesam's had given me a letter to the representative of the Government there. I found the man in his office, surrounded by his idling cronies. There was, it appeared, only one person in Natanz who spoke anything other than Persian—an Iranian engineer who had spent six months in Germany and who is installing the new electric plant in the town. While he was being fetched, the Government official and I exchanged politenesses.

'The air here is good,' I said.

The Ark, Tabriz
(p. 166)

Governor of the Shrine, Mahan
(p. 198)

Passenger on the Afghan bus
(p. 119)

'It is just as well; we live on it.' (I was pleased at getting the point of this little joke.)

When conversation grew thin, he took a pencil and made a little drawing.

'Guess what it is!'

'A tree?'

'*Bha, bha,* very good!' He was happy as a child. He doodled in a few little apples, then handed me the pencil and paper. I drew a dragon, and passed it to him.

'An animal. I do not know it. An English animal, no doubt.'

The engineer arrived, and his German proved to be remarkably good. Impossible, he said, for me to get to Na'in at the moment; but there was a van going that afternoon to Isfahan— would I care to go with it? I would—even though it means sacrificing Na'in. From Isfahan it will be easy to get to Yazd. In Isfahan there will be Pepsi-Cola. . . .

He took me to see the Friday Mosque and its adjoining buildings, which date from the early years of the fourteenth century. A big plane tree threw flickering shadows upon the lovely portal of the *Khanqah* (monastery), now scaffolded for repair, and the turquoise-tiled inscription that records the construction, in A.D. 1325, of the hundred-and-twenty-foot minaret. We climbed the hazardous stairs of this minaret to enjoy, from its crumbling summit, a glorious view of the pretty, green little town and the surrounding mountains.

'And now,' said the friendly engineer, 'we will go and see the electric plant.'

It was already one o'clock. 'Is it far?' I asked.

'No distance at all.'

After twenty minutes' walk along a shadeless road we arrived at the ugly concrete building that housed his new toy. 'Is it not fine?' he said.

Like Charles Lamb, 'in everything that relates to science, I am a whole Encyclopaedia behind the rest of the world.' When confronted with a piece of machinery that I am expected to praise, I am always rendered speechless. Horses and babies are difficult enough, but one can at least pat them, give them sugar, dig them in the ribs. Machinery does not respond to such treatment. Moreover, babies like me; electric motors do not.

7—PS

'Very fine,' I said.

'And very beautiful?'

'Very beautiful.'

'No doubt you understand how it works?'

'Well, not exactly.'

It was a fatal error. He proceeded to explain.

When someone with an empty stomach makes it plain to me that he knows little about pictures and cares less, I refrain from subjecting him to an hour's monologue on aesthetics. Rarely so the mechanically minded, who too often assume that everyone is capable of understanding, and, moreover, eager to learn how their miserable machines work. It was two o'clock before I sat down to what at Natanz passed for lunch.

The van was to collect me at three. . . . No, you are wrong: at three precisely it arrived, and at three-five it left.

At a tea-house where we made a short halt, the driver removed his trousers and prayed; I did not, and did not. An officer drove up in a car to which a trailerful of women was attached; they were herded in it like cattle being taken to market. He left them there in the sun while he enjoyed his tea in the shade.

It was abominably hot; by the time we reached Targh-Natanz I was again in the grip of lager-hallucinations. A prettier place I never saw than this little walled town, cliff-borne and tree-girt, backed by purple mountains and fronted by a turquoise lake. Could it be a mirage? I plunged my hands into the blue water—and found it wet. But as I walked back to the van, suddenly I *knew* that I must be 'seeing things': for it appeared to be loaded from tip to toe with Pepsi-Cola bottles. . . .

The driver threw them down to me—bottle after bottle. They exploded as I opened them, fountaining three-quarters of their contents high into the air. Greedily I swallowed the inch or two of hot liquid that remained in each.

Isfahan. The Irantour being full, I was obliged to go to the lesser Sirüs.

In the dining-room, which is hung with pictures of Mohammad, the Virgin Mary, the Shah, Churchill and Cleopatra, I was joined by a rosy-cheeked little Swiss geologist dressed in pink knickerbockers. He speaks Turkish and seems surprised that no one can understand a word he says. I was able to be of some small assistance to him in the matter of beer and stamps. He is utterly lost.

He has just been climbing Mount Ararat; good work, for he must be nearly sixty.

'And did you find Noah's Ark?' I asked.

Or rather, that is what I intended to ask. But, alas, *Arsche Noahs* is Noah's behind; I had, of course, meant *Arche Noahs*. He corrects me as detachedly as though he were a schoolmaster going through a German prose with a pupil.

The Swiss went off to an early bed, leaving me briefly to enjoy the company of three drunken Chinese who were beginning to smash glasses and throw whisky bottles at one another. The Persian waiter looked on contemptuously, but dared not interfere. I don't blame him : they are ugly customers.

The sound of breaking glass continued far into the night.

May 15th

Day after day of these cloudless skies; and so it will continue —week after week, perhaps month after month. I find myself instinctively commenting on the beauty of the weather, upon which the Persians look pityingly at me. One can say, 'It will be fine tomorrow' with the assurance that one can say, 'It will be Wednesday tomorrow,' and it makes equally poor conversation. Some of our official weather-prophets ought to spend a summer out here; a little success might hearten them.

As I waited for a bus outside the blacksmith's forge opposite the hotel, the small infant who works the bellows came out, thrust a big red rose into my hand, laid his hand upon his heart, salaamed, and returned to his work. He cannot be more than five, and is black as his eyes from head to foot. He had no thought of a reward, and vanished almost before I could thank him. I shall treasure the memory of that little moment, perfect as the final curtain of *Der Rosenkavalier*.

But where are *'Les roses d'Ispahan'*? Conspicuous for the most part by their absence. I wish I were now in Herat. Or, better still, somewhere not merely green and flowering, but also cool.

I would like to be walking round Tintern Abbey in the rain. . . .

This afternoon there was a fire in the bazaar. A red, uproarious fire-engine charged frantically through the dim tunnels of shops, scattering purchasers, upsetting bales of fruit, scaring camels and mules. A large crowd rushed in pursuit. A moment later it was rushing back again—or was it a different crowd? Chaos reigned everywhere. Nobody seemed to know where the fire was. The scene reminded me of an ant-hill into which a child had thrown a large stone; the surging and resurging crowds were like shots from an old film of *The Last Days of Pompeii*. Half an hour later I came upon the fire-engine, melancholy and deserted, in a remote corner of the bazaar.

A photographic shop near the Chehel Sotun is displaying some deliriously improbable groups. Group photography, occupational disease of athletes in the West, seems in Iran to appeal principally to the criminal classes. One photograph shows what at first sight appears to be a College Eight holding its oars—or should I call them blades?—in the air; closer inspection reveals eight brigands clutching lances crowned with human heads.

'Not for sale,' says the shopkeeper firmly.

May 16th

An idle day. To tell the truth, I am rather bored. I don't feel like revisiting, in this heat, the sights with which I am already familiar.

After wandering aimlessly, clinging to shadows, I realized that I was lost, and stopped at a shop to ask the way. The proprietor, anxious to air his English, detained me for the duration of three thimblefuls of tea.

'Have you seen our big mosquitoes?'

'No. But surely, with DDT . . . ?'

'Not the royal mosquito?'

'No.'

'Not the Friday mosquito?'

'Ah! now I begin to understand.'

The tea had merely increased my thirst. A little tea-house with a garden full of roses enticed me to a Pepsi-Cola. Suddenly there was an explosion : the heat had shattered a bottle of *dugh*. 'Isfahan atom bomb!' said the waiter as he gathered up the fragments.

Having slept the whole afternoon, I called on my friend Peter Wild, who had cured me of lumbago; he increased my debt to him by insisting upon my staying the night at his house. His garden also is full of roses, but there are sweet peas too that speak of England. He gave me introductions to two friends at Kerman and telegraphed to one of them to expect me.

I start for Yazd at dawn tomorrow.

13

Yazd, Kerman and Tehran

May 17th

To Yazd by bus—an all-day journey. Good bus, good driver, and for the most part a tolerable road.

Outside Isfahan we stopped at the first beggar, to whom the driver threw a coin to propitiate the god of the road. 'Elevenses' at a wayside tea-house whose walls had been gaily decorated by an itinerant dervish with figures, lions, goats, roses and holly-hocks. This kind of thing, naïve though it is, is a hundred times better than the bogus miniatures of the Isfahan professors. A Persian colonel from Kerman—fellow-passenger—made me show my passport, and then stood me tea while someone else plied me with biscuits.

As we approached the mountains, the plain was strewn with a pale yellow eremurus about two feet high. There are sixteen species of eremurus in Iran; how can these plants, which flourish in the pitiless desert, survive in our English gardens? There were lavender irises in abundance too, and the remains of white narcissi.

The bus swept relentlessly through Na'in, where there is some superb tenth-century plasterwork in the Mosque. Maddening it was to have nothing of it but the blue flash of a dome like any other, then to be rushed the wrong way round the inevitable superfluous roundabout and carried off again into the wilderness.

Rivers of dried salt, white as new-fallen snow, traversed the desert. The distant mountains were veiled in a haze of dust. Nothing relieved the utter monotony but a rare, crumbling village with its handful of palms, and its domed *abanbar* (cistern) and *badgirs* (wind-towers) masquerading as a mosque. Before Avergan(?) the ground was for miles like a hard tennis-court, making the road redundant. At Maibud, where we stopped for lunch, a handful of wild boys were attempting to bathe in a tepid hip-bathful of roadside water.

The mountains began to close in from the north—hazy, fantastic. Big drifts of sand engulfed the road, forcing us into the desert. The bus became a furnace. I slept.

Perhaps it was five o'clock when someone more wakeful than I cried out that Yazd was in sight. Of the town we could then see little more than the tall, minaret-crowned façades of the Friday Mosque and the entrance to the bazaar, rising from the plain like the legs of an inverted table.

'Point Four' took me in—and very friendly it is. I have no claim on it whatever.

What is 'Point Four'? The words are on everyone's lips: 'Point Four will put you up,' 'He's working in Point Four,' 'Just get in touch with Point Four when you get there,' and so on. When I first arrived in Persia I had never heard of it. It appears that it is an American plan for aiding backward countries. What do the Americans get in return? I can't imagine.

The manager is a Russian-born Armenian whose parents were killed in the Revolution; a wandering life (described to me in infinite detail) has landed him, for the moment, in Yazd, but his one ambition is to emigrate with his family to America. The cook (charming—but a little mad?) picks me a pink La France rose from the garden; his two-year-old son, goldenly beautiful, sleeps all day in the veranda. There is—at a price—unlimited Pepsi-Cola.

I appear to be the only guest. And probably the only European in Yazd except George Hiller, who has arrived, a day ahead of the ambassadorial party, to pave the way. He and Mr. Mu'in, a rich Yazdi merchant, collected me in a car and took me to the bazaar. Sunset was gilding the minarets that crown its tall portal; the garden before it was scented with tobacco plants and stocks; a gay crowd surged inquisitively round us.

They propose to demolish this lovely although relatively modern gateway. Why? Because, they say, it is unsafe, and they cannot afford to repair it; in fact, because it blocks the advance of a half-constructed boulevard. This mania for driving, in the name of Progress, unnecessarily broad thoroughfares through the hearts of the old cities of Iran is a disaster. One day, too late, they will regret it.

From the bazaar we were taken to the big new spinning

factory on the edge of the town. Here is true Progress. The vast rooms are equipped with up-to-date machinery and are water-cooled, the water flowing out into an onyx-rimmed tank a hundred or more yards long. And there, by moonlight, I bathed —nylon-panted, for lack of more orthodox wear—in water at 95 degrees Fahrenheit. It was too hot to stay in long. The manager of the factory fed us afterwards with cucumbers and pistachio nuts on an emerald lawn surrounded by night-scented flowers—an Arabian Nights dream of a place to find in the heart of the desert.

Oh, the beauty of these southern nights! Sirius-stars are three a penny here.

May 18th

We saw the sights of Yazd at high level this morning and at higher speed, for George, as forerunner of the Ambassador, was given an impressive military and civil escort that whisked us from mosque to mosque with great dexterity and defended us from the fanaticism of the inhabitants. There is much to see; I wish I was to have more time here, but I have arranged to leave tomorrow.

The Friday Mosque, dating mainly from the fourteenth century but recently much, and skilfully, repaired, ranks among the finest buildings in Iran. The cutting of a new street through a labyrinth of squalid mud hovels has opened up a magnificent view of the tall portal, over a hundred feet in height and surmounted by two slender minarets. (Clearance of this kind is quite justified.) Byron shrewdly compares its narrow tapering arch to the chancel arch at Beauvais.

Our escort conducted us to five or six other buildings—mosques and ruinous domed mausoleums decorated with painted friezes of immensely stylized Kufic which the dry air of Yazd has preserved even where domes have fallen. In the modern Zoroastrian temple (for no longer may the Zoroastrians expose their dead to the vultures on their Towers of Silence) the undying flame burns in a setting of tubular metal chairs labelled with the names of the donors. The place, which smelled of incense, reminded me of Woking Crematorium.

But the most characteristic feature of the town is its battery of wind-towers, which collect and convey air into the subterranean rooms that alone make summer in Yazd bearable. I had already seen one or two on the way; but here and at Kerman they are as numerous as television aerials in a London suburb. They look like large radiators on the tops of chimney-stacks.

It was George Hiller's idea that we should visit a *hammam* (bath-house), but the unexpectedly early arrival of the Ambassador made it impossible for him to come with me.

It was of course my fault that I had imagined Turkish and Persian baths to be identical. I had vague recollections of a Turkish bath in Munich nearly thirty years ago, and on this I let my fantasy play. There would, of course, be the domed *caldarium*, with dusky figures half glimpsed through clouds of steam, ghostly as pedestrians in a London fog. There would be the *frigidarium*, with its elegant blue-tiled pool and plashing fountains. There would be a dozen different kinds of massage to choose from, and, being ignorant of the subtleties of the language, I would have to dab at random and hope for the best. Then, lapped in some exotic gold-embroidered robe, couched upon priceless Kerman rugs, I would await the cup of Turkish coffee, the plates of pistachio nuts and *halva*, the bowls of pomegranates, the jug of iced sherbet and the friendly hubble-bubble brought by some elegant youth and set upon tables inlaid with mother of pearl.

The reality, judged by any standards, was disappointing. The proprietor of the *hammam*—a spherical man of unprepossessing appearance—fired a long question at me, the only word of which I caught was 'soap.' Feeling clean enough after my bathe, I said 'no' and awaited a further and a happier suggestion. The man conducted me in silence along a dreary passage which smelled like the corridors of my private school, then ushered me into a small room containing a broad tiled ledge, a couple of towels and a row of cheap coat-hangers. Adjoining this room was a second and rather warmer one with a shower; it was roughly what one might expect to find in a Paddington bath-and-brush-up-for-tuppence establishment for the disinfection of tramps.

'What do I do?' I said.

He waved a puffy hand at the shower.

'How long?' I said; 'five minutes?' I wanted to get the ritual right. But for only answer he grunted non-committally and left me.

The shower proved capricious—now too hot, now ice-cold, and always irresponsive to rational tap-manipulation. After enduring five minutes of shock treatment I dried myself and returned to the outer room to await further instructions. None being vouchsafed, I went in search of the proprietor. I found him deep in conversation with two skinny, naked clients; he appeared to resent interruption.

'What now,' I asked; 'massage?'

With obvious distaste he abandoned his cronies, led me back to my cell, manhandled me brutally for a minute or two and then disappeared without a word.

Sad and disillusioned, I dressed and crept out again into the bright sunlight.

The bus to Kerman, scheduled to start at dawn tomorrow morning, is now said to be leaving at 2 a.m. because its passengers have revolted against day travel in this heat. Chancing to pass the bus office on my way back from the baths, I called in to check. The bus is leaving at eleven o'clock tonight.

Dinner with and much kindness from the ambassadorial party in a garden pavilion surrounded by sentries. The Ambassadress loaded me with welcome English cigarettes. At ten o'clock, as I was strolling back towards the hotel, a frantic busman, sent in search of me, told me that the bus was leaving that instant. But for the reflected glory of the Ambassador I should have been left behind.

And now I began to pay the penalty for my over-indulgence in the *jub* water of Kashan.

I would not wish my worst enemy the miseries of acute diarrhoea on a nine-hour nocturnal bus-journey. I stared out at the dead, moonlit plain and prayed that my travelling companions—they were mostly soldiers—would stop asking me questions, stop singing, stop being hearty, stop being friendly; prayed that the bus would stop soon, and again soon. . . .

As the sun rose, we drew up at a tea-house for breakfast.

The driver, who was a wag, looked at my coat—new when I left England but now rather shabby—and said :

'That coat of yours, it looks as though it dates from the time of Shah Abbas. It would just do for me to drive in. May I have it?'

This sally was greeted with peals of happy military laughter. Spurred on by success, he continued: 'Those shoes: Shah Tahmasp, I should guess. And those trousers: obviously Hulagu Khan.' (More laughter. 'The driver is a very good man,' said someone.)

'And that hat?' (It really was a rather battered object, and thick with dust.) 'Straight from Takht-e-Jamshid!' Takht-e-Jamshid is the Persian name for Persepolis.

And then, to show that there was no ill feeling, he paid for my tea.

May 19th

My arrival at Kerman was inauspicious.

Mr. A., to whom Peter Wild had telegraphed, was away. The lodge-keeper of his house, whom I must put on record as the only rude Persian I met in all my time in Iran, threw me, and my luggage after me, into the street, where I was eventually rescued by the Kerman fire-brigade and taken to Point Four.

Mr. Carroll [1] was away. Mrs. Carroll was most sympathetic, but powerless to help. I was not American; I had no special recommendation. Yazd must be different. Her husband had left strict orders . . . Of course if he were here, no doubt . . .

'I also have a letter to Mr. Fasovaher,' I said.

She telephoned him. He was away.

So I had to go to the Hotel Akhavan.

Yet I was glad to have my freedom. When one is not feeling well, being the perfect guest—especially in a Persian house—is something of a strain.

Moreover, the Hotel Akhavan had great and curious charm. It was built round the customary courtyard, with the customary pool in the centre, and set about with pomegranate bushes, mulberries, acacias and clumps of tall hollyhocks. The white, one-storey Iranian building had honeycombed doorways and prettily patterned brickwork; it was simple, but completely

[1] Mr. and Mrs. Carroll were murdered by bandits in March 1957.

satisfying. The rooms were high; and behind each was concealed a second and unfurnished room, lit only by a hole in the ceiling, for use in the heat of the day. There was also a series of underground rooms. These cooler retreats, however, I did not discover until after I had spent a long, intolerable afternoon in my west-facing outer room.

Odd people kept popping in and out, including a man who announced that the other bed in it was his. He is welcome to it, but they might have warned me. (In fact, he never appeared again.) In the courtyard, an old woman was incessantly washing, one-handed, miscellaneous nether-garments in the pool; with the other, she conscientiously held her *chador* across her face. There was also a vast woman, twice the size of an average Isolde, who wandered aimlessly around, veiled and bored to tears. They were a friendly crowd. Impossible to lock my room; but, as in Shiraz, I am confident that nothing will be touched.

The three students who accosted me that evening outside the hotel seemed to be about nineteen or twenty years old. They were dressed in rather shiny Western 'spiv' suits, clock socks and brown shoes. Two of them were brothers. The elder, who was dark and good-looking, wore a convincing imitation of an Old Etonian tie. The younger—a lanky, spotty lad—might have been English, and spoke English passably; he reminded me irresistibly of a boy I was once at school with, called Conyngham.

The third was a jolly youth, very suave, very sure of himself. He had, he said, a jeep—right there where we were standing. 'My father is rich,' he added, in Persian. 'His father is rich,' echoed Conyngham (for I cannot call him anything else), in English. 'My father is also rich. He has much rice. Where do you go now?'

'I'm going to see the Friday Mosque.'

'We will go in Mahmud's car,' said Conyngham.

We bundled into the ramshackle machine and bounced down the pot-holed street at the breakneck speed of youth showing off before age. Old women leaped aside to avoid certain death; donkeys brayed their disgust. A camel with the face of a philosopher advanced imperturbably to meet us; Mahmud drove full tilt at it. At the eleventh hour the camel threw dignity to the winds and with a snort of rage jumped the *jub*. The youths thought it the best joke in the world. For my part, I was thankful when the Friday Mosque came in sight and the jeep screeched to a standstill.

Until quite recently, the main portal of the Friday Mosque was surmounted by two minarets; it must then have resembled a broader version of that at Yazd. It is dated 1459, but photographs taken some thirty years ago reveal how extensively the tiling has recently been repaired and restored. Much of the modern work is a good deal coarser than that which it replaced. Inside is a fine *mehrab* which Robert Byron believed to be Yazd work of the fourteenth century; it is in fact signed by an Isfahani artist, and dates from about 1550.

Conyngham and his friends took me over the Mosque, encouraging me to photograph even the *mehrab* (which I thought must certainly be forbidden) and to help myself to handfuls of the tiles that have been ruthlessly stripped from the northern portal. I wept to see how much had been wantonly destroyed.

'And now,' said Conyngham, 'let us go to the cinema.'

I could not face it, but took them back to my hotel and gave them tea. They sat in my room, fingering everything; wanting to know what I had paid for this shirt, that vest, those socks; asking a thousand questions. Conyngham—most curious, most eager of them all—jotted down every unfamiliar English word in his notebook.

'You must go,' he said, 'to Mahan. It is beautiful. It is cool there.'

Mahan is a famous shrine about twenty-five miles from Kerman. It was already on my list. I said I would.

Conyngham, for whom I am apparently the most exciting thing that has happened in Kerman for years, promised he would come and collect me at the hotel early tomorrow morning. I said good night to them and settled down, in the courtyard, to a delicious meal of rice and raisins, yoghourt, coffee and brandy. I felt much restored.

Then, suddenly—guiltily, it seemed, as though late for an appointment—up popped the moon: not the inquisitive English moon that peers into forbidden shrubberies and prods the dark corners of back alleys, but a gentle, placid, all-pervasive moon to flood the whole courtyard with diffused radiance. . . .

Night is surprisingly cool here, and indescribably beautiful. Cicadas chirp in the trees. From the pool comes the sound of trickling water, and over the roof-tops the distant, plaintive throbbing of Eastern music. Moonlight still paints the courtyard, where most of the guests have chosen to sleep. The hens, too, are asleep; only the cats are vigilant.

I go down to the pool and wash a nylon shirt.

May 20th

Last night I could not sleep. Was I too tired? Was it too beautiful? I remembered the advice of Mr. Tatchell,[1] who recommends as a soporific the full-throated singing of 'Why do the Nations' from *The Messiah*—'and when I want to give myself a special treat, I muffle myself up in the bedclothes and halloo for all I am worth. A couple of minutes of this is just splendid. Then I compose myself for sleep, feeling at peace with all men.' Very possibly—but what about the rest of the hotel? I preferred the misery of a *nuit blanche*.

Conyngham, after all his protestations of undying devotion, did not show up; I therefore went off on my own to explore the town.

There is, so far as I can discover, little of interest here beyond the Friday Mosque: Jenghiz Khan, Tamerlane, the Afghans, Nader Shah and the Qajar eunuch have seen to that. The present town dates from the early nineteenth century; the Friday Mosque, and three miles of mud ruin to the south-east of it, are all that remain of the earlier and once famous city. The Madraseh of Ibraham Khan has some amusing tilework showing ducks and peacocks, and a turret containing a large English clock. The Madraseh of Ganj-i-Ali Khan is worth a passing glance. The bazaars differ not at all from those elsewhere, but are being proudly extended in corrugated iron. I bought some biscuits; the shopkeeper refused payment.

It is too hot to explore further. One loses so much time by being cooped up indoors from twelve to six o'clock.

Cooped up, and hallucinating again. . . .

For the worst thing about Kerman is the drink situation. It is

[1] *The Happy Traveller*, by the Rev. Frank Tatchell, M.A., Vicar of Midhurst. (Methuen, 1923.) If this glorious man is still alive, I would like to spend an evening 'yarning' with him.

outside the Pepsi-Cola zone. The properties of the water are such that one has to go slow even with tea, of which I put little driblets aside to sip when they are tepid. I have bought a bottle of wine and another of brandy; but what I want is a dozen bottles of iced lager and twenty gallons of pure cold drinking water.

After tea I set out to try to find the garage that was alleged to run a bus to Mahan. Outside the hotel I ran into Conyngham.

'You never came this morning,' I said.

'My mother is ill. I could not come. Where do you go now?'

'To the Garaj Popoli, to try to book a seat for Mahan on Tuesday.'

'I will go with you to Mahan tomorrow.'

'But I want to go on Tuesday.'

'I cannot go on Tuesday. My mother is ill.'

'Why should your mother be well again tomorrow and ill again on Tuesday?'

'I will go round the world with you.'

'But I am not going round the world.'

'I will come to England with you. My father is rich; he will give me much rice.'

I paused to visualize my arrival at Eton with Conyngham in one hand and a sack of Conyngham's father's rice in the other.

Conyngham continued: 'I will come to Mahan with you on Tuesday. I will tell my mother you are my teacher, then she will let me go. You are a very good man.'

'I hope so.'

'You are my father. I will tell my mother that you are my father.'

'I wouldn't do that; it would only muddle her.'

May 21st

There is a recurrent type of small boy here with hawk-like face and tragic, piercing eyes. They all look exactly the same; at the sight of my camera they all burst into tears.

I had my lunch in one of the underground rooms of the hotel. The adjacent room was occupied by a visiting party of ten Persians—men, women and children—who on my arrival set

about erecting a barrage of curtains to prevent their womenfolk
from being seen by a male and an infidel. From what I glimpsed
as I entered, this was a pity.

This evening, a German-speaking Tabriz carpet-merchant
joined me in the courtyard. I offered him some brandy. 'I
daren't,' he said. 'My companion is a fanatic. He would kill me.'

But he continued to gaze longingly at the bottle. 'Perhaps I
might take a little in a tea-glass,' he volunteered at last. 'If my
friend comes out, then he will not know.'

I was sorry for him; there is nothing in the world so irritating
as having to live up to other people's principles.

The carpet trade in Kerman, he told me, is steadily declining.
That there is a certain national guilty conscience about sweated
child labour is implied by the obstacles (beyond Stygian gloom)
put in the way of the photographer. Moreover, the Americans
have imposed their designs on the weavers. He has found little
to justify his long journey. He hates Kerman, and talked incessantly of the flesh-pots of Tehran and Tabriz. He finds the hotel
terrible, the food uneatable. 'In Tabriz there is ice. . . .' I too am
looking forward to a return to civilization.

His friend appears—a sinister individual who might easily
slit a throat or two. He surveys my brandy bottle with infinite
disgust. The carpet merchant introduces me and smiles guiltily.

Suddenly the lights fuse, and we are plunged into moonlight.

May 22nd

Conyngham said he would pick me up at the hotel at half
past five this morning; I waited for him till a quarter to six and
then set off alone for the garage. I never saw him again. I dare
say he was a little mad; nineteen Kerman summers might easily
affect the brain. Or had he been telling his father that I was his
father . . . ?

The 'good' seat I had been promised proved to be over the
wheel and hopelessly inadequate for my legs. But the journey
was only an hour and a half; I thought I could endure it. And
the morning was so deliciously fresh; if only one had the energy
always to get up at five! We passed a long train of mules laden
with snow from the mountains towards which we were heading.
Tonight there would be snow in Kerman. . . .

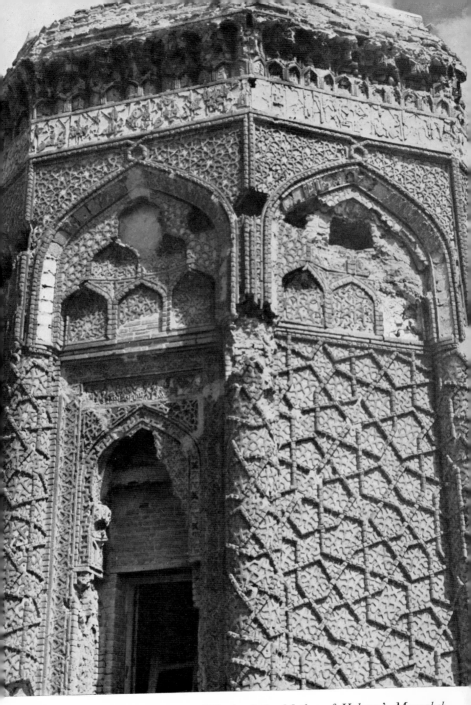

'Tomb of the Mother of Hulagu,' Maragheh
(p. 167)

Zur Khaneh, *Tehran*
(p. 204)

(Above) *In the Elburz Mountains*
(p. 158)

(Below) *Wild tulips in the Elburz*
(p. 159)

Friday Mosque, Yazd
(p. 188)

(Above) Wind towers, Yazd
(p. 189)

'Mahan!' cried someone at last.

In the distance—five, or it might be ten miles away; who could measure that unvarying desert?—I could see a little fleck of deepest green crowned by a pin-head blue dome and a cluster of needle minarets.

The saintly Ni'matollah, whose bones the Shrine at Mahan encloses, was a Sufi protégé of Shah Rokh. He was nearly eighty when, in 1406, he settled in Mahan for the remaining twenty-five years of his long life. The 'Nostradamus of Iran,' as he has been called, had a happy gift for prophecy, among his luckier shots being—so it is alleged—the Indian Mutiny. Fred Richards, in *A Persian Journey*, adds that Ni'matollah, after climbing Demavend (18,700 feet) and spending eighty days among its eternal snows, settled down to a forty years' diet of dust. (I wish I knew where travel writers find these colourful stories; the *Dictionary of Islam* makes Ni'matollah's career sound as un-eventful, and his diet as nourishing, as those of an Anglican bishop.) But be that as it may, his Shrine and the gardens which surround it are a paradise to those who in summer have won them at the cost of dust, sweat and toil.

The Shrine consists of three courts. From a garden full of rose trees smothered with single white flowers, the pilgrim passes beneath the house of the Governor of the Shrine into the first court. Lofty cypresses and pines here stand guard over a pool in the shape of a cross and edged with pots of geraniums. Gay though these flowers are, they contrive to suggest the approach to a luxury Riviera hotel; to judge from Robert Byron's photographs, it must have been a pleasanter place before these 'improvements' were carried out.

The pool reflects two minarets and the blue dome that covers the yellow marble tombs of Ni'matollah and his grandson. A white, honeycombed portal, hung with what may well be the ugliest lamp in the world, leads to a lifesize portrait of the saint by moonlight, and thence to the tomb chamber, which is sur-rounded by cool white galleries. A smaller, cypress-shaded court is succeeded by a large Qajar court terminating in two very tall minarets. Of the giant plane tree which once stood beyond the last gate, only the sprouting stump now remains.

So factual a description can give but little idea of the magic of Mahan: its cool, shady precincts; its silence; its glitter of tiles ever mirrored in still waters; the ever-present lavender curtain of mountains. Its charm was enhanced for me by the kindness of the people. A one-legged, English-speaking student appointed himself my guide and took me to see his uncle, the Governor of the Shrine, who offered me tea on the veranda of his house. The Governor allowed me to take photographs, and consented to pose for his own; he let me wander over the roofs; he encouraged me to smoke. It was as delightful as it was unexpected to find such liberality in so holy and so remote a spot.

They had said in Kerman that there was a return bus at eleven o'clock. Mahan denied its existence. It arrived, punctually at eleven, but was full. The student, having business to attend to, handed me over to an electrician who also spoke English. This man said he was sending a truck to Kerman at one o'clock, and offered me a lift in it.

I lunched in a dirty tea-house whose walls were decorated with peasant-art pictures of Noah's Ark and the ascent of Mohammad into heaven, and posters advertising Aureomycin ('Prevents Calf Scours') and Nuffield Tractors. A man with a rose in his mouth was roasting *kebabs* on charcoal which he fanned to a glow. There were chickens everywhere—yet I was warned that the eggs were uneatable; I therefore limited myself to yoghourt and tea, for which the electrician insisted upon paying. I tried to get cigarettes; he went out and bought me a packet. Then he conducted me to an underground room that houses Mahan's electric-light generator, and in the cool gloom of this vault plied me for hours with tea and conversation.

'I have seen a picture of London when Victory was King of London,' he said.

And the truck? Still not ready. Would I like to see the Shrine again? The local school? Did I understand how the generator worked?

Hastily I assured him that I did. So we saw the school, and little boys with shaven heads who were copying a curiously distorted drawing of a cup and saucer which the teacher had made on the blackboard. We saw the Shrine once more. We wandered round the town. All the inhabitants of Mahan, I noticed, wore comic little hats perched on the tops of their heads, and looked like theatrical tramps.

We returned to the power station.

And the truck? Not quite ready yet.

'Now you must meet the Governor,' said the electrician.

I had no great desire to meet anyone. But the electrician had been so kind; I had to submit.

At that moment, the Governor came round the corner. He was on his way to his office, and carried us along with him.

'His Excellency is a famous poet.'

'Indeed!'

The electrician explained to the Governor that he had told me that His Excellency was a famous poet. His Excellency made deprecating gestures with his right hand.

The Governor's office consisted of a pavilion, fronted by a spacious veranda and set in a delightful garden full of roses and Madonna lilies. After the usual *ta'arof*, we sat down in the shady veranda and exchanged the usual civilities : 'Mahan is very beautiful. . . . The people of Mahan are very good, etc., etc.'

The Governor suddenly became abstracted and pregnant with thought. He stared at the roof. I stared at it too, thinking that, like so many Persian ceilings, it might be about to collapse.

Then he turned and said something to the electrician.

'His Excellency asks if he may write a poem for you.'

'Please convey to His Excellency that I am deeply honoured.'

We sat for a minute or two in silence, awaiting the descent of the Muse. Then the Governor seized a pen, flourished a quatrain, subscribed it and handed it to me.

I asked the electrician to translate. At his dictation I wrote :

'This village whose name is Mahan is a place that sleep there the King Ni'matollah. In the next time will become better than now by the King of Iran.

'I give this note to my dear friend Mr. Weelfreed Blint, who is writing a work here in the College of England.

'Shahrdar Mahan

'Azarpu.'

'Is it not beautiful?' said the electrician.

شماره ....

تاریخ ....

پیوست ....

وزارت کشور

استانداری هشتم ـ فرمانداری شهرستان کرمان

بخشداری ماهان

این قریه که نام و شهرتش ماهان است   آرامگه شهنشه عرفان است

در آثار آثاری و عمران و نقاش   برخاسته نفس اهل ایران است

تقدیم به تیمی دیلفرد بنت استر عم نقاش در کالج اتون در نگلستان

۳ر۳۵

شهردار ماهان ـ آزاد پور

'Please thank His Excellency; it is very beautiful.'

The Governor bowed.

I bowed.

'His Excellency says, you now please to write poem.'

I gazed at the ceiling. The Governor gazed at the ceiling. The electrician gazed at the ceiling. But my mind remained a blank. I asked permission to walk round the garden in search of inspiration.

It was then that I discovered a rose of surpassing loveliness,

unlike any I had ever seen. A tight cluster of small, deep
magenta petals was surrounded by a fringe of large, paler petals.
It looked like a double hollyhock.

But there was work to be done. What rhymed with Mahan?
Kerman, of course, and Iran—as god-given as Tomsk to Omsk.
I wrote:

> *She said, 'If you go to Kerman*
> *You must certainly visit Mahan,*
> *For its gardens and Shrine*
> *Are just simply divine:*
> *My dear, it's the pearl of Iran.'*

The Governor made me read it aloud. It sounded, I thought,
a shade thin, but he expressed himself delighted and took down
a translation. 'English,' he said, 'is a very beautiful language.'

'Persian,' I answered, in Persian, 'is also a very beautiful
language.'

The Governor bowed.

I bowed.

Peasants now began to arrive—summoned, it appeared, to a
conference. 'His Excellency will talk of water-ditches,' said the
electrician. It was our cue to leave.

But not until *ta'arof* had once more been duly honoured. Not,
also, until I had asked permission to take cuttings of the magical
rose.

'The garden is yours,' said the Governor.

I only took the cuttings. I got them back to Tehran; by then,
unfortunately, the heat had reduced them almost to charcoal,
and I do not think they can strike.

The truck? Yes, there it stood, outside the power station.
Beside the driver sat a woman, veiled from head to foot; the
space was cramped, but there was just room for one more
person.

'You may not go,' said the electrician firmly.

'But why ever not? Because there is a woman?'

'No!'

'Then why not? I *must* go.'

'Because she is ugly woman. If it is beautiful woman you may
go. It is bad to go with ugly woman.'

'But I couldn't care less. Anyway, I can't see her face. *Please* let me go in it. I *must* go.'

'No. It is bad. You must not make a bad thing. Soon will come the bus.' He signalled to the driver; before I could decide what to do next, the truck had started.

At that moment I could gladly have killed the kind electrician. 'And just *when*,' I asked, 'does this bus of yours leave?'

'At four hours.'

I looked at my watch; it was ten past five. I turned on my heel and walked away, too angry to speak.

Miracles can still happen : at six o'clock, just as I was resigning myself to a night at Mahan, the bus appeared.

We drove away in golden dust, the sinking sun a red ball of fire. It seems that ugly women do bring bad luck, for in mid-desert we came upon the broken-down truck. The woman was sitting in a black, dejected heap by the roadside; the driver beckoned to us to stop.

Our driver waved him the mercy of Allah and left him with the oncoming night.

It wasn't for nothing that they brought that snow from the mountains. In spite of the warnings of the Tabrizi carpet-merchant, I am now drinking red Kashan wine allayed with it—and delicious it is, if one does not think of it in terms of claret or burgundy.

May 23rd

To Tehran !

The car drew up in mid-desert, a quarter of a mile from what will one day be Kerman's airport waiting-room but is still a mere chairless husk. Yet for the sake of the shade of its walls I struggled there. My only companion was a German zoologist who was taking a 'royal desert fox' back to Tehran. It smelt.

The plane came at last; but there was a further hour's delay in getting away, for, a couple of seats had been sold twice over. A dog-fight ensued : '*Ensha'allah* Airways,' mutters someone. It was stifling in the plane. An elderly *shaikh* was fanning another elderly, dying *shaikh* with a folded vomit-bag. An Indian woman was having the first stages of what I suppose was a heart attack.

She concluded it at Yazd. They carried her out of the plane and laid her, writhing in agony, on the ground under the shade of a wing. The passengers watched her spasms unmoved. Her daughter massaged her. Suddenly she stopped moaning and lay so still that I thought she might be dead. Then she sat up, stood up, and walked back in a kind of trance to the plane. So, nineteen hundred years ago, must it have seemed to the Jews who saw a sick man take up his bed and walk.

There was an hour's delay at Yazd too, for someone had mislaid the petrol. At last it arrived, in battered tins, and was pumped into the tanks by means of a hand-pump. Some of it was spilled upon the sand. Smokers moved a few feet farther away from the plane.

The desert lay below us again—an incredible, cruel, blinding white like a sea of molten metal. Curtains were drawn. The *shaikh*-fanning ceased. Perhaps he was dead. Perhaps we were all dead; it was too hot to know, too hot to care.

May 24th. British Embassy, Tehran.

Oh the joy to be back again in civilization! A cool bedroom, a bath, water you can drink, coffee and poached eggs for breakfast, a refrigerator, martinis, letters from home, people who speak real English, a *green* garden. . . .

But

> *I've a mouth like an old potato,*
> *And I'm more than a little sick.*

May 25th

But not much more. Dr. Shabani says that I'm 'dehydrated,' and has sent me to bed for twenty-four hours. Orders: to drink a very large glass of something cold every half-hour. Everybody —even the Ambassador himself—calls to inquire. Really, the kindness of these busy people is immense!

May 26th

Recovered, but for a weariness about the knees as though I had recently climbed Everest once or twice.

We were standing outside the Russian Embassy.

'A man was bastinadoed here the other day,' said my companion.

'What—here in the street?'

'Yes—the scene of the crime. He threw papers over the Embassy wall; but the wind blew them back and he was caught.'

Gosh! It makes one think.

The entrance to the Russian Embassy is in the Avenue Churchill. This street runs along one side of the British Embassy, which in its turn backs upon the Avenue Stalin. Now just outside my bedroom window, in a British tree overhanging the Avenue Churchill, sits a nightingale which, unmindful of motorhorns and screeching brakes, nightly and impartially serenades these two antagonistic diplomatic bodies.

It is no ordinary nightingale, but the veriest full-throated Flagstad of the feathered tribe. It hates a moment's silence as cordially as does the B.B.C., and is as little considerate of its audience's powers of endurance as is an Oxford Philosophy don on the Third Programme.

At first I was charmed by the attentions of the romantic bulbul. Then, by degrees, I began to wonder whether it might not be straining its voice; ought it not to take a rest from time to time? In the end I shut my window upon it and got at last some much-needed sleep. Norman Douglas, I seem to remember, had a similar experience at Olevano.

'Of course you will see *zur khaneh* before you leave Tehran.'

'What is *zur khaneh*?'

'Gymnastics.'

'Why on earth should I want to see gymnastics? By walking a hundred yards I can see it all day and every day for eight months of the year.'

'But this is religious gymnastics, and wrestling too; it's very interesting. It takes place in the National Bank.'

To an Englishman, the concept of sport as merely another manifestation of religion could cause no surprise, but there was something Erewhonian in the choice of battleground. Of course I must see it; and I am very glad that I did, though even now I do not quite know what it was all about.

The team consisted of ten young bank clerks (?), dressed only in breeches. And what breeches! Every square inch of them was embroidered in rainbow colours. But the artist had reserved his most intricate, his most daring arabesques for the seats. His talent was not wasted : buttocks, throughout, were excessively in evidence. Club-swinging, chain-waving and posterior-posturing were conducted by a young man with a dust-sheet round his waist, seated on a dais, who throbbed a drum like a giant egg-cup and intoned from the *Shah Nameh* in a monotonous voice. In front of him was an electric fan, above his head a bell by means of which he started and concluded the various events.

There seems to be nothing about *zur khaneh* in Curzon's *Persia*, and little elsewhere, though Byron devotes a couple of pages to it. The tradition is extremely ancient, and probably Zoroastrian. The exercises were almost certainly intended to keep men fit for military service, and the wrestling (which I did not see) follows the pattern of the various combats described by Ferdausi.

The little lieutenant, who is back with his regiment in Tehran, came to dinner. He seemed, if possible, even smarter than before. And even smaller : I had half a mind to carry him home with me in my pocket.

14

Damascus and Jordan

May 27th

Farewell to Persia, speeded by a large contingent from the Embassy who were seeing various people off. We were just in time to witness the magnificent dog-fight that ensued when the Swiss Minister called the bluff of the airport officials by refusing to pay the outrageous tax levied upon all travellers who use the Tehran airport.

Western Persia, seen from the air, added little to what I already knew. Over Mesopotamia I was not this time deprived by darkness of a sight of a surprisingly blue Tigris, a muddy Euphrates, and between them a most unhorticultural Garden of Eden. A new dam has created a big turquoise lake in the yellow desert. Beyond Baghdad the sand becomes almost pink.

Then there lay spread below us an emerald carpet splashed upon its northern fringe with a dab of white—Damascus, asleep in its green oasis.

An American vice-consul from Iran, who was on the plane, took me along with him to the New Semiramis Hotel, the best in Damascus, where he had booked a room. But they had no place for me. My unlucky star guided me to the Hotel X. Of this den of thieves I shall have more to say in a moment.

The vice-consul had only one afternoon in which to see Damascus; having lunched—excellently—together at the New Semiramis, we therefore took a guide (an admirable young man) and a taxi (less admirable and far less young) and set out on an indigestibly rapid tour of the town. I minded this the less for having tomorrow in which to repair the damage.

Impressions crowded quickly: stone again—so much stone after Persia's tiles and mud; a Western air to the buildings, but the passing flash of a minaret; biblical Pharpar, now called the Barada, caged between high stone parapets. Then came the older town, the narrower streets, the brighter dresses. Straight street : it only has one little kink in it, so hardly deserves Mark Twain's famous jibe about the street which is *called* Straight. And suddenly we were driving among the ruins of the Temple of Jupiter, right up to the door of the Great Mosque of the Omayyads.

You buy your ticket, pull on over-slippers, and find yourself in a splendid court—a court stone-paved, stone-faced, exquisite in colour and intricately carved. But there was barely time to glory in that bright air a-flutter with doves, to gape at the superlative series of Byzantine mosaics, to marvel at the beauty of the little eighth-century treasury and to pay homage at the shrine where once the Baptist's head was laid—before our inexorable guide swept us up and drove us breathless through Jupiter's golden temple into the *suqs* (bazaars). I will of course come back tomorrow.

What are those itinerant vendors crying? Baedeker says, of the tinkling water-seller rattling his brazen cups, *'ya 'atshan, es-sebil'*—'O thirsty one, the distribution'; of the fruitjuice-seller, *'balak snunak'*—'Take care of your teeth'; of the hawker of nosegays, *'salih hamatak'*—'Appease your mother-in-law'; of the cress-seller, 'Tender cresses from the spring of Ed-Du'iyeh; if an old woman eats of them she will be young again next morning.' How I wish I could understand! My helplessness here (though much French is of course spoken) makes me realize the value of my few words of Persian.

We stopped just long enough in the *suqs* for the vice-consul to buy a hideous embroidered table-cloth for his mother, and then came the little white-domed tomb of Saladin; Kaiser Wilhelm laid a wreath upon it in 1898 and paid for the restoration of the building. Very odd of him.

Next, I think, the Azem Palace, now a folk-lore museum. This I remember more clearly—the large flowery courtyard, the polychrome stone, the painted ceilings and furniture and the elaborately dressed wax figures posed for a wedding reception.

At the Kisan Gate, in the walls of the city, is what my guide-book grandiloquently styles 'St. Paul's Cathedral'—an oratory built upon the supposed site of St. Paul's escape from Damascus. How he managed to get away from a window exactly over a city gate, which must have been guarded, the experts can doubtless explain. The modern gate is a pretentious affair made of toy stones and decorated with sacred monograms; within is a depressing little chapel.

Did we also see the house of Ananaias? Very likely; but in next to no time we were on the slope of Salhiyeh, and the sun was setting over the green-girt town, and the vice-consul was agreeing that we had had enough.

I did not see him again. I can remember only three things that he said: that two shillings and sixpence was too much to pay for a glass of orangeade (at the New Semiramis; he had stood me one); that as I was interested in painting I ought to go to the States to see the 'Impressionistics' there; and that there were only two important dates in the history of Persia—the introduction of Islam and the introduction of Pepsi-Cola. He is right, all along the line.

The dining-room curtains of the Hotel X are made of 'shrunketized' cotton.

The Member of Parliament for Bosra, who is staying—or at all events drinking—in the hotel, says it would be madness to visit Syria and not see—Bosra. Aleppo is 'very dull.'

Conscious that my total ignorance of Arabic was going to be handicapping, I took to bed with me a small English-Arabic conversation manual which I had picked up for a penny in a second-hand bookshop in Windsor. Perhaps I would be able to memorize a few simple phrases.

Entitled *The Eastern Traveller's Interpreter; or, Arabic without a Teacher*, by Assaad Yakoob Kayat, published in the same year as Kinglake's *Eothen*, the book seemed designed to assist the Frank in the delectable occupation of brow-beating the Syrian natives. The good old days! There is conversation for the inn ('O Caravansary Keeper! what have you for food?' —followed by a brisk demand for fried eggs); for the conversion of the pagan ('Let me hear you read the third chapter of John'); on education ('I will teach your children. I will open a school gratis, and my wife will teach your girls'); for putting an Eastern Bishop in his place ('It is deplorable to see Christians divided into so many sects; I hope you will preach the love of Christ. Are your clergy educated?'); for deflating a ship's captain ('How old is your boat?'); for keeping a Pasha up to the mark ('This is a fine country; it wants good roads. Printing-presses would promote many blessings'). The traveller is assumed to be incapable of recognizing the simplest object unaided ('Are these the cedars of Lebanon?'). We will leave him with the phrase which he probably found the most useful: *'Fârjeene dârb ckânessât al-ânghleez'*—'Show me the way to the English church.'

As for me—I shall have to muddle along with French.

May 28th

I stood early outside the entrance of the Omayyad Mosque, a Jupiter column for shade, waiting for a foreground to my photograph. There soon emerged a superb old greybeard, wear-ing his tattered garments like a king's robe. He stood a moment before the great bronze door, magnificent, blinking at the sun-light; I raised my camera and released the shutter. Immediately I felt myself seized roughly by the arm.

He was so blond a youth he might almost have been a German, extraordinarily handsome in anger; little sweat-drops of fury had formed and glistened on his forehead, his cheeks, round his eyes. And suddenly I saw myself as he saw me: a rich, idle, odious European come to mock the poverty of the East. A hostile crowd began to collect. 'The police!' cried the youth—'fetch the police!' Someone snatched at my camera, but I managed to keep hold of it; another tugged at the case, but the strap held.

'Should you be attacked by a mob in the East,' says the Rev. Frank Tatchell (whom God preserve) of Midhurst, 'hurt one of the crowd and hurt him quickly. The others will gather chatter-ing round the injured man and you will be able to slip away.' Yes, but who?—or rather, whom? Mr. Tatchell does not say. Someone one's own size? I saw, with considerable relief, that there was nobody who answered that description. The youth was the tallest, but I recoiled from the idea of damaging a work of art. Also he looked the sort of boy who might hit back, or even first—and Mr. Tatchell had not provided against such contingencies.

Fortunately it was a decision that I did not have to make. For as suddenly as anger had arisen, it subsided. The crowd,

thinking perhaps that I had learned my lesson, left me, *haud
ingratum*, in peace. I shrank away guiltily into the shades of the
suqs, thankful to find myself still more or less unlynched. But
the memory of those hate-filled, flashing blue eyes went with me
all the day.

My tail between my legs, my wicked camera burning my back,
I wandered through the old town, admiring the tribal splendour
of swaggering *shaikhs* such as Eric Kennington drew, but I
might not photograph. At last I could not resist a balcony:
surely they could not mind my photographing a balcony.

'Why take that? It's ugly,' said a decoratively dressed young
man in impeccable English.

'Then may I photograph you instead?'

He bolted down a side street and was not seen again for dust.

Back in the modern town, I visited a travel bureau to inquire
about Petra and Palmyra. Petra is too laborious, too expensive
in time and money. The much advertised weekly aeroplane to
Palmyra does not exist. So Petra and Palmyra are 'off.'

The splendid new Museum here is constantly being enriched
by fresh finds. In accordance with a general plan for displaying
the antiquities of the Near East, Aleppo specializes in the pre-
Classical antiquities, Antioch covers the Classical, and Damascus
chiefly the later collections. The Damascus Museum contains,
among much else of interest, a complete fourth-century Jewish
Synagogue, a necropolis from Palmyra, and rooms from the
Omayyad desert palace of El Heir whose entrance gate has been
reconstructed on one of the outside walls.

Near to the Museum is the Tekkiyeh Mosque, built by
Suleiman the Magnificent in the Turkish style. With its elegant
pencil minarets and flat grey domes, its striped stone cloisters,
and its enchanting pooled garden full of cypresses, pines,
oleanders and bright flower-beds, it is a charming and a peaceful
spot. Adjoining the Mosque is a decayed and aromatic cloister
which serves as a school. Its pupils chatted amiably to me, did
not try to smash my camera, and did not beg; I began to think
I must be back again in Persia.

But as I came out, and was taking a photograph of the

Mosque from the street, a shower of stones from some street arabs greeted me. I knew that I was in Syria after all.

There was one sight in Damascus that I was determined on no account to miss—the tomb of my old hero Abd el-Qader, which is in the Mosque of Shaikh Muhaddin al-Arabi. Towards sunset, and with infinite difficulty, I found a tram to take me up to Salhiyeh. Not knowing the fare, I offered the conductor a paper note; he returned me twenty-one small copper coins, and a most minute box of matches for the odd halfpenny for which no coin exists.

They are nicer in the suburbs. Somebody found the Mosque for me, and did not beg. The *molla*, when I spoke of my admiration for the Algerian, let me enter. I stood, not unmoved, before the last resting-place of the great hero of the Algerian resistance in the middle of the last century. He was considered a patriot then; today he would be termed 'rebel' and 'murderer'; there are no longer 'patriots' among the ranks of the enemy.

I promised to describe the Hotel X, which describes itself as 'the most firstclass well reputed hostel' in Damascus. That is untrue. Each room is said to have a private bathroom with hot and cold water, and for the price charged it ought to have half a dozen; there is, in fact, a shower, with two taps from both of which cold water ultimately emerges. The bells remain unanswered. The food, at its best, is indifferent; generally it is cold, and not infrequently uneatable. The New Semiramis, on the other hand, really is first class, and well worth the extra money; probably the New Omayyad, the Cattan and the Orient Palace are almost as good. (The Cattan, I see, has 'luminous signals' in every bedroom.) If one cannot afford the best, it is always advisable to go for something that does not pretend to be anything but second class.

I appear to be almost the only inhabitant. The manager says that the hotel is actually brim-full of thirty-five Persian footballers who are playing today against Lebanon at Beirut and will be back soon; it was such an ingenious lie that it quite took me in.

The manager is probably 'the most firstclass well reputed'

brigand in Syria. He is a benign-looking, spectacled little man who might pass for a rather down-at-heel archaeologist. 'You are an artist, *Monsieur*?' he said. 'Damascus is a city for artists. Yes, *Monsieur*; I too love beautiful things. My little collection . . . Once I was rich, now I am poor. But I still have a few pieces left: some coins, some bronzes, some pottery . . . of course they are not for sale. I will show them to you; it is always a pleasure to show one's treasures to a connoisseur, a fellow artist. . . .' He beamed so amiably at me through his glasses that I longed to go straight off into the town and buy him some little antique trifle to augment his attenuated collection and restore his faith in humanity.

'You will visit Jerusalem, *Monsieur*? No? But you should. A little tour. I will arrange it. Of course you must see Jerusalem. The Dome of the Rock, the Church of the Holy Sepulchre— they are very beautiful. The Y Tourist Agency will arrange a car. You will travel in comfort. A first-class hotel in Jerusalem. An excellent guide will show you round. You will see everything. You will visit Bethlehem . . .'

(The only thing he forgot to mention was that the manager of the Y Tourist Agency was the second most firstclass brigand in Syria, and that he was hand in glove with him.)

And so—and because I had been robbed of Petra and Palmyra —I fell. Each time I passed the office, little improvements in the itinerary (with little additions to the cost) were adumbrated. 'You must see the Dead Sea, *Monsieur*; you must visit Jerash. . . . That will be a little more money . . . twenty pounds, *Monsieur*. You will not regret it.'

Weakly I agreed. After the wear and tear of Iranian travel it would, I felt, be good to journey for once in comfort and privacy; and twenty pounds seemed a fair price to pay for the privilege.

May 29th

'The car is ready,' said the manager; 'I hope you will enjoy your trip.' Then he vanished—rather guiltily, I thought—into the bowels of the hotel.

The car was not merely ready; it was full. Occupying all but a negligible fraction of a front seat were eight Saudi Arabian pilgrims. Three of these were howling infants, three more were

Mr. R. and Hesam
(p. 176)

(*Above*) *Peasants near the White River*
(p. 162)

(*Below*) *Roman bridge in the Leba*

heavily veiled women. Two rather seedy-looking males, and the chauffeur and myself, brought the carload up to ten. And it was not a large car.

Now in fairness to these two brigands it must be admitted that they had never actually said, in so many words, that I was to have a car to myself. Yet everything—the modified itinerary to enable me to see Jerash, the suggestion that I would be wise to spend two nights at Jerusalem instead of one at Amman and one at Jerusalem, and indeed the high price I was paying —all combined to give the impression that I was to travel alone. There was, however, nothing to be done but to grin and bear it, and to make a vigorous (though doubtless unavailing) protest on my return.

The infants' howls accompanied us through the long green oasis, and though the driver turned the wireless on at full blast he lamentably failed to drown them. 'Much trouble, I am sorry,' said the father next to me, as he tried to stifle the shrieks of the child on our knees; he seemed a nice man.

The palm groves yielded at last to arable land golden with corn—a Salisbury Plain with camels and snow-topped Hermon thrown in for luck. At Dera'a we crossed the hot frontier into Jordan. It was at Dera'a that Og, the King of Bashan, met his death. How often on my travels had I envied him his thirteen foot iron bedstead (see Deuteronomy iii, 11)!

Shortly after midday we saw below us on the red-tawny plain the scattered remains of Jerash, the Roman Gerasa. The Saudi Arabians remained like baggage in the car while I went to see the ruins.

'Take your time. Stay ten minutes if you wish,' said the chauffeur.

'I shall be an hour," I answered.

I believe that the temperature should be exactly 85 degrees Fahrenheit for viewing Classical remains in open country. I have had, before now, to turn my coat-collar up at Paestum, to take my shirt off on the Acropolis: to shiver and to roast. Jerash was precisely right; and even had the ruins been dull, they would have seemed bewitching in that vibrating heat which transformed the landscape into a *pointilliste* painting. Figs, pomegranates and walnuts; gold corn among the weathered

8—PS

stones, and everywhere flowers converted by the heat into a *hortus siccus.*

But the ruins were far from dull—they were splendid: the great oval Forum, the Temple of Artemis that dominated the town, the Nymphaeum, the Thermae, the Temple of Zeus, the Theatre, the Triumphal Arch, the Street of the Columns. . . . Don't ask me to describe them: you may read about them all in Mr. Lankester Harding's well-written, jaunty little guide-book published by the Department of Antiquities at Amman, of which he is (or was?) the Director.

The car—you might call it an oven—greeted my tardiness reproachfully, for the driver had been sounding his horn for the last twenty minutes. The children howled their disapproval —or perhaps just howled. The shrouded women looked more than ever like over-cooked *dolmas*—that delectable dish composed of meat wrapped up in vine leaves.

Enchanting country, sometimes like Provence, sometimes Italianate, now opened before us. Came olives against the red soil, then pines, and always the oleander-fringed streams in the valleys. The scenery was endlessly varied, for sometimes the road kept company with the winding valley, sometimes climbed briskly the brow of a barren hill.

But finally it plunged in earnest. A notice announced 'Sea Level,' and a further descent of nearly thirteen hundred feet brought us to Jordan's banks. Reeds and tamarisks encompassed the muddy little stream, which was crossed by Allenby's Meccano bridge. A tame soldier followed me down to the water's edge to prevent my photographing this important military object, and various touts attempted to sell me phials of Jordan water which, unlike most of the objects hawked about the Levant for the delectation of tourists, was probably genuine.

Jericho—my guide-book describes it as 'the lowest, *geographically speaking*, inhabited town in the world' (my italics)— lay sweltering in the afternoon heat, surrounded by its banana plantations and groves of palms. There were Arab refugees from Israel squatting in more than Persian squalor in clustering booths hardly larger than dog kennels and far less solidly constructed. We stopped for tea at a wayside café sheltered by a tree flaming with scarlet blossom; but there was no time, of course, to see the recent excavations of ancient Jericho.

The Dead Sea glittered beside blinding white shores dappled with dead yellow grasses and burnt sienna weeds. Beyond it rose pale violet hills, shimmering in the heat. It had, of course, its Lido ('Undressing outside the baths forbidden') with the usual tourist-trash for sale; but the place at that hour was deserted. I dipped my finger in the salt water and touched my tongue with it; it burned like acid.

A feature of the landscape between the Dead Sea and Jericho is the curious agglomeration of ivory-coloured hillocks, distasteful as the heads of very bald old men. Every two or three hundred yards along the road here, and continuing over the scorched hills to Jerusalem itself, there lay a shoddily dressed sleeping soldier. Since half the male population of Jordan is in uniform of a sort (even children of ten can be seen handling Bren guns), this barely surprised me; I supposed they had been posted there not so much to guard the road as to keep them out of mischief. But there was in fact a particular reason : Jordan's Old Harrovian ruler was returning from Jerusalem to his capital, Amman. I missed, by inches, seeing him.

Past the Good Samaritan inn (now a police station), past an odious signboard inscribed 'WELCOME TO THE HOLY LAND! Ask for ——'s Biscuits' (I positively refuse to give them this free advertisement), and suddenly the walls and towers of Jerusalem crowded the crest of a hill before us. We drew up outside Herod's Gate ('Parking place for City Taxi Company'), from where I was conducted by my appointed guide to the Hotel Azzahra—an agreeable, quiet establishment outside the city walls.

It was five o'clock. The guide said he had to go back to Bethlehem immediately or he would miss the last bus, and could therefore show me nothing that evening; he would collect me at eight o'clock tomorrow morning. There was so little to see in Jerusalem that one morning, he assured me, was ample. He seemed an unpleasant young man, and although I was paying about a pound a minute for his services, and suspected (rightly, as I discovered) that his 'last bus' story was a lie, I was happy for the present to dispense with them.

But though I was free of him, I was not free of his breed.

There were touts everywhere in the town, trying to sell guide-books, trying to lure one into King David's Store or the Queen of Sheba's Souvenir Shop. 'Stop, look, listen! Here is the Petra Bazaar!' 'This way to Schmidt's Girls College.' 'You want a guide, sir?' 'Ashtrays made from genuine olive wood from olive trees from the Mountain of Olives.' 'You want a guide, sir? You want to see Holy Sepulchre? I show you Pool of Bethesda. You want nice souvenirs. . .?'

'*Yehudi! Yehudi!* (Jew! Jew!)' shouted the children, swarming round me like gnats. (They really ought, in Jerusalem, to know what a Jew looks like.)

And yet, in spite of all that is done to make Jerusalem into an oriental Polperro, how lovely it is! For the moment I was content to wander aimlessly up and down the narrow, winding streets till I reached the death-wall that bounds the Arab city. There is a no-man's-land between this and the Jewish town. The dresses are splendid as ever, and in the bazaar the old way of life continues uninterrupted. The grey stone still surprises after the bricks and tiles of Iran. From a balcony I looked down upon the Temple area and the Dome of the Rock, shut at this hour to infidels. The sites must wait until tomorrow.

It was almost dark by the time I reached my hotel.

At the next table to me at dinner was a Jordani engineer. He told me that on one occasion he gave a lift in his car to a Beduin woman. After a while the woman asked if she might stop; she returned a few minutes later, carrying the child to whom she had just given birth. This, at least, is one embarrassment which the Good Samaritans of the English road are spared.

May 30th

Breakfast was ruined by the political propaganda of the engineer. He tried so hard to be broad-minded. All his sentences began, 'Believe me, I have nothing against the Jews, *but* . . .'

The guide arrived punctually at eight o'clock. A night's rest had only increased his truculence, the morning light underlined the distastefulness of his appearance.

'I show you everything you give me very good tip?'

Looking back, I see now what I should have done: I should

have taken him to the Pool of Bethesda—or rather to the town sewer, if there is one—and pushed him in.

We passed through Herod's Gate and so, by way of the narrow Via Dolorosa, to the Church of the Holy Sepulchre.

'Go inside, have a good time, have a good pray,' said the repulsive youth. Then he sat down on a tombstone and lit a cigarette.

After the splendour of the Persian mosques, the first view of the holiest site in Christendom filled me with infinite depression. Darkness, dankness and decay; narrow gloomy passages and perilous winding steps; not so much a church as a labyrinthine cave whose gloom was punctuated by occasional expensive over-crowded candle-lit antique shops (H. V. Morton, I see, compared them to 'exotic jewellers' shops'). An icon took my fancy (it would need cleaning of course, repairing), and 'How much?' I almost asked of the black servitor who was trimming the candles. Such was the *visual* impression; the heart creates its own images. Whether the site be authentic or not, it is impossible to stand unmoved in a place so long hallowed by tradition.

I found the guide blasphemously impatient, and his pile of cigarette stubs told me how long I had remained inside.

'Hurry please, very hurry,' and he stepped off briskly in the direction of, perhaps, the Wailing Wall (where they may wail no more).

For it would be a mockery if I attempted to describe the buildings that I saw in that one brief ill-tempered half-morning; five hundred better pens have done the work already. Nor, indeed, can I recall the details; only that now we were plunging down ill-lit steps into some sacred subterranean cavern, now I was stubbornly refusing to be dragged into King Solomon's Antiques or Herod's Carpet Store. And always :

'*Yehudi! Yehudi!*'

'Hurry please. You give me nice-a big tip no?'

'*Yehudi! Yehudi!*'

'Wait a moment while I take a photograph of St. Stephen's gate.'

'No—it is forbidden.'

'. . . of this street.'

'No—they Musselmens; they not like it.'

'. . . of this wall.'

'No—it is military wall. It is not allowed. How much tip you give me?'

'Go to blazes!'

And once more the cry of the children went up: '*Yehudi! Yehudi!*'

One site, however, will remain clearly fixed in my memory: the Temple Area and the Dome of the Rock. After those claustrophobic grottoes, suddenly there was space, and light, and air, and colour; not the strong colour of Iran, but gentle, melancholy shades of exquisite beauty. The guide found a stone, a crony and a cigarette, and left me alone with my thoughts.

'Now we go to Bethlehem. Hurry please!'

I could not understand his enthusiasm to take me to Bethlehem; but on our arrival the reason became only too apparent, for before I could say 'Saudi Arabia' I found myself inside the souvenir store of

Canavati and Sons
Milk Grotto St., near
Milk Grotto Church,
Bethlehem, oppo
Chapel of St. George

'You no like nice-a prayer-book, made of olive wood from Mountain of Olives?'

'No, I don't want anything.'

'You no like nice-a camel made of olive wood from Mountain of Olives?'

'No.'

'You no like old dagger, old crusader cross, old crusader jacket—all very old?'

'No.'

'You no like ashtray made from Dead Sea stone?'

'No.'

'You no like scarves, shawls, blouses, all done with hand?'

'No.'

'You no take anything home as souvenir from Bethlehem?'

'No. I no take absolutely nothing. I want to see the church, and then I want to go straight back to Jerusalem.'

'You no like nice-a music-box play "Green hill, green hill far away"—very cheap, very beautiful, all made from olive wood from Mountain of Olives? You give me very good tip?'

'NO!'

He put me down in Jerusalem, outside the office which inflicts his services upon defenceless visitors.

'You will tell them I very good guide, I show you everything?'

'No.'

'You now give me very good tip?'

I gave him a piece of my mind instead, and left some more of it in the office.

After a brief siesta I took a bus to the top of the Mount of Olives. On my way down, uncertain of the path, I asked a soldier the way.

'Are you a Jew?' he asked.

'No.'

'Then I will help you.'

'Why should you imagine I'm a Jew?'

'We think all foreigners are Jews.'

That explains much.

I was glad that he did not accompany me. I preferred to walk alone down the rough perilous pathway, half eyes for the road, half for the long-familiar prospect of the Holy City— for which Baedeker wisely advocates an early-morning light. But Jerusalem was lovely enough in the dusty *contre-jour*, and hazy-golden behind the black olives.

The track became a provincial road, the olive trees more ancient, and I was in the Garden of Gethsemane with its flowery, self-conscious little parterre and spacious modern church.

'You will also wish to see the Tomb of the Virgin?'

Once more I found myself plunging down a hundred steps into the bowels of that sacred earth. . . .

Near me at dinner were the Financial Advisor to the Director of Education of the Philippine Islands, and his wife. During the Japanese occupation they exchanged their grand piano for two eggs. Since both could eat and neither could play the piano, this apparently reckless transaction was probably sensible.

May 31st

We left Jerusalem as the early-morning sunlight was gilding the city walls. It looked incredibly beautiful at that hour. If only it belonged to friendly people like the Persians, what a pleasant place it might be!

A stop was made at Amman—ostensibly for me to see the Roman theatre, in fact for the driver to transact some business. At Jerash, where there was much to see, I was hustled; here I was deposited at the theatre and told that I would be collected in a few minutes, but it was more than two hours before, parboiled, I was rescued.

What is left of the theatre can be seen at a glance. It is exactly like any other, but duller and more decayed than most. There are no inscriptions to read, beyond the reiterated DDT painted on the walls and seats (for until recently it was full of refugees). You have to be an expert before you can profitably spend two hours on such a site.

There was no sign of the manager when I reached the hotel in Damascus, but the manager of the Y Travel Agency was in the hall. I opened the attack. He sat there, a brown slug, fabricating lie upon lie to explain away his extortions. I called him a liar and a robber, but he did not recognize these as terms of opprobrium : brigandage and mendacity were his professions; as well call a doctor a doctor, or a dentist a dental surgeon, and expect fur to fly. In the end I paid, as I knew I must, and then gave notice to the hotel that I was leaving early tomorrow morning.

I did not see the hotel manager again. Perhaps it was just as well.

15

Aleppo to Tortosa

June 1st

By taxi to Aleppo. This is a good and a cheap way of getting about in Syria.

With me in the car were several Syrians and one Lebanese —nice, friendly people, but too painfully anxious to make propaganda for their respective countries. First I was subjected to the usual anti-Jewish set-piece, which I begin to know almost by heart. Thereafter my attention was continually being drawn to cars, garages, factories, mechanical reapers and other such symbols of Progress. 'You must go to Beirut,' said the Lebanese wistfully, 'to see the cars in the street.' (Ultimately I did, and was almost killed by one.)

To the right of the road I suddenly saw—or thought I saw— about a thousand camels, and rather maliciously (for camels are not 'progressive') pointed them out to my fellow travellers. They looked embarrassedly down their noses : 'There are very few camels in Syria now,' said one. 'Oh, do look at that lovely sugar factory !'

Just a mirage, no doubt.

At Hama are the famous *na'uras,* the giant waterwheels of the Orontes. I was pleased to find that the Syrians did not attempt to deny the existence of these obsolete machines (which, as a matter of fact, are represented on some of the bank-notes), but even came with me to see them. The expedition was, however, ruined for them by some small boys who were bathing naked in the river; for bathing in the nude is not 'progressive.' They tried to make a big detour to avoid my witnessing this scandalous scene, but I was obdurate. 'How happy those children look !' I said. The Syrians averted their eyes; 'They are young,' said one; 'they do not know any better.'

I was sorry that there was no time to explore Hama further; Robin Fedden, in his *Syria,* makes it sound attractive. In particular, I regret having missed the Azem Palace there.

The last stages of the road to Aleppo were dull but for the curious beehive houses which are still being built in the villages, and for a boisterous wind-blown sky.

I found a room at an hotel called the Ambassadeur, though I do not see high-ranking diplomats making much use of it. False economy again; Baron's Hotel, next door, is the right one. Walking into the town, I was soon picked up by a boy who turned out to be a tout and who took me to a brigand who sold silk (?) dressing-gowns. When I had thrown the boy off, I fell victim to a plausibly amiable man who also turned out to be a merchant's pimp, and soon I was back again in the same brigand's den.

'I am the official guide to the *suqs*,' said a third. Oddly enough, I believe he really was. He took me through the mazy tunnels of the bazaar, where he was everywhere greeted with respect, and showed me much that I might otherwise have missed: little mosques, baths, and *khans*—the fine old warehouses which date from the days of Aleppo's mercantile prosperity.

'Perhaps you might be interested,' he said at last, 'in buying a silk dressing-gown. . . .'

That old brigand must be the best spider in Aleppo.

June 2nd

I had kept the principal sights of Aleppo up my sleeve for today; there is much to see, and I set out early.

A stone's-throw from my hotel is the Museum, whose contents are for the most part Hittite—which seems to be tantamount to saying that they are devoid of aesthetic value. Hittite objects would appear to be second-rate, ponderous or comic, but intensely interesting of course to archaeologists. Even the official guide-book comments upon the 'incredibly fatuous expression' of a certain lion, and what is left of the face of King Lamgi-Mari (who is briefly dressed in a South-Sea-island palm-leaf petticoat) is not encouraging. Are these things Hittite? I do not know, I do not greatly care; life is too short to get all those pre-Classical civilizations sorted out. I want to see the town.

First, the Citadel. With the possible exception of the greater pyramids, this must surely be the largest man-made object on earth. Abraham may or may not have milked (as they say) his cows on the summit;[1] in any case the hill was fortified at least a millennium before Abraham's time and is therefore roughly coeval with its rivals. Baedeker, usually so lavish with his figures, does not mention the height of this vast truncated oval-based cone of earth, but the little moat—now dry—is nearly seventy feet deep. The scale of it all is staggering.

The Citadel is not merely big; it is breasted and crowned by magnificent buildings, mostly erected between the thirteenth and the fifteenth centuries. The approach is by way of a gate-house, a lofty bridge, and a tremendous fortified gateway that straddles the once stone-faced glacis. Over the gateway is the great throne-room. A twisting passage and two further gates lead to the interior of the fortress, and so, past many ruins and the little twelfth-century chapel built to the glory of Abraham, to the square-minaretted Mosque. One should, of course, climb to the top of the minaret; but I had climbed enough, and remained satisfied with the view already at my feet.

Of the religious buildings in Aleppo, the principal is the Great Mosque of the Omayyads, with its spacious, airy court (to which the unshod infidel has free access) and superb square minaret dating from the eleventh century.

The Madraseh Othmaniyyeh has the tallest minaret and the largest number of cats in Aleppo. The philanthropist who endowed the college left a special legacy for the care of stray cats. There they were, in a little railed enclosure—the living, the dying and the dead all huddled together in this feline Black Hole of Calcutta. Some kittens only a few hours old were crawling blindly over the decaying corpse of a large tabby, while children—till I drove them off—prodded them with sticks. The Moslem may not put a dying animal out of its misery (which shocks the Christian, who refuses euthanasia to human beings); but the *mollas* might at least remove the dead. A horrid spectacle. . . .

Outside the town is the Madraseh el-Ferdaus—an agglomeration of buildings dating mostly from the thirteenth century and interlaced with figs, pomegranates and vines; it was built by

[1] 'Aleppo' in Arabic is 'Haleb'; 'milk' in Arabic is '*halib*.' So what?

Saladin's daughter-in-law. The portal is splendidly honey-combed, the brown and grey stone *mehrab* magnificent. But above all, the place is outside the tout zone, and consequently there is a sense of peace that enhances the excellence of the architecture and the natural beauty of the setting.

One should not miss the Madraseh Halawiyeh, built by the Empress Helena and until the twelfth century the cathedral of Aleppo. Its marble columns with their wind-blown acanthus capitals are pure Byzantine, and the thirteenth-century wood and ivory-inlay *mehrab* a technical miracle.

I would like also to have seen the Jami' al-Tutah, or Mulberry Mosque, for the sake of its name : there was no time.

Aleppo was the rich mart of Syria, and many fine old private houses and *khans* of the merchants still remain. There are also the *khans* of the Frank factors, clustered together for mutual protection in those perilous seventeenth-century days. The pattern of the *khan* is almost invariable. A handsome zebra-striped stone doorway leads past a porter's lodge into a small academic quadrangle where Time has stood still. A lazy vine straggles over the crumbling stone; a pomegranate tree leans drunkenly over derelict bales. That donkey cannot have stirred for a decade; that man has been sleeping there for a century, and the clamour of the *suqs* will never reach to waken him. The College of St. Ichabod.

The private houses also conform to a type. A humbler entrance leads again to a court, but fountained here and set about with flower-beds and tubs of orange trees or lemons. The principal reception room is open to the court and watered by its own fountain; its roof is fretted and honeycombed and, like the panelled walls, painted in bright colours and gold. The chimney-piece may be of 'scented' stone—but scented only to the nose of faith. The court itself is richly walled with warm stone exquisitely carved in a free rococo around the windows. A musicians' gallery is concealed by an iron grille that invites the honeysuckle or blue convolvulus to climb. Two of these buildings are now used as Armenian schools, whose children look as fish-out-of-water as did the wartime Malvernians in Blenheim.

The al-Labbadiyyeh baths, with their handsome black-and-white façade, date from the fourteenth century but are now used as a felt manufactory.

I am ashamed to have to admit that I did not know that felt was *made*. I thought that 'felt' was the same word as 'pelt' and the German *Pelz* (but I find it is not : never safe to jump to these etymological conclusions). I thought it was—well, the skin of some animal. (To tell the truth, it is not a matter to which I have ever really given much thought.) Admittedly there is no animal called a 'felt'; but then there is no tree called a 'deal.' Presumably some obliging creature lent its anonymous skin for the happiness and comfort of us all—Homburgs off to it !

So I went to the baths to learn how felt was made. And for another reason also : there was a passage in M. Saouaf's *Visitors' Guide to Aleppo* which had aroused my curiosity. He writes : 'The jerky movements and the unintelligible sounds of these half-clothed felt-makers as they work in the deceptive shadows of the old bath may remind the educated visitor of a scene from Dante's *Inferno.*' Would I prove to be educated, or would I not?

I would. I was. It would not be precisely accurate to say that I was reminded of Dante's poem, of which I have never succeeded in reading more than six consecutive lines; but I could at least see a resemblance (after M. Saouaf had put the idea into my head) to Doré's illustrations to the *Inferno*. It was a ghoulish place—a twilit dank prison full of kneeling, groaning, quarter-clothed dwarfs (they seemed) laboriously soaping, rolling, kneading, hammering, pummelling and generally bullying some kind of hair—operations that in the West are, I learn, quickly performed by large steam-heated rollers and vibrating flat-irons. Had M. Saouaf been as well educated as I am, he might also have been reminded of the Nibelungs in the third scene of Wagner's *Das Rheingold*.

So much for the buildings. The people I like less.

'Why not photograph the clock tower in the Place Bab el-Faradj?' shouts someone as I tip my camera towards the top of a minaret.

'Because,' I want to say, 'it looks as though it were knocked up about 1890 in Birmingham from bits left over from the

Brighton Pavilion. And anyhow, the faces show different times : would you like the British public to know that?'

Here are one or two other experiences in Aleppo :

I try to take a general scene in the bazaar. A soldier informs me, quite politely, that photography is forbidden in the *suqs*.

I try to photograph the elegantly carved stone doorway of a private house. A man rushes up and plants an unshaven chin between the lens and its objective. 'Why,' I ask, 'mayn't I photograph that?'

'Because it is old.'

'You would rather I photographed the new Post Office?'

'Yes.'

I try to photograph another gateway, which leads into the courtyard of a *khan*. Once again I am stopped—not, this time, because it is old, but because a hundred yards away, in the remote and shady recesses of the court, there is visible the head of a donkey. 'Gate yes, animal no.'

Can they not understand, these good people, that it is no secret in Europe that there are donkeys still in Aleppo, that Beduins wearing their splendid traditional dress are still to be seen in the streets? I have been photographed at Eton by Orientals of every shape, size, colour and creed—and I rejoice to think that my picture now adorns a hundred scrapbooks from Scutari to Shiretokozaki; anyone who stalks the streets in medieval fancy dress, whether cap and gown or *keffieh* and *abayieh*, must expect to be photographed. Can they not understand, too, that we appreciate that they have not yet had time to destroy all their old buildings and replace them by modernistic monstrosities? Can they not understand that if anything were likely to expose them to the ridicule of the West it would be photographs of some of their contemporary architecture (for, as Mr. Robin Fedden says, 'It is difficult to think of modern buildings in Syria calculated to give pleasure either now or in the future')?

And finally, surely they must understand (for it touches their precious pockets) that it is precisely to see this thing of which they are so ashamed—the rich and fabulous life of an ancient oriental city—that Europeans might be willing to submit themselves to the discomforts and discourtesies that a visit to Syria now involves, and that if they impede and insult us beyond endurance they will not have us there to rob. They will have killed the goose that lays the golden eggs. God, they make me angry!

It should, however, in fairness be added that this extreme obstructive attitude is principally that of the man in the street (indeed, the official Handbook to Syria contains a photograph incorporating an animal suspiciously like a donkey). The authorities respect and try to preserve their ancient monuments. Very broadmindedly, they allow photographs to be taken in the courtyard of the Great Mosque itself; nor was I stopped at the Citadel, which I feared might be scheduled as a military object. Such other scenes as I recorded in Aleppo were 'snapped' surreptitiously and at the risk of my liberty.

June 3rd

I went today by car to Kalat Seman, to see the church erected in honour of St. Simeon Stylites round the pillar upon which he stood for more than forty years.

I can sympathize with many forms of eccentric behaviour to which I am not personally attracted—polar exploration, for example, or playing golf; but the whole gamut of avoidable and unprofitable (to self and others) discomforts and mortifications, ranging from sitting for an evening in an unnecessary draught to sitting for a lifetime on an unnecessary pillar, lies beyond my comprehension. I had not been greatly tempted even by the rich selection of auto-flagellation chains on sale in the Meshed bazaar (price 1s. 9d. upwards). *A chacun son goût*; doubtless I have missed something. The career of St. Simeon, prince of fleshly mortifiers and pioneer of column-squatters, is so remarkable that I may perhaps be excused for recapitulating it here.

Simeon, a poor Cilician shepherd boy, was born at Sis in the year 386. Encouraged by some local ascetics he entered the monastery of Teleda where he remained for ten years. At first he was content to practise the conventional austerities and fastings; but gradually he embarked upon a campaign of self-torture which began to alarm the good monks. The monks fasted every other day; Simeon now ate on Sundays only. The monks were satisfied with mild little mortifications and discomforts; Simeon was always devising something new, improbable and painful, such as corseting himself with cords made of palm-leaves until the wounds that they made turned septic. Seeing that he was setting a pace that they were unwilling, if not indeed unable, to sustain, the monks summarily ejected him.

Simeon roamed the countryside in search of somewhere uncomfortable to install himself : the bottom of a fairly dry well exactly met his requirements. A few days after he had moved in, however, a deputation arrived from the monastery to beg him to return. This he did; but the experience had unsettled him, and soon he was off again.

We next find him in a cell at Telanisos, near Kalat Seman, still busy improvising fresh ways of tormenting himself. His favourite pastime now was to have himself walled up for forty days at a stretch; but after he had performed this feat for the twenty-eighth time, he found that it was losing something of the charm of novelty, and something indeed of its rigours. Abandoning the cell, he climbed a neighbouring hill and had himself chained to a large rock.

Simeon was becoming famous. Pilgrims began to pour in : the paralysed, the impotent; souvenir-hunters who snipped away little bits of his meagre skin tunic; the idly curious and the genuinely devout. It was now that, in order to escape the importunities of his devotees, he hit upon the happy notion which was to assure his immortality : he constructed a pillar upon which he could stand unmolested by the crowds.

The various authors to whom we are indebted for our knowledge of St. Simeon give different figures for the height of his column, of the series of taller ones to which he successively withdrew, and of the number of years which he spent upon each. Roughly, we may say that the final column (which was composed of three drums, to symbolize the Trinity) was some sixty feet high, and that the greater part of his forty and more years as a stylite was spent upon it. Clad only in the most meagre garb (but permitting himself the luxury of a hat), exposed alike to winter storms and the blazing suns of summer, standing always, he set an example of almost superhuman endurance. When he prayed, he bowed low; through constant practice (one spectator counted 1,244 prostrations and then gave up) he could touch his feet with his forehead. On festival days he would stand from sunset to sunrise with his hands raised. It was his custom to preach twice a day, and his sermons, though they dealt chiefly with spiritual matters, sometimes took a more practical turn—as, for example, when he urged incurable swearers to swear by their slaves rather than by God, or when he fixed six per cent. (per annum?) as a fair rate of interest for moneylenders. From his pillar-top he settled family disputes, cured the sick, or directed the policy of an emperor, as occasion demanded.

On rare occasions a visitor might be invited to ascend to the top of the pillar. A pilgrim from Ravenna, who had accused Simeon of having the unfair advantage of being an angel, was provided with a ladder and allowed (like St. Thomas) to verify that the saint was made of flesh and blood, and to explore with his fingers the hideous ulcers that were the by-product of sanctity. They came, these pilgrims, from Persia, Arabia and Armenia; from Spain, Italy and Gaul. Idolaters were converted by the thousand. Not infrequently, disputes and even pitched battles took place around the foot of the column, from whose summit the indignant saint strove in vain to restore order. Theodoret, who has left us the best account of St. Simeon, nearly lost his beard in one of these scuffles. When at last Simeon died, armed forces of Christians and Saracens rushed the pillar to dispute the possession of the corpse. It was finally secured for Antioch, where it was interred with tremendous pomp.

St. Simeon's example was followed by innumerable disciples and imitators. The golden age of the stylites extended from the fifth to the tenth century, but long after that time the practice continued. Brosset saw a pillar-saint in Georgia as late as 1848. The cult, too, was widespread, stylites being found in places as far separated as Egypt and Russia. In the West, however, there is mention of one pillar-saint only—a man named Wulflaicus, who in the sixth century erected a column at Carignan in the Ardennes. Some bishops who happened to be passing destroyed the pillar and thus nipped in the bud a practice which they considered 'unsuited both to the Western way of life and the Western climate.'

Yet is our climate really so unsuitable? Southern England is little colder in winter than many parts of Syria, and infinitely preferable in summer. Pillar-squatting is notoriously conducive to longevity. The publicity value of the pillar is undeniable.

Let Nelson make place on his column for a modern St. Simeon who shall become an example and an inspiration to us all, and who will be conveniently situated to guide the deliberations of Downing Street as Simeon once guided the policy of an emperor.

My driver was intelligent, well read, *simpatico*. The price that he fixed for the journey to Kalat Seman and back was extremely reasonable. 'Syrians,' he said (in French), 'think of nothing but money.'

'Aren't you a Syrian?'

'Certainly not. I am an Armenian.'

Always the same story here: if anyone turns out to be nice, ten to one he turns out to be Armenian also.

We drove among silver-grey hills, crossing a Roman stone-paved road in better repair than our own. For a while the earth at our feet was red as wine; there were cemeteries planted with white irises, and beehive villages watched over by the sad ruins of Rome. Then, as we climbed higher, the ground about us became stony and barren, where goatherds and bright peasants fed flocks on air and reaped an invisible harvest. Smiling children conjured a flower or two out of the wilderness and thrust them upon us—but the emptied hands lingered for their reward.

'Our great national hero is Michael Arlen,' said the driver.

'You read much?' I asked.

'Yes. For many years I read novels—everything I could get hold of. Then poetry. Now, *Monsieur,* I have been ill . . . *une légère fluxion.* So I study medicine. A man can soon become his own best doctor.'

My heart went out to this genial philosopher.

'The younger generation,' he said, 'lives only for pleasure. The youths spend their nights in brothels. Every evening they get drunk. I too drink, *Monsieur.* I smoke: we can only die once —*Ah, je vous remercie, Monsieur!* But true pleasure lies in moderation.'

And there, ahead of us on a sallow spur of rock, Kalat Seman sprang into view as we were talking.

It would be hard to picture a more exquisite spot. But for the pretty girl who opened the gate to us and pressed a flower into my hand, we were alone there with the stones and the sky; with larkspurs and big purple thistles, the fig trees and the pomegranates, which somehow contrived a livelihood in that reluctant soil. Wide were the views of the rolling sherry-coloured plain, flecked here with russet, there with the gold of stunted corn. Such was the *mise-en-scène*; but the buildings called us. 'Us'— for the driver had never before been to Kalat Seman, and was as excited at least as was I.

'That, *Monsieur,* must surely be the baptistery; the church and monastic buildings lie there to the right. Permit me to look a moment at the guide-book. Here, of course, a dome has fallen. How beautiful is the Syrian stone . . . !'

The church itself, writes Mr. Fedden, is 'the largest remaining Christian monument that antedates the tenth- and eleventh-century cathedrals of the West, and perhaps the finest building put up between the Roman monuments of the second century and the creation of Santa Sophia in the sixth.' It covers an area considerably larger than Wells or Lichfield. For the church consists in fact of four basilicas, united under an open octagon to form a Greek cross. The eastern basilica, with its triple apse, constituted the church proper, the remaining three serving as *promenoirs* for the pilgrims. Beneath the dome which formerly crowned the octagon once rose the lofty column of the saint; now time and souvenir-hunters have diminished the precious relic to a crumbling square base and an amorphous fragment, too big to steal, of the pillar itself, standing forlorn among giant tumbled stones.

The buildings, ruined though they are, are majestic still and exquisitely proportioned; where it is yet in place, the richly carved stonework is surprisingly well preserved. The monolithic pillars of the arches bear Corinthian capitals, some of which show the exhilarating 'wind-blown' acanthus leaf. To the beauty of form must be added the beauty of texture and craftsmanship, of colour from grey to sorrel, of the greater silence, and of the hill-high setting under the glory of a Syrian sun.

I found it hard to tear myself down from the top of a high wall that I had climbed in order to take a photograph. A little longer, and I too might have become a stylite.

Tailpiece to Aleppo. From Dr. Julian Huxley I learn that all known golden hamsters—those prolific, pretty pets and valuable laboratory 'guinea-pigs'—derive from a single female which, with her twelve young, was captured near Aleppo in 1930. The only other scientifically recorded specimen was found in 1839.

June 4th

I must write it more worthily : JUNE THE FOURTH!

As I lie in my not uncomfortable bed in the Hôtel Ambassadeur, I think of Eton.

It will be almost lunch-time here when the first fine cars begin to park themselves on the giant NO PARKING sign beneath my window at Baldwin's Shore. Closing my eyes, I seem to see those fresh, eager, overscrubbed Lower Boys, being worn (as Dylan Thomas might have said) by large, overpriced carnations, who wait so hopefully by Barnes Pool Bridge for the arrival of tardy parents. Older boys, Fourth-wise boys, remembering the long hours that lie ahead, have fixed a later rendezvous. And though I am more than two thousand miles away, I think I hear a bright, brittle, upper-class voice saying : 'Ronnie dear, tell John to tell Angela that the caviare is in the boot of the Bentley.'

In Upper School, where it is rather uncomfortable and probably very hot, a Colleger in knee-breeches is now reciting Euclid in Greek. Although it has not understood much, the audience claps loyally and wonders how the match is going on Upper Club. I see myself, in imagination, at the Drawing Schools, talking to a parent whom I cannot place, about the water-colours of her son that I cannot remember. Someone is saying that the boys' work is too modern, and someone else is saying that it is too old-fashioned. A large Leanderthal man with a rather bushy moustache is asking why there aren't any pictures of Henley.

It is one o'clock. In the Hind's Head and the Café de Paris, corks are popping. Beside the river, under shady elms, the great luncheon cornucopias burst open to disgorge their treasures of salmon and strawberry. A happy satiety descends.

But how to bridge the broad gulf that stretches till night turns blue and the first golden rocket may cleave the darkening sky? There is always the cricket, sprawling on; and oh, how deck-

chairs ease the aching feet! Green and white, green and white.
'Diana! How lovely! You know Michael? And Alister? And
this is Tom's sister. Where's Arthur?'

At last, a movement towards the river bank, where the pale
slim boats glide softly by and straw hats are wreathed with
flowers. A crew is standing, swaying crazily. 'They'll go in!
They're going in! THEY'RE IN!'

It is half past eleven; I can stay awake no longer. But in the
night I stir. Now the rockets must be rising, to tumble in their
golden rain. One! One, two! One, two, three! One, two, three,
FOUR!! 'Sit down! SIT DOWN, CAN'T YOU!' 'George,
what the devil have you done with the whisky?'

But before poor George can find the whisky, I shall have fallen
asleep again.

So I mused, little guessing what tribulations the day had in
store for me. Then, having dressed, packed my luggage and paid
my bill, I left Aleppo by taxi for the coast town of Latakia
(Laodicea), from where I hoped to find transport to Tortosa
(Tartus). Tortosa is the centre for visiting the picturesque Island
of Ruad, and Krak des Chevaliers—most splendid of Crusader
castles and almost certainly the finest surviving medieval castle
in the world.

My companions were friendly Syrians, the driver again an
Armenian. At first we followed the familiar road towards Kalat
Seman, then climbed steeply to two thousand feet. Wild hollyhocks, oleanders, yellow daisies and yellower broom kept us
company. Descending by flowery ways among pine-covered
slopes, we reached at length a little tea-house and halted. A
natural arbour of trees, their stems painted in rainbow colours,
had been supershaded with bamboos and dead branches into a
cool little paradise; for want of a refrigerator, in a fountained
pool several hundred bottles of 'sinalco' (orangeade) mounted
welcoming guard. A giant Turk he seemed presided. My companions, the kind Syrians, stood me coffee and asked a billion
questions about my salary, pension and future prospects in this
world and the next.

Then down, down to the sea. Latakia is like a little Riviera
townlet, set about with bougainvillaea, oleanders and hibiscus,
scented of sunshine and the sea. I was deposited in the taxi

office; a car would be going to Tortosa soon. But now became apparent the snag of the travel-by-taxi system : the Tortosa taxi would not fill. Half a dozen times we drove round the town, crying our wares to deaf ears.

But at last we were considered replete enough to be a paying proposition. The driver was a vivacious young man, filled with an exuberance that gin alone in northern climes engenders. He sang the whole way, letting go the steering-wheel to conduct, to clap the rhythm, to wave to friends and acquaintances. We lurched perilously, the sea-drop at our feet. But such *joie-de-vivre* is infectious; though all my efforts to make him drive sensibly were fruitless, I could not bring myself to be angry with him.

The Banias terminal of the Iraq Petroleum Company, with all those absurd and ugly pipes. Drowsy heat. Crickets chirping. 'Why not come on with me to Beirut?' said the sportive youth, waving all his hands towards the horizon.

'But I want to get off at Tortosa.'

'I shall not,' he said, 'stop.'

But he did; and would he had not! He put me down at the Hotel X.

The Hotel X proved to be a provincial little affair with Persian sanitation. I was given a room full of someone else's clothes, and that someone else—who proved to be the manager—was to wake me from my midnight sleep to collect his best trousers. The hotel provides no meals—not even breakfast; but this is no great hardship, for not far away there is the Restaurant Aida, 'ready to offes [*sic*] you all kinds of dishes and meats. Fishes, chickens, doves, etc. . . . Pay him a visit once and you will be its eternal guest.'

Having deposited my luggage, I asked the manager to point me the way to the police station. He seemed surprised : what, he asked, might I want with the police? Only a permit to visit the island of Ruad? Ah well, then he would tell me. . . .

The charming children of Tortosa accompanied me through the town, the more athletic showering me with stones, the more avaricious clamouring for money. I stopped for a moment to enter the old Crusader Church—a lovely cool empty building made of golden stone. But it was being repaired, and piles of delectable missiles tempted the childhood of Tortosa to more vicious attack. Unwilling to end my days as a second St. Stephen, I pressed on to seek refuge in the kindlier arms of the Law.

'Please show me your passport. Where is your permit to visit the military zone?'

'What permit?'

'All the coast towns of Syria are in the military zone. No one may visit them without special permission.'

'But how could I know that?'

'The British consul in Aleppo would have told you. Why did you not ask him?'

'But why should I think of asking him?'

'I am afraid this will bring you much trouble.[1] What is that book in your hand? Show it me.'

It was Robin Fedden's admirable *Syria*, in which I had just been reading of the beauties of Ruad and the glories of Krak. He took it and thumbed it through, then turned to the endpapers, which showed a map of the country—a map that betrayed, by means of a stylized little ship, the terrible secret that Syria is bordered on the west by the sea.

'Where did you get that map?'

'I got it with the book.'

'Where did you get the book?'

'In England.'

'What did you pay for it?'

'Twenty-five shillings.'

'How much is that in Syrian money?'

'About twelve pounds.'

'Have you any other books about Syria?'

Indeed I had. Almost burning my pocket was a highly incriminating notebook in which I had put down (you have already read it) exactly what I thought of the Syrians. A good spy would doubtless have contrived to eat it; I just hadn't the stomach.

I answered, quite truthfully, 'I have the official handbook,' and wondered when they would start searching me.

'Where did you get it?'

'In London.'

'What did you pay for it?'

[1] In the light of subsequent events, it seems probable that the first consignments of Russian arms were already arriving at Latakia. No doubt the weekly aeroplane to Palmyra had been discontinued for military reasons.

'Nothing. It was given me at the Syrian Consulate.'

He was now convinced that I was lying. No Syrian would give anyone anything for nothing. And since I was a liar I was clearly a spy also—a dangerous spy. He began to put little questions designed to trap me. For example (suddenly): 'How old are you?' followed by an examination of my passport and an elaborate subtraction of 1901 from 1956.

But I was not to be caught. And it was he who first began to flag—partly because French was more of an effort to him than it was to me, partly because (as he had rashly admitted) he 'worked twenty-four hours a day,' and stronger heads than his could not stand that pace indefinitely.

Though reluctant to divide his prey, in order to give himself time to recover he began to assemble other and more important police officers, to each of whom in turn I had to repeat my story. 'If I were a criminal,' I said for the twentieth time, 'would I be likely to go straight round to the police station the moment I arrive?' But this was too subtle for them. Finally, a car was sent to the barracks to fetch representatives of the military.

After another two hours of cross-examination too futile to relate in detail, I was taken under military escort (but not handcuffed to a policeman, as is, I had noticed, the custom still in progressive Aleppo) to the colonel in command at the barracks.

The colonel was both pleasant and sensible. He was humane too, and sent for coffee. I could see that he was morally certain that I was harmless. He readily agreed that, had I been a spy, I would hardly have gone voluntarily to the police. But I had put myself in an awkward, a very awkward position: I had trespassed into the military zone. I must return under escort to Latakia. There, if the authorities thought fit, I would receive a permit to visit the coastal towns, the island of Ruad, and Krak des Chevaliers; if not, I would be sent back to Aleppo.

I was now possessed of one single, simple desire: to get across the Syrian border with the minimum conceivable delay. Was there any chance, I asked, of my forgoing the wonders of Ruad and Krak and leaving directly for Beirut? He thought it was just possible; but first he must telephone to Latakia. Meanwhile he ought really to detain me overnight at the barracks; provided, however, that he could keep my passport he was ready to take a risk and let me return to my hotel. Which did I prefer?

I almost chose the barracks. But there was the question of my luggage. There was also something to be said for bearing known ills. So I returned to the Hotel X. There I found the manager in a state bordering on panic. What had I been doing with the police all that time? What had I been saying about him? No doubt he would have slept better had he known that it was I who was the criminal in the eyes of the Law.

Then, locking the door of my room, I took out my notebook and a rubber and doctored the text until it read as though the Syrians were the nicest people in the world.

June 5th

While I was breakfasting at the Restaurant Aida, an orderly returned with my passport and instructions for me to proceed at once to Beirut : in other words, I was being expelled from Syria as an undesirable alien. Within half an hour I had secured a place in a car and was on my way to freedom. Never again shall I set foot in Syria.

16

Beirut to London

THE coastal road, with its clusters of wild rose and convolvulus, its oleanders, sugar canes and waving palms, was a continual delight; empty beaches, a sea bluer than in the posters of Bognor Regis, would have seduced the most chicken-hearted bather. But not until I had exchanged the Syrian frontier post for the welcoming Lebanese could I fully enjoy the beauties of Nature.

Passing through Tripoli, a large and thriving place with a square bright with jacarandas, we reached immemorial Byblos (I must return here) and soon after the Adonis river. Then, where the Dog river gushes out between precipitous cliffs, the mountains come down to the sea. Here, on the vertical rock-face, conquerors from Rameses II to General Gouraud have recorded their triumphs in hieroglyphics, cuneiform, Greek, Latin, Arabic, English and French: more than three thousand years of Syrian history upon unperishing stone.

We were approaching the outskirts of Beirut when a car bore down upon us on the wrong side of the road. Its driver swerved just in time. As he passed us he relinquished the steering-wheel and, without pausing in his singing, waved both hands to me.

Beirut's much recommended Hotel Normandy being full, and the hideously splendid Saint George too expensive, I went to the Z—internally a dreary, old-fashioned affair, but which attempted to disguise its decrepitude by means of a crude lick of paint on the façade, a so-called 'American Bar,' and a sun terrace dominated by a vast signboard informing its guests that

Men of Distinction use
ARISTOCRAT
Ideal for the Hair
(Agent: Noubar Nadjarian, Beirut)

The place reminded me of an elderly trollop whose faded charms had been injudiciously over-restored. It serves no meals beyond breakfast; but at the Restaurant Albert I look like putting back a part at least of that stone of flesh that Persian cuisine robbed me of.

A bathe in the sea, and the Albert's admirable French cuisine, have done much to restore me to good humour.

June 6th

Beirut is a typical Mediterranean town : except for a few Beduins and a few tarbooshes, one might here be in Naples— but a Naples almost devoid of antiquities. The people are pleasant and civilized, though there is rather more street-touting and begging than I really care for. The climate is hot and moist, but, as at Tehran, the mountains are at hand.

I walked this morning through the town, failing to get inside the Great Mosque (once a Christian church), and frequently losing my way among streets that, in an outburst of American modernity, have abandoned names for numbers which are not shown on the newest town map.

There is an elderly English spinster—I will call her Miss Jelf —staying in this hotel. As soon as I show up on the sun terrace, she and her 1906 Baedeker appear from nowhere and settle, as if by chance, at the table next to mine. She is 'frightfully interested' in Eton, where her father was; since (as she happened to mention) he died in 1902, I have no very clear recollection of him. She is also frightfully interested in the Phoenicians, Sumerians, Mittanians, Hurrians, Assyrians and all the rest of them. Indeed, it isn't easy to find anything ancient in which she is not interested—except, perhaps, the Romans. She thought Baalbek 'very decadent.' It seems that she takes an annual jaunt from Tunbridge Wells in search of the Hittites or whatever it happens to be at the moment. A sporting old girl.

After she had given me a twenty-minute lecture on the antiquities of Byblos, I asked her how she managed to be so fully informed.

'Oh well,' she answered modestly; 'you see, I always go to bed with the guide.'

The Museum, which lies a good mile from the centre of the town, is well worth a visit. There one may study the origins of our alphabet, and worship many and strange gods. In one gallery is a row of twenty-six 'sarcophagi in human shape,' looking like a Henry Moore air-raid shelter or a plump dormitory of petrified schoolboys.

Outside the Museum is a reconstructed Roman colonnade. There is a story current in Beirut of two Americans who hired, at great expense, a car for Baalbek and were successfully fobbed off with this puny trifle, the hoax being exposed only when they proudly displayed their photographs.

But there is another story about Beirut that I like even better:

The Dragon for the first performance of *Siegfried*, manufactured in Birmingham, was dispatched in three large crates—head, body and tail—to Bayreuth. Head and tail arrived safely; the body was shipped to Beirut!

Perhaps it is there still, in some dusty warehouse—rare prize for a *Wagnerverein*. Or even yet on its way: one of the tapestries sent from Paris for the French Embassy in Kabul took fourteen years on the journey.

I really thought I was going to get through my holiday without running into a former pupil. But I was wrong. This afternoon, as I was standing outside the Great Mosque, failing for the second time to effect an entrance, I heard behind me a fresh, educated voice:

'Fancy meeting you here, sir!'

I turned. Before me stood a large, nice, pink, stupid, good-looking young man with a moustache, whom I remembered at Eton a few years back as a large, nice, pink, stupid, good-looking boy without one. I could not recall his name, nor even whether it was upon water or upon grass that he had so distinguished himself. But somewhere, certainly, he had been tremendous. I could see him standing outside Chambers one distant June day, the sunlight filtering through the leaves of the lime trees and dappling his splendid 'Pop' waistcoat; and I could hear someone saying to me that he was probably one of the nicest, and certainly one of the stupidest boys who had ever stuck the course at Eton. He had the large, soupy, trusting eyes of a spaniel; I felt that at any moment he might lick my hand.

In London we would each have run a mile from the prospect of spending an evening in the other's company, but here we seemed to one another like breaths of home. Having commented upon the surprising smallness of the universe, he said :

'How are things at Eton? Any changes? One's so cut off out here.'

'Oh, all right. No, I don't think so—except the new swimming pool; it's being opened this month.'

A far-away look came into his big brown eyes. He was back, I knew, upon those smooth green fields (or gently gliding waters), hitting that unforgettable six over the Pavilion (or winning the School Sculling by unprecedented lengths). He turned away his head, and I had the uncomfortable feeling that he might be going to cry, or break into the Eton Boating Song. But, with an effort, he pulled himself together.

'How's m'Tutor? Has he still got m'Tutor's?'

'It's very stupid of me,' I said, 'but I can't for the moment remember where you boarded.'

He could hardly believe it : it was like asking the Queen her address. And had I added that I couldn't even remember his name, he would have known I was joking.

Yes, his Tutor, I told him, still had the House.

He seemed amazed.

I asked him what he was doing at Beirut, and he asked me what I was doing there. But he didn't want to talk about Beirut; he only wanted to talk about Eton.

'Anybody been sacked lately?'

'Not that I know of.'

There was a silence. Then : 'Do you know, my last year at Eton was the happiest time in my life.'

I could not doubt it. His life, for practical purposes, was over. It had finished five or six years ago. For the next fifty years he would live in the past—in a past that memory made ever sweeter, where it was ever June and ever green, where life was free of care and no day ever long enough for all the pleasure that had to be squeezed into it. I pitied him from the bottom of my heart.

That evening, after a very good dinner at the Albert, we sang the Boating Song together, arm in arm, on what is left of the beach.

June 7th

To Baalbek by car, with an agreeable driver who had been for three years with the British in Egypt.

The roads climb splendidly above Beirut, past the luxury hotels and the showy, ugly summer villas of the rich Lebanese, to the five-thousand-foot pass of Dahr el Baidar, then descends dramatically into the broad, green and tawny village of the Beqaa that divides the Lebanon from the Anti-Lebanon. By the vineyards of Ksara we paused a moment to offer thanks to the Jesuit Fathers for their heartening wines. It is not until twenty miles beyond Ksara that the vast columns of the Temple of Jupiter at Baalbek first become visible against the western foothills of the Anti-Lebanon.

Whatever he may have read beforehand of the magnificence of Baalbek, the visitor must surely find that the reality surpasses his preconception. And if he is sensitive to mood, his pleasure will be doubled. Perhaps I was lucky in the day I chose; at all events, I found few tourists and fewer touts. There are no litter baskets, yet no litter; no notices discouraging one from inscribing one's name, photographing, trespassing or urinating. There is no barbed wire; there are no arrows, no barricades, no edifying inscriptions announcing that one is 'now entering the COURT-YARD OF THE SACRIFICES.' No zealous municipal hand has run amok with Poulsen roses. One bought—and reasonably —a ticket at the entrance; thereafter one had the sensation of having come upon something that the hand of man had not defiled for a long millennium. In fact, man has been hard at work. Those blocks of stone that make it so easy to climb to a viewpoint have not fallen so conveniently; they have been artfully coaxed into position.

I will not attempt to describe the buildings—'the * temple of Jupiter Heliopolitan; the *** temple, so called, of Bacchus; the ** *pronaos* of the temple, in front of the ** monumental gate . . .' Messrs. Hachette have run riot with their asterisks, but there is not a star too many. I was not, as at Kalat Seman, alone among the ruins: one could hardly have expected to be. Two black-robed priests there were, with a handful of bright-eyed pupils; there were a couple of blond, honeymooning young Norwegians who soon forgot, among the tall-growing hollyhocks, that Constantine had here suppressed the cult of Venus, and three plump, *ach-wie-schön*ing, middle-aged Germans who looked embarrassedly the other way; there was a bearded French archaeologist measuring fallen columns with a metre-rule : just so much humanity as was needed to give scale to the giant columns of the Temple of Jupiter, and to infuse again these dead stones with life. And as once the patch was used to enhance beauty, so the black priests served as a foil to the golden skin of the marbles.

Then the ruins themselves—so grandiose and so radiant, decayed to the perfection of picturesqueness, overgrown by just the right amount of wild flowers. The great columns were never tired of framing new vistas of tiger-coloured plain, green slopes and snowy peaks. And over all ruled the unbroken blue of the sky. The Mosque—which until recently uprose prettily from a crop of Indian corn—and the little Temple of Venus (there is a copy of it at Stourhead, Wiltshire) lie outside the main enclosure. Near 'Papa George's Store' may be seen one of Baalbek's few concessions to the vulgarer kind of tourist : a tame Arab *shaikh* and camel, both ornamented up to the eyes and at the disposal of lady photographers at a shilling a time.

And finally there is the Hotel Palmyra, offering the perfection of courtesy and simple clean comfort and where, for the sake of the bread alone, I would gladly have stayed a month.

After dinner, Miss Jelf buttonholed me and told me, at greatest length, how she had once met someone who had once met someone whose great-aunt (I think it was) had (once) met Marie Antoinette. 'Frightfully interesting, don't you think?' she said.

There are about a hundred versions of this tiresome 'links with the past' story—all tedious and almost all, I suspect, untrue. I have known dull hostesses to produce one, in cold blood, to help a sticky dinner party along. Suicidal tactics ! I have invented my own version, about a man whose first wife was painted by Sir Joshua and second wife by Augustus John : 'This man, when he was only twenty, married (for her money) a widow of eighty who, as a girl of two, . . . etc., etc.' Foolproof, baffling, intriguing ! And who (except John) dares dub it a lie ? Miss Jelf noted it for future use; but I am not sure that she believed it. She was soon off again with her Hittites.

June 8th

Alan Trott, who is in charge of the Middle East Centre for Arabic Studies at Shemlan, in the mountains above Beirut, has kindly invited me to stay with him for a couple of days. Mrs. Trott fetched me this morning in the car.

One could not wish, at this time of the year, for a more delightful spot than Shemlan. The airy house commands a dazzling view of the Mediterranean and the red seashore. Beirut sparkles to the right, and in the foreground the land falls terrace by flowery terrace, gay as a rock garden. There are oaks and olives, and everywhere big scented bushes of broom.

June 9th

We drove this afternoon higher into the hills to collect an oncocyclus iris (*Iris sofarana*?). Trott proves to be not only an expert orientalist but a knowledgeable botanist as well.

In the evening a madrigal party for the students and some friends from Beirut. For Trott is not only an orientalist and a botanist but a musician also. An American professor who was present explained to me at some length how refrigerators work; I still do not understand. He then asked me to explain the intricacies of the tutorial system at Eton. He still does not understand. I begin to wonder whether I do.

June 10th

Mrs. Trott and her daughter left this morning for Jerusalem, by way of Damascus. Miss Trott, I heard later, was turned back at the Syrian frontier—for having the Christian name of 'Rachel'! This sort of anti-Semitism is even madder than the spy mania of the first World War.

I too left, hiring a car to Beirut by way of Beit ed-Din—a fine drive with a view of the Cedars of Barouk, poor relations of those of Lebanon.

Beit-ed-Din, the mountain palace, the oriental eyrie that hangs between earth and sky in the lower Djebel Barouk, was built at the beginning of the nineteenth century by the Emir Bechir. Bechir, with his black beard and sparkling eyes, his passion for

Hollyhocks, Byblos
(p. 246)

Baalbek
(p. 242)

public justice and private revenge, was a brilliant enough figure to dazzle Lamartine and to re-emerge today as a national hero. For forty years, undisputed, he ruled the Lebanon.

The austerity of the mountains restrained his Damascene architect from excessive ornamentation, though not from uttermost luxury. The arcaded court, the terraces and fountains, the sumptuous *hammam*, might yet find favour with those who cannot stomach full oriental rococo. And no one responsive to beauty could stand unmoved before the sublime severity of the mountain setting.

Beit ed-Din, though now a summer residence of the President of the Lebanese Republic, is also a National Monument, presided over by courteous and efficient guides. English visitors will enjoy among the exhibits in the admirable museum a most offensive letter from Lord Palmerston to the Emir, which either innocence or extreme liberality has persuaded the authorities to display.

Miss Jelf told me this evening that, though she never forgets a face, she can't ever remember a name. As she hopes to get my book in due course from the lending library, this is a relief. Little use, I fear, her describing my face to the girl behind the counter at W. H. Smith's (Tunbridge Wells Branch).

After a quick bathe, dinner with Sir Desmond and Lady Cochrane in a fabulous Lebanese palace with a Villa d'Este garden. 'Tante Isabelle,' who is ninety-four, was the life and soul of the party. She left later for three or four hours' bridge at the Aero Club, specially founded to afford an outlet for her inexhaustible energy.

On the way home I ran into the Old Etonian again. He has asked me in for a drink tomorrow evening.

'What do you think is happening at Eton at this very moment?' he said.

I looked at my watch. 'Quarter past eleven: that means quarter past nine in England. And it's Sunday. I don't suppose they're rowing, or playing cricket at that hour. I should think that a nice earnest boy with slight spots is reading a paper to the Archaeological Society on the Roman Wall in Britain.'

June 11th

Without telling Miss Jelf, I booked a place in a car for Byblos.

The only other passenger was an American woman who said, 'Oh my, what a bee*oo*tiful location!' as she arrived, and spent most of her afternoon photographing me against walls and columns 'to show the scale.' I recommended the guide, who was about five foot one, as a better foil; but she said she preferred me.

There are, I think, two possible ways of briefly visiting a place such as Byblos, where more than six thousand confused years of unfamiliar history are unrolled upon stone : you may toil round with the guide or the guide-book, being forced to admire the traces of a neolithic village or fruitlessly pursuing the 'formless vestiges' of a temple 'a little further to the E' of the obelisk of Abishmoo, King of Byblos (nineteenth century B.C.); or, at peace with the world, you may wander among the flowery ruins, enjoying the 'splendid* panorama,' pausing here to admire the rare beauty of a clump of wild hollyhocks against a wall of exquisitely weathered stone, or there to fraternize with a lizard which, unmindful of the sacrilege, is frisking sunnily upon the sarcophagus of Ahiram's aunt.

In short, Miss Jelf's way, and—on this occasion—mine.

It was too beautiful, it was too hot, I was too weary, I was too lazy, to chase after the tomb of Ibishmoo, father of Abishmoo, which Miss Jelf had so warmly recommended to my notice. Except when I was being propped up against columns for American photographic purposes, I roved as the spirit moved me, drinking in (the correct phrase, I think) the golden beauty of that happy place. And long after Miss Jelf has forgotten the name of Ibishmoo (whose face she never knew), I shall remember those oleanders rosy against the white stone columns, and how the wild grasses and the pink hollyhocks sloped down to that gentle, shining sea.

None the less, I am, of course, heartily ashamed of myself.

We sat on the veranda of the Old Etonian's flat, watching, as night fell swiftly, the lights of Beirut twinkling at our feet.

'I've just been to Byblos,' I said.

'Where's that? What's there to do there, anyway? I take it you've heard the news,' he added before I could answer.

'No—what?'

'Harvey and Archer look like saving the follow-on.'

'Follow what on?'

'Ha ha!' he said. 'Very funny!'

'But I honestly don't know. Is it the Test Match or something? And anyhow, I thought you were a wet-bob. The Boating Song the other evening—you remember?'

'Fancy that!'

It was all he could bring himself to say. He pitied me from the bottom of his heart.

June 12th

'Time, gentlemen, please!'

Must I, this warm and scented morning, exchange Lebanon and its six thousand years of history for cold and wet (I hear) *modern* little Eton?

'Time, gentlemen, *please*!'

Yes, my time is up; I must go back. And, happy though I have been, I shall be glad to be home again. Glad to see once more certain faces, to hear again some half-forgotten voices; glad to be back again in that curiosity shop that does me service for a study; glad to tread again a countryside that God painted before He ran short of green; glad to find shelter once more in the old, cosy, rosy, delectable groove.

Sun upon Beirut, as we leave the seashore runway.

Sun upon Cyprus, land of Death.

White toy-clouds over Turkey, framing vignettes of rolling plain and snow-streaked mountain, with here and there a lake the blue of an early John.

Beside me sits an Iraqi lady missionary, full of goodness. Her weary, bloodshot eyes take refuge, behind gold-rimmed pince-nez, from the cruel world; her lips form and reform the words of the typescript she holds in her hand:

'ALCOHOL IN THE HOME

'Madam Chairman, ladies and gentlemen.

'I want to tell you a true story. In my home city of Baghdad,

Iraq, I know a family blessed with all good things; wonderful children, a responsible position, and many earthly possessions.

'The father, we shall call him Hassan, had well-deserved self-respect and was proud of his ancient family.

'Then tragedy struck . . .'

Grey cloud over Istanbul and the un-Golden Horn. They serve us with Turkish coffee at Yesilkoy ('Grey Village') airport in a grey-washed waiting-room full of tired waiters.

Rain over Frankfurt—an unrepentant, German rain. A dripping toy tram pretending to be a dripping toy train carries us from the plane to a waiting-room walled with glass cases crowded with little luxury knick-knacks too fragile to use, too costly to buy, too ugly to tempt. There is an obese German with a cough like a cow's.

Wrapped in grey, we travel blindly on.

We must be over England now.

'Fasten your belts, please! No smoking, please!'

We plunge steeply. And suddenly there are visible the great rectangular reservoir of Staines, the lines of little red suburban houses, the long blue busy riband of the Great West Road, and distant Windsor watching still over Eton.

As the air hostess, beautiful as wax, hands us out on to the dripping tarmac, a solitary horizontal ray of sunlight strikes through the sunset clouds in welcome.

> And they, too, are there to welcome me.
> They have not failed me.

17

Postscript

This afternoon I took a few of my photographs round to show to poor old Mrs. H., tied to her dreary little bed-sitting-room by her 'various' veins and other depressing hang-overs from charring days.

'What's this one?' she asked.

'A mosque.'

'What's a mosque?'

'A sort of church.'

'It looks all newfangled to me. Why can't they make 'em same as ours?'

It seemed to her that everything out there—the buildings, the dresses, the camels—were perversely determined to be different from Christian England.

'That bus don't look safe,' she said, 'and they ought to mend the road.'

'It wasn't, and they ought; I told them so at the time.'

'Did you meet the King of Africa?'

'Which one?'

'The one that came over here: the Queen of Africa.'

I paused a moment, perplexed. 'Do you mean Queen Salote?' I tried.

'Yes, that was her.'

'No, I didn't, I'm afraid.'

She seemed disappointed; she thought I had been moving in the highest circles. 'And now,' she said, 'I'll make you a nice hot cup o' tea. Do they drink that in—wherever it was you were?'

'Oh yes, all day, every day.'

'Well, that's *something* anyway.' She gave an approving little nod: it was the first good thing she had heard about those nasty black heathen.

IRAN (Persia)

This brief summary is intended for the use of readers who are unfamiliar with the Persian background.

THE COUNTRY

Iran is roughly three times the size of France, and is believed to have a population of about 18,000,000 inhabitants, some ten per cent. of whom are nomads. The country consists chiefly of a high and arid tableland, 4,000 to 7,000 feet above sea level. The Elburz range, culminating in the 18,000-foot Mount Demavend, separates the northern part of the plateau from the sub-tropical, wooded shores of the Caspian Sea. The Zagros range lies along the south-western border. To the east are the immense deserts of the Dasht-e-Kavir and Dasht-e-Lut. The coasts of the Persian Gulf and the Gulf of Oman, to the south-west and the south, have a tropical climate. Iran is bounded on the north by Russia and the Caspian Sea; on the north-west by Turkey; on the west by Iraq; and on the east by Afghanistan and Pakistan.

HISTORY

The MEDES were the first Aryan peoples to gain ascendancy in Persia, which they began to occupy in the eighth century B.C. In the sixth century B.C. the PERSIANS, a nomadic tribe, settled in the country and, together with the Medes, overthrew the Assyrian Empire. In 550 B.C., Cyrus II (the Great) captured Ecbatana (Hamadan), the Medean capital, and founded the ACHAEMENID dynasty. Under Darius I (521-485 B.C.) the Persian Empire reached its greatest extent, and the ruins of Persepolis still bear witness of the magnificence of Achaemenid architecture. In 333 B.C., the Greeks under Alexander the Great defeated the Persians at the Battle of Issus and so brought the Achaemenid dynasty to a close.

To the SASANIANS (A.D. 226-658) we owe the remarkable rock-carvings at Shapur, Naqsh-e-Rostam and elsewhere, and some fine embossed silverware. In A.D. 642, the ARABS, under the Caliphs of Baghdad, conquered Persia and introduced the religion of Islam. The SELJUQ Turks, from the central Asian steppes, ruled the country from 1037 to 1197. The MONGOL invasions in the thirteenth century under Jenghiz Khan and Hulagu Khan, and under Tamerlane in the fourteenth century, wrought immense destruction. But the Mongols also built splendidly where they had destroyed. Tamerlane's descendants, the TIMURIDS, reigned for several generations and encouraged the arts.

The second ruler of the SAFAVID dynasty (1501-1722) was Shah Abbas the Great, who made Isfahan his capital; he was a wise administrator and a great patron of architecture. He defeated the Ottoman Turks and with English help drove the Portuguese from Hormuz. In 1722-29 the AFGHANS invaded and laid Persia waste, but they were expelled by Nader Shah (1746-47), who also conquered India. Karim Khan (1751-99), who called himself the *Vakil* (regent), restored order and prosperity in the south, after the disorders that succeeded the death of Nader Shah. In 1794, Agha Mohammad Khan, a eunuch, established the QAJAR dynasty (1794-1925).

During the first world war, Persia was occupied for a time by both Britain and Russia. In 1925, the last effete Qajar was ejected by an army officer named Reza Khan, who as Reza Shah founded the PAHLAVI dynasty. He did much to Westernize Persia, which now, at his wish, readopted its ancient name, 'Iran.' In 1941, after Iran had been occupied by the Allies, Reza Shah abdicated. He was succeeded by his son Mohammad Reza, the present ruler. In 1951, the Iranian Parliament nationalized the Iranian oil industry, which, by mutual agreement, had been controlled by a British company. A new agreement with British and other oil companies was made in 1954.

RELIGION

The Persians are Moslems and, since the sixteenth century, adherents of the Shiah sect. The Shiahs hold that the lawful successors of the Prophet were his son-in-law Ali, and the twelve 'imams'; the rival Sunnis are partisans of the soldierly Abu Bakr and the succeeding caliphs. Iran's neighbours are for the most part Sunnis.

Besides Jews and Armenians, there are also in Iran some ten or fifteen thousand adherents of the pre-Islamic Zoroastrian faith, and about a hundred thousand Bahais—followers of Abdol Baha, and his forerunner, the 'Bab,' who founded a new religion in the middle of the last century.

LANGUAGE AND LITERATURE

The Persian language is Indo-European, but has incorporated many Arabic words and is written (from right to left) in a slightly augmented form of the Arabic script. Turkish is much spoken in north-west Iran, and Persian in north-west Afghanistan which is culturally a part of Iran.

The Persians show great independence of mind, and have a considerable interest in poetry and mysticism. Thanks to Edward FitzGerald, the *Rubaiyat* (quatrains) of Omar Khayyam are better known in England than the greater poetry of Ferdausi, Nizami, Sa'di and Hafez.

THE ARTS

The finest remains of pre-Islamic architecture and sculpture are the great ceremonial palaces at Persepolis, and the Sasanian rock-carvings at Naqsh-e-Rostam (near Persepolis) and Shapur (accessible from Shiraz).

Early Islamic architecture is mainly of brick, with stucco decoration; it is simple and monumental. In the twelfth century began the development of the faience tile, which was to play so great a part in Persian post-Mongol architecture.

The characteristic features of a mosque are the rectangular court, the arcaded walls broken by immense portals (*ivans*), the domed chambers, and the minarets. Usually the surfaces are almost entirely covered with tiles, a turquoise blue predominating. The greatest age of Islamic architecture in Persia was under the Timurids in the fifteenth century.

In the minor arts of calligraphy, miniature-painting, book-binding, ceramics, carpet-weaving, and metal-engraving, the Persians have shown themselves to be second to none.

PRINCIPAL TOWNS

TEHRAN. Made the capital by the Qajars at the close of the eighteenth century, Tehran is now largely Westernized and contains, outside its Museum, little of interest of a date earlier than 1800, though the ancient ruins of Rai (Rhages) lie just to the south.

TABRIZ. The second largest city in Iran, famous for its Blue Mosque and citadel. It lies near the Russo-Turkish frontier.

ISFAHAN. Made the capital by Shah Abbas in 1598. The splendid mosques and bridges, the famous Maidan (Square) and Chahar Bagh avenue, are largely his work.

SHIRAZ. Long famed for its wine, roses and nightingales, Shiraz is at the moment the most progressive town in Iran. Sa'di and Hafez are buried there. Persepolis is thirty-five miles distant.

MESHED. Meshed, the holiest city in Iran, lies in the north-east corner of the country. In the magnificent Shrine is buried the eighth Imam.

QOM. The second most sacred city in Iran. In the Mosque is the tomb of Fatima, sister of the eighth Imam.

YAZD and KERMAN. Desert towns with fine mosques.

ABADAN. Centre of the oil industry.

Other towns of architectural interest include Qazvin, Nishapur, Hamadan, Kermanshah, Ardabil and Maragheh.

FURTHER INFORMATION, compact but comprehensive, will be found in *The Persians*, by Sir E. Denison Ross (Clarendon Press, 1931).